Merry Christmas
1986

From
Rick + Rose

Bob Larson

Your Swabian Neighbors

 Schwaben International Verlag

FOREWORD

Dear Reader,

With such a large number of Americans living in Baden-Württemberg, I have gotten to know many of them well – even well enough to know that when an American says "damn Yankee!" he means a baseball player, not a Down Easter.

Speaking of Yankees, it is Bob Larson's theory that the Swabians share many characteristics of the Yankee, although most of them emigrated in times of hardship to New York, Pennsylvania, and Ohio. (A member of LaSalle's crew named Hiens was the first Swabian to reach Texas back in 1687!) A member of Columbus's crew – according to an old joke – allegedly went AWOL on his first night in the New World to look up a kinsman from Böblingen.

But most of the Swabians have remained here in the land of their birth. Their attitudes and characteristics have been shaped by a fascinating and eventful history, which Bob Larson manages to compress into three short chapters. They are the heaviest part of a book that is otherwise light-hearted, reflecting how much the author enjoyed writing it. He has done his best to present the Swabians from all angles and aspects so that his fellow Americans get to know them better.

After you read this book, I hope that you will never have any reason to say (or even think) "damn Swabian!" The great Will Rogers was fond of saying "I never met a feller I didn't like." I hope you will be able to say the same thing about your Swabian neighbors. Enjoy the pages that follow and your stay with us in Baden-Württemberg. We promise to be not just good, but the very best of neighbors.

LOTHAR SPÄTH
Minister President
of Baden-Württemberg
Federal Republic of Germany

3

Printing History:

1st Printing: March 1980
2nd Printing: August 1980 (revised)
3rd Printing: September 1981 (revised and enlarged)

© 1981 Verlag Schwaben International
        Charlottenplatz 6, 7000 Stuttgart 1

Photo credits: Stuttgart Tourist Office, cover, pages 18, 49, 77;
Federal Photo Office, Bonn, pages 58, 79, 116, 161;
State Photo Office, Baden Württemberg, page 93;
Stuttgart City Archive, page 107

Cartoons: Richard G. Kurman, Biberach

ISBN 3-9 800 351-0-7

Table of Contents

For my favorite Swabians:
Margot and Miriam
and Lord Mayor Manfred Rommel

In Memoriam:

Wilhelm Schreiber
(23 XII 1920 – 7 VIII 1981)

I   Swabia and the Swabians

Who am *I* to talk about the Swabians? My qualifications are two-fold: I have lived longer in Stuttgart, the capitol of Swabia, than any other place at home or abroad; and: I'm married to a Swabian.

At the outset I think it is safe to say that if the Bavarian is the Texan of Germany, then the Swabian is the Yankee. Shrewd, thrifty, inventive, and conservative, the Swabian is initially skeptical of all things foreign, be they as remote as Manitoba or as near by as Munich. ("Foreign" includes Prussians, Bavarians, Hamburgers, people from the Palatinate *and* from Baden – in short, just about anyone who's not *a true Swabian.*) He even has a word for such outsiders, calling them *"Rei'geschmeckte"* ("those who have tasted their way in"). I guess our word "nipper" comes closest, even though it is limited to small eaters and small kids.

An old Swabian proverb defines the Swabian as a person who speaks Swabian. That sounds like a magnificent grasp of the obvious until you discover how different Swabian is when compared to standard or so-called "High" German. The sound system, the word order, the syntax, and the vocabulary of the Swabian set his language apart from all others – domestic and foreign – and immediately betray his origin whenever and wherever he opens his mouth.

In moments of tenderness, that happens rarely. In moments of anger, it happens often. Asked to make a declaration of love, the Swabian will stammer a few non-committal syllables. Provoked, he will give full vent to his ire with a richness of invective that would make Richard Pryor blush. Volatile and easily aroused, the Swabian can swear "like a grenade" *(granatenmäßig),* to borrow one of his favorite adverbs. *"Leck mi am Ärschle"* ("Kiss my ass") is so frequently on his lips – to convey anger, disgust, or insult, but also surprise or joy – that the phrase is known throughout the Federal Republic as "The Swabian Greeting."

Dr. Hans Bayer, who died on 6 July 1980, published a "Swabian Cussword Calendar" under his pen name of Thaddäus Troll. Born in Bad Cannstatt, educated in Tübingen, and a resident of Stuttgart (how Swabian can you get?), he wrote a book called *Deutschland Deine Schwaben (Germany Thy Swabians).* It was published in 1967 but unfortunately is not available in English. If you've tried the

Swabian specialties at the *Stüble* in the Graf Zeppelin hotel in Stuttgart, you might have seen his explanatory notes on the menu.

Dr. Bayer claimed that the trained ear of the Swabian enables him to classify the origin, intelligence, tact, and self-confidence of fellow Swabians by the way they handle the dialect. He made the interesting observation, however, that the Swabian is in a dilemma with respect to his language. The Swabian's characteristic pronounciation of the sounds *au* and *sch,* his lilting intonation, his addition of *-le* to every other noun, his complete disregard of the *ge-* on past participles and the final *-n* on infinitives – all of these expose him immediately as a *Schwob* (= Swabian) whenever he tries to speak standard German. Unable to disguise his accent completely, he is embarrassed by his "imperfect" High German. If his fellow-Swabians hear him try to speak High German, on the other hand, they accuse him of snobbishness.

The Swabian dialect is as diversified as Swabian geography. Professor Ernst C. Helmreich of Bowdoin College calls Swabia "an indefinite area in southern Germany, bounded by the Rhine in the west, by the Lech River in the east, by Vorarlberg and Switzerland in the south, and by the Palatinate in the north." A true *Schwob,* such as my friend Dr. Rudolf Wandel in Göppingen, takes exception to that broad description. He claims that based on similarity of dialect, the area from Heilbronn in the north to Tübingen in the south, and from Calw in the west to Geislingen an der Steige in the east (see map above) is the *real* Swabia or *Schwabenländle,* as it is lovingly called by the natives. Outside of that nucleus there are many scattered enclaves with regional variations in speech.

All of these dialect distinctions are meaningless, of course, when it comes to the essentials of swearing, which brings us back to Dr. Bayer's "Swabian Cussword Calendar". He selected a cussword for each day of the year, beginning with *Häfelesgucker* (one who gapes into the cooking pot) for January 1 and ending with *alter Krauter* (old cabbage-grower) on 31 December. Although highly specialized, this profanity is readily understandable by all true Swabians. When outsiders are on the receiving end of it, they might not recognize that they are the targets, unless the tone of voice and body language of the swearing Swabian make it perfectly obvious.

In the first edition of this book I translated *Häfelesgucker* as one who gapes into the chamber pot. It was an honest philological mistake. I know that *Gucker* means one who gapes, and I assumed that *Häfele* meant chamber pot in this context. But Dr. Reinhold Aman, President and Founder of Maledicta, the International Research Center for Verbal Aggression and the world's leading authority on cusswords, caught my error and wrote to me that a *Häfelesgucker* is "the kind of fella who always snoops around in the house, in the kitchen, looking into every pot to see what's cooking, and thus being a real pain in the ass for his wife. Just ask Margot: she'll tell you how annoying a *häfelesgucking* husband is!"

My wife is fond of calling our eight-year-old daughter Miriam a *wurmiger Blitz* (literally "wormy flash"), which is the word of the day for August 26 on Dr. Bayer's calendar. That wouldn't offend me, but it always draws a mean look from Miriam. Similar "swear" words, which wouldn't make me mad either, include *Tropf* (drop), *Schtöpsel* (stopper), *Ripp* (rib), *Nachtwächter* (night watchman), *Hasafuaß* (rabbit's foot), *Dragoner* (dragoon), *Maikäfer* (May bug), *Zipfel* (edge, point, or tip), or a *Jodler* (yodeler). But if you think that's the

9

best profanity the Swabian has to offer, you're very much mistaken.

Dackel (dachshund) is a favorite insult with several combination forms readily available: *Schmalzdackel* (lard dachshund), *Allmachtsdackel* (omnipotent dachshund), *Granatedackel* (grenade dachshund), *Saudackel* (sow dachshund), *Grasdackel* (grass dachshund), *Halbdackel* (half dachshund). Like finding just half a worm in an apple, being called a "half dachshund" is a worse insult than being termed a "dachshund" (and you *know* which half the Swabian has in mind!)

The word *Sau* (sow) is even more popular, and not just as an insult. It's a good gap-filler. When the Swabian forgets the words to a song, he sings "la-la-la." When he can't think of an apt comparison, he often says *wie't Sau* (just like a sow), regardless of the context. Thus one hears such strange comparisons on Swabian lips as "cuss like a sow," "sweat like a sow," "hurry like a sow" (*sauen* is the verb for this), and even "speak the Swabian dialect like a sow." *Sauglatt* means "very funny" in the sense of strange or peculiar. *Saumäßig* also means "like a sow." You will hear the Swabian use it to describe his health (when it's bad) and the weather (when it's unseasonably hot or cold). Combinations with *Sau* in cusswords are:

saudummes Geschwätz (drivel)	*Sauklob* (sow log)
Sauluader (sow wretch)	*Saurammel* (sow snot)
Saumaul (sow's mouth)	*Saulalle* (sow simpleton)
Sauhund (sow dog)	*Saulomp* (sow rascal)
Sauigel (sow hedgehog)	*Drecksau* (filthy sow)
Saumaga (sow's guts)	*Baurasau* (peasant sow)
Saukerle (sow-of-a-guy)	*daube Sau* (stupid sow)
Sauviech (sow beast)	

and *Säule* (little sow), which the non-Swabian might mistake for column or pillar.

Animals play a prominent part in Swabian profanity. In addition to dachshund and sow (with variations mentioned above), one hears *Aff* (ape), *Palmesel* (palm jackass), *Goiss* (goat), *Kuah* (cow), *Wendhond* (greyhound), *Ochs* (ox), *Hornochs* (old ox), *schtercher Bock* (thieving ram), *Brommbär* (growling bear = a grouch), *daube Henn* (stupid hen), *Gockeler* (rooster) and *Trampeltier* (dromedary). I don't dare mention another "sow."

The multitude of barnyard animals is hardly surprising, when you consider that just about half of Baden-Württemberg (especially Swabia) is devoted to farm land, on which 1,988,100 tons of vegetables (mostly white cabbage) 884,900 tons of grain, 105,200 tons of potatoes, 256,800 tons of sugar beets, and 425,900 tons of fruit were harvested during the 1978/79 farm year. Dr. Hans Bayer summed it up nicely when he said in his *Germany Thy Swabians:* "One need only go back three or four generations to find a farmer" in every Swabian family tree.

In addition to the 365 cusswords in Dr. Bayer's calendar, I have learned several more from my father-in-law, who rents apartments to Americans. When his American tenants occasionally depart without leaving the apartment in the condition in which it was occupied, he makes use of this rich vocabulary to express his dissatisfaction. But after every profane tirade against the "sloppy Americans," he throws his arms around me and pleads: "The Americans must stay here forever to protect us against the Russians, no matter how mad your countrymen make me!"

When the Swabian is upset or feels wronged, he will gripe out loud to himself. This practice is known as *bruddeln*. My father-in-law and my wife do it frequently. No sublimation of feelings, no pent-up emotions, no knot in the stomach. With my wife, I find it an excellent early warning system – for me to get out of her way!

II   Swabian Ideals

Q. What is the geological origin of Grand Canyon?

A. *A Schwob lost a Mark there.*

There is also an old joke that the Swabians were kicked out of Scotland for being too thrifty.

Part of that thrift can be attributed to the Swabian's agricultural past (and present). Farmers the world over are noted for their economy. A much larger part is due to the Swabian love of hard work and the acquisition of property. *"Schaffe, spare, Häusle baue"* ("work, save, build a house") are the words of a popular song about the Swabian. He is the first to admit that they are his lifetime goals.

As an old friend of mine in the real estate business was fond of saying, Swabians are "land-lushes." Acquiring real estate and building houses-the great game of *Monopoly*–are the Swabian's bag. But it takes bags of money to do it. According to the *Baden-Württemberg Statistical Pocketbook (1980 edition),* the average price for residential property in 1978 was DM 78.15 per square meter. According to my Swabian father-in-law, who keeps his ear to the ground when it comes to *"Bauplätzle"* (building plots), the going price for residential real estate in the cabbage patches of Filderstadt, where the both of us live, is about DM 900 per square meter. Since it takes about 300 square meters of land to put up a one-family house, and about DM 300,000 to build the house itself, the total price tag can come to at least DM 570,000 or to $237,500 at an exchange rate of DM 2.40 to the dollar. (Now you know why rents are so high around here!)

Considering the average price for the same-size house in the United States-about $200,000 less-one wonders how the land-aholic Swabian can afford to feed his habit. Hard work, thrift, saving, the Building and Loan Associations, and the widespread use of family members, relatives, and friends for the construction work are the answer.

In the Federal Republic the Building and Loan Associations are called *Bausparkassen.* Some of the largest are the *Öffentliche Bausparkasse, Bausparkasse GdF Wüstenrot,* and *Bausparkasse Schwä-*

bisch Hall. At a low interest rate of 4½ percent, a German citizen can open a building savings account with the *Bausparkasse* for a specified amount of money. Once he has saved 40 percent of the total, the *Bausparkasse* will advance him the remaining 60 percent as a loan at an interest rate between 4½ and five percent. Depending upon the size of his family and of his income, he can also obtain premium savings credits from the government and from his employer.

The ins and outs of such complicated financial arrangements, including tax breaks and mortgages, are best known to the Swabian. He also knows how and when to reinvest his savings in order to double his money. Once that first house is up, he has excellent credit and collateral to offer in exchange for more money – to build more houses. No wonder the Swabians have more savings deposits per capita in *Bausparkassen* than the residents of the other states of the Federal Republic.

The Swabian has another edge on his neighbors in other states. According to the latest count, there are 62,329 bricklayers, 15,506 carpenters, 5,405 roofers, 8,798 tile-layers, 29,320 house painters, 5,766 plumbers, and 30,740 electricians in Baden-Württemberg. Even if these highly skilled workers aren't all Swabians themselves, the vast majority of them are either related to – or friends of – Swabians. The shrewd and thrifty Swabian house builder *(Bauherr)* will round up as much as he can of this talent, plus the skilled and unskilled members of his family, to build his *Häusle* during vacation, after office hours, on weekends (but never on Sundays or religious holidays). It's all in accordance with the Swabian philosophy of "sell the dog and bark yourself."

My father-in-law, who describes the Swabian as *"rau, schaffig, und sparsam"* ("rough, industrious, and thrifty"), is a Super-*Schwob* when it comes to house building. A retired precision tool maker, he can do masonry, carpentry, roofing, painting, plumbing, tile and wire-laying himself. Despite vertigo, I have helped him put new shingles on the roofs of his houses (by holding the ladder steady). I have assisted his carpentry when building new houses (by holding the boards steady for sawing). I have rendered full support to his tile and wire-laying (by holding his tool bag).

When it comes to thrift, my father-in-law is a Super-*Schwob,* too.

Last spring, when he noticed that the rust from all salt the Germans dump to melt the winter's ice was beginning to get to his ten-year-old Mercedes 200 Diesel, he decided to replace the fenders himself. Working in the seclusion of his garage, including Sundays and holidays, he made steady progress. The day before he was about to make the finishing touches, he told me he was saving at least a thousand Marks by doing the work himself.

When I happened to pass by his house the next day, I saw him and my mother-in-law frantically pushing the smoking car out of the garage and into the street. He had applied a fresh layer of undercoating just before making the last of the welds with his acetylene torch. When the undercoating caught fire, he discovered that only one of his four fire-extinguishers was in operating condition. The entire inside of the car was gutted by the time he extinguished the flames. His Rollei 35 S in the glove compartment looked like an overdone hamburger. But instead of taking the car to a Daimler-Benz garage, he bought new seats, carpeting, dashboard, and wiring, and went right back to work. When the repairs were finished, several weeks later, he confessed to me that he had spent twice as much as Daimler-Benz would have charged, not including labor. *"Aber sag's bidde moiner Alde net!"* ("But don't tell my old lady!") he whispered urgently into my ear.

Although he spends a lifetime working and saving for property and houses, even the *Schwob* knows that he can't take it with him when he goes to meet his Maker. So why does he knock himself out and deprive himself of so many luxuries and pleasures? He claims he is doing it for his children, but he threatens to cut them out of his will every time they do something out of line.

A German proverb says that material goods provide satisfaction, but only ideals that have been achieved deserve to be called the content of life. For the true Swabian, material goods *are* the ideals. Hard work is the content and the way of life of the *Schwob*.

Despite enforced retirement after a severe heart attack, my father-in-law is still the hardest-working Swabian I have ever known. He is only happy when fully exhausted, having re-roofed, re-wallpapered, re-painted, or renovated completely the interior or exterior of one of his houses. He knows that he is literally killing himself, but that is the way a Swabian would prefer to go.

Thaddäus Troll told the story of a Swabian who tried to do so by committing suicide. It didn't work out the way he intended, and he survived the attempt.

His wife was most critical of his behavior.

"You'd like that," she chided at his bedside. "Just to lie down in your coffin and take it easy!"

III   Swabian Wine

Ask a true Swabian for a two-word definition of his favorite past-time, and chances are the answer will be *"Viertele schlótza"* – which cannot be rendered in English as briefly. It means "suck on a quarter-liter glass of wine." Suck *on,* not up. He takes his time, contemplating the color with his eyes, smelling the aroma with his nose, testing the sweetness by rolling his tongue around in his mouth, enjoying the full bouquet with all of his senses.

He does this usually after a hard day's work (*schaffa* or *wuhla*) in one of those half-timbered inns (*Wirtschäftle*) "which must smell of cigars, roast, and fresh pretzels." This description of the proper surroundings comes from Th. Michael Schweizer's guide to fifty *Wirtschäftle* in Stuttgart and vicinity. The Swabian calls his favorite inn his *Boizle.* That cosy hideaway, where he can sip quietly and say nothing, join in the conversation, or get into heated argument at the *Stammtisch* with his buddies, is not to be confused with a *Boiz.* That's what the Swabian calls a dive or a joint.

There are hundreds of jokes and anecdotes about the Swabian's love of wine. Th. Michael Schweizer tells the story about the *Schwob* who had been warned by his doctor to cut his consumption down to one *Viertele* a day. Not willing to accept that rigid constraint, he con-sulted four other doctors. All issued the same warning. One night his friends found him in high spirits, sipping his third glass of wine in his *Boizle.*

When they asked for an explanation of his new lease on life, he said:

"I've seen five doctors now, and every one said the same thing: one glass a day. But they didn't say anything about the night."

At a dinner party in Stuttgart, a prominent Swabian bragged to me that he drinks two bottles of Württemberg red wine a day and feels fit as a fiddle.

"How are your liver and your blood pressure?" I asked him.

"As sound as a dollar," he responded. A moment later, when he realized his poor choice of words, his florid face turned pale.

Every time I think of him I visualize the advertising logo for Würt-temberg wines–a man with his head tilted back and his eyes half closed in rapture as he sniffs the aroma of a half-filled glass of wine.

In a circle around his head is the slogan: „*Kenner trinken Württemberger*" ("Those who know drink Württemberg wines"). That must be just about everyone in Swabia, because very little of the 2,484,000 liters of red and white wine grown in Baden-Württemberg in 1979 was exported out of the state. Most of it was and will be consumed domestically.

The high quality of the Swabian wines is due to the development of the wine-growing industry here. One hundred years ago the Kingdom of Württemberg (as Swabia was then called) had 49,420 acres of vineyards. Today only 17,297 acres-the very best-are used to grow wine grapes. These are the slopes along the Neckar River, the *Schwäbische Weinstraße* from Bad Cannstatt in the south to Gundelsheim in the north.

The white grapes are pressed the same day they are harvested. The juice of the grapes, calles *Most* in German, is often served as "new wine" or "cider" in the fall, together with hot onion cake. (In my neck of the woods, where there are more cabbages than onions, we prefer the tastier hot cabbage cake.)

Red wine gets its color by allowing the skin of the grapes to ferment along with the trampled mash from three to four days before pressing. *Rosé, Weißherbst* and *Schiller* (now legally referred to as *Rotling)* are names for a blend made of red and white grapes. Pressing a day after harvest produces a pale pink color.

All wines must ripen for a certain time before they achieve full maturity and optimum flavor. The Swabian speaks of "young" wines which acquire their best flavor in about six months. These are the Müller-Thurgau varieties from the valleys of the Kocher, Jagst and Neckar rivers and the early burgandy wines *(Burgunder)* from the *Schwarzriesling* grapes that ripen early in the Heilbronn area and in the lower Weinsberg valley.

When the Swabian talks about "ripe" wines, he means the ones that ripen late and reach their full flavor only after a year. These are the *Trollinger, Lemberger, Riesling* and *Silvaner* grapes that grow in the upper Weinsberg valley, in the Heilbronn area, on the slopes of the Heuchelberg and the Stromberg, in the Bottwar and Rems valleys, and in the Stuttgart region.

Late-blooming burgandy wines *(Spätburgunder),* including *Samtrot ("velvet red")* and *Clevner,* are produced from *Schwarzriesling*

grapes. If you're trying them for the first time, be careful! After just one *Viertele* you feel like an amateur wrestler: your head's in a hammerlock and your legs in a scissors.

Whether young or ripe, red, white, or rosé, all wines should be stored in a cool place, with the bottles lying down on the shelf. Several hours before serving, the wine should be brought to the proper temperature: 51 to 54 degrees (Fahrenheit) for young white wines; 54 to 57 degrees for ripe, heavy and high-quality white wines; 61 to 64 degrees for young red wines; and 64 to 68 degrees for ripe, heavy, and high-quality wines. Rosé should be chilled just like a white wine.

The label on the bottle is a wine's birth certificate. It tells you its vintage (in general the odd years are best and 1971 fabulous), vineyard, city and the quality rating. A recent wine law draws a formal distinction between ordinary table wines (*Tafelweine*) and quality wines (*Qualitätsweine*). The very best are quality wines with high mark (*Qualitätsweine mit Prädikat*), such as *Kabinett* (cabinet), *Spätlese* (late selection), *Auslese* (best selection), *Beerenauslese* (best selection of berries) and *Trockenbeerenauslese* (best selection of dry berries). There is an informal vocabulary for praising the best wines, with words such as:

anregend	animating
aromatisch	aromatic
ausdrucksvoll	expressive
blumig	nice bouquet
edel	noble
elegant	elegant
erdig	earthy
feinduftig	fine fragrant
feinherb	fine dry
feinwürzig	fine fragrant
fruchtig	fruity
füllig	full-flavored
gediegen	solid, of splendid character
gefällig	pleasing
gehaltvoll	full-bodied, racy
harmonisch	harmonic
herb	dry

herzhaft	hearty	*rezent*	piquant, pungent
kernig	pithy	*samtig*	velvet
körperreich	rich in body	*süffig*	tasty
kräftig	strong	*warm*	warm
mild	mild	*wuchtig*	heavy
rassig	noble, racy	*würzig*	fragrant

The Swabian calls a wine that is over-ripe or has lost its full bloom *firn* (meaning old or seasoned in a negative sense). If it's simply sour, he'll call it a "throat cleaner" (*Rachenputzer*), or a "belly tightener" (*Ranzaspanner*) if it's very sour. The wine-growers of Tübingen (popularly called *Gogen* or *Raupen*) and the wine-growers of Reutlingen (popularly called *Huser*) are rivals of long standing when it comes to producing sour grapes. There are myriad jokes about the *Gogen,* called „*Gogen-Witze*" or simply „*G-W*"). The first collection of these was published in 1916 with the permission of King William II of Württemberg. Like all Swabian humor, they are extremely earthy.

Several *G-W* refer to the rivalry between Tübingen and Reutlingen, such as the story about the wine-grower from Reutlingen who was kidding a wine-grower from Tübingen.

"Your grapes were so hard," he said to the *Gog,* "that you had to call in the elephants from Hagenbeck's circus to trample them."

"We did write a letter," the *Gog* replied, "but they turned us down. The elephants' feet are still sore from tramping Reutlingen grapes last year."

Schorle (white or red wine diluted with carbonated water) is a Swabian invention or, to be honest, a theft from the French. I am indebeted to William L. Chew III, a budding philologist at the University of Tübingen, for telling me the origin of the word. During the Napoleonic wars, Bill explained, the French soldiers brought their peculiar habits to southern Germany. (See also Pages 43 and 44.) The Swabians considered the French habit of mixing wine with water a most peculiar custom, preferring to drink theirs neat. When French soldiers clinked wine goblets in public inns, they loudly proclaimed *"toujours l'amour"* as a soldier's most appropriate toast. The Swabians thought that was the name for the diluted wine. In the course of time and phonetic evolution, "toujours l'amour" became *Schorle-Morle,* and finally just *Schorle.*

IV   Swabian Food

When I married my Swabian wife Margot in April 1971, I weighed 131 pounds – soaking wet. Today I weigh 155. According to medical experts, I can only attribute 11 pounds of that weight gain to having quit smoking in 1972, shortly after our daughter Miriam was born. The remaining 13 pounds I owe to Margot's skilled and delicious preparation of Swabian food.

One of the oldest and most fattening of Swabian specialties is *Spätzle,* which can only be translated as "Swabian noodles." The word actually means "little sparrows," although they look more like something color-blind sparrows might mistake for worms. (Don't let that thought spoil your appetite. It hasn't spoiled mine.)

Germany's oldest law book, the *Sachsenspiegel (Saxonian Mirror),* written between 1220 and 1235 by Eike von Repgau, represents the Duchy of Swabia by a knight who is holding a *Spätzle* board and scraper, the two implements required to make the noodles properly. Swabian girls still make them that way, having learned the proper flick of the wrist from their mothers. No true Swabian housewife would ever buy the ready-made *Spätzle* in the supermarket, but she might cheat once in a while, when lots of guests are coming for dinner and time is tight, by using one of many mechanical devices that make the job easier. As a going-away present we usually give the best of these, a *Spätzlesmühle (Spätzle-grinder),* to our departing American friends. It looks and works like a meat grinder.

Here's how to make 'em (for six people): Sift a pound of wheat flour into a bowl and make a dent in the middle of the flour. Pour into the dent 2–3 eggs, one teaspoon of salt, and a bit under ½ pint of water. Beat the dough until it loosens from the bottom of the bowl or begins to form bubbles. Spread a bit of the batter on a wet *Spätzle* board (any flat wooden surface will do) and scrape long, thin strips from the board into boiling salt water with a wide knife or a scraper (called *Spätzlesschaber* or *Spatzenschaber* in German). Keep the water boiling and bubbling as long as you scrape in the *Spätzle.* When they rise to the surface, remove them immediately with a skimming ladle, rinse them in fresh, hot salt water so they don't stick together, drain well and serve on a warm platter. When Swabian housewives want to impress their guests, they use as many eggs as the flour will absorb and no water at all. When you pour gravy on your meat, add some to the *Spätzle*. A real Swabian is one who can eat *Spätzle* with potato salad with lots of gravy on top!

An equally fattening Swabian dish is *Maultaschen*. The literal translation is "snout pockets." They look like giant ravioli but are prepared and served differently. It has often been said that there are as many recipes for *Maultaschen* as there are Swabian housewives. Most Americans first make their acquaintance with *Maultaschen* when they find them swimming in a bouillon soup, but there are several other delectable variations.

The first step in making *Maultaschen* is to prepare a noodle dough. This is done by folding four eggs into a pound of flour with a knife. Add a pinch of salt and about ¼ of a pint of water and knead until firm. The second task is preparing the filling. If you plan to serve six people, take six rolls and cut them into thin slices. Soak them in water, squeeze them out and tear them apart. Bring a pound of (German) spinach to a boil and let it come to the surface several times. (As you have probably discovered already, German spinach tastes quite different from ours.) Chill the spinach in cold water, rinse it thoroughly, and chop it up together with a handful of parsley and a bunch of chives.

Mix those ingredients with three eggs, ½ a pound of skinned pork sausage or fine-chopped boiled beef, and ¾ of a pound of ground beef. Season well with salt and nutmeg. Place this mixture in small, even piles on top of one half of the noodle dough, which has been flattened with a rolling pin. Lay the other flattened half on top and press down the edges between the piles. Use the edge of a thick porcelain plate to divide the dough into squares and separate them with a knife. Boil the "snout pockets" for ten to twelve minutes in salt water, then remove them with a skimming ladle and serve in a homemade or ready-made bouillon. Garnish with chives and serve piping hot. (NB: Be sure to use German flour *(Mehl)* in the above recipes.) *Guten Appetit!*

Maultaschen can be prepared with smoked meat instead of skinned pork sausage, or removed from the soup and served with onion rings fried in fat, potatoes and salad, or cut into strips when cold and fried in hot butter as leftovers. If this sounds like too much work, go to your local butcher shop or supermarket meat counter and buy ready-made *Maultaschen.* They come in transparent packages of four and are sold by the weight.

As has already been mentioned, the word *Maul* in German means "snout," which is considerably less refined than the word *Mund* for "mouth." *"Halt's Maul!"* ("Shut your snout!") is just as offensive as our "Shut your trap!" But those inoffensive, overgrown ravioli are called "snout pockets" (no one knows exactly why) for better or worse. The former Chief of Protocol of the Baden-Württemberg government told me that when the Queen of England visited Stuttgart a few years ago, a state dinner was given in her honor. The best of Swabian food and wine was served, but the printed menu read *"Mundtaschen,"* not *Maultaschen* so that Her Majesty might not take offense!

(Was it jealousy that motivated an Irish girl to tell me that *Maultaschen* enabled the Swabians to eat meat on Friday during the Middle Ages without getting caught by the clergy?)

Speaking of leftovers, a favorite Swabian soup is made of thin pancakes, called *Flädle,* which are left over from light lunches with pancakes, salad, or fruit. (The Swabians don't eat pancakes with syrup for breakfast. They eat them with cherries for lunch.) Swabian pancakes are made out of a mixture of ½ a pound of flour, one pint of milk, two eggs and salt, baked on a griddle greased with bacon until bright yellow on both sides. As the main ingredient of a bouillon soup, *Flädle* are rolled up, cut into small strips and allowed to simmer in the boiling bouillon for a while before being served garnished with parsley or chives.

The Latin word "Vesper" means a late afternoon religious service. To the Swabian *Vesper* means a meal between breakfast and lunch or a light supper (or both). *Vesper* is a serious Swabian pastime, second only in importance to drinking wine, with which it is often combined. The Swabian has a choice of a warm or a cold *Vesper.* Sausage cooked or grilled, *Leberkäs* ("liver cheese," a kind of spam that contains a dab of liver but no cheese), and all edible parts of the pig are popular warm dishes.

Cold "liver cheese" (also called *Fleischkäs* or "meat cheese"), sausage and (real) cheese are the possibilities for a cold *Vesper.* It ain't just baloney, either. Each Swabian butcher competes for the best reputation for sausage-making. It comes in a dozen varieties, but most of it is too fatty for American tastes. The Swabian absorbs the fat by eating *Weckle* (rolls), *Laugenbrötle* (rolls made of pretzel dough), or *Bretzle* (pretzels) with the sausage.

Despite the risk of goiter, the Swabians are fond of eating organs or "innards," such as liver, heart, brains, intestines, and kidneys. There is no need to share these recipes with Americans, although I hasten to point out that once you successfully steam the smell out of the kidneys, there is nothing more delicious. The Swabians call this specialty *Saure Nierle* (sour kidneys).

They sure are!

V   Swabian Humor

Scholars might argue with me, but I like to trace the word "humor" back to three Latin words, all of which have something to do with its nature.

Humus means earth, and humor is often earthy.

Umor means damp, like our tears when we laugh too hard.

Humanus means human, and only that can be its essence.

Swabian humor, like humor the world over, covers all aspects of "the human comedy" – stupidity, greed, ambition, thirst, intoxication, hunger, food, illness, doctors, money (of the lack thereof), students, professors, the clergy, sex, children, relatives (especially mothers-in-law), the discomforts and disappointments of travel, the law and lawyers, bureaucrats, life and death, God and the devil. As German humor, it sometimes displays that trait of enjoying the other guy's misfortune. There is a special German word for that sickness called *Schadenfreude* (meaning pleasure in harm).

But several aspects of Swabian humor make it not only distinctive. They add to its delight. Unlike the Prussian – and much like the American – the Swabian is able to laugh at himself, not just at others.

Swabian humor is dialect humor. That doesn't make it exclusive or esoteric. It just makes it twice as funny.

Lastly, Swabian humor reflects pride in and calls attention to typical Swabian attributes: thrift, hard work, love of domesticity, saying very little (when the occasion might warrant more being said), yet thoroughly enjoying gossip (which the *Schwob* calls *schwätze* or *babbele),* and coarseness. The latter is particularly characteristic of the humor of the *Gogen,* the winegrowers of Tübingen, whom I mentioned already in chapter three. No less than 63 of the jokes in Heinz-Eugen Schramm's anthology of *Tübinger Gogen-Witze,* published in 1975, have to do with urination, defecation, flatulation, and inverse peristalsis. Permit me the Swabian coarseness of stating that again in plain Anglo-Saxon as pissing, shitting, farting, and puking.

Many of the *Gogen* jokes stem from the turn of the century, when cesspool cleaning was a profession and the product sold to winegrowers as fertilizer. (Try not to think of that before you enjoy your next *Viertele.* Instead, just remember that fermentation kills everything but the taste!) Being Swabian, the *Gog* used his own excrement as fertilizer, as the joke about Carl and Caroline shows.

Winegrower Carl and his wife Caroline emptied the contents of their cesspool into two barrels and carried them up to the top of their hillside vineyard. Then Carl tripped and the contents of his barrel spilled over the retaining wall. "Oh, oh," Caroline wailed, "are you an idiot! We spent half the winter shitting for nothing!"

The value of human fertilizer in those days can be found in the advertisements in old issues of the newspaper *Tübinger Chronik*. The owner of the *Gasthaus Löwen* also advertised the contents of his cesspool in that paper. A winegrower, who had exhausted his own outhouse, read the ad and went to the inn. The owner asked him: "What will you offer?" The *Gog* replied: "Give me a pole first." After stirring around in the pit for a bit he said: "I won't give you a damn thing, cause this is students' shit, and it's worthless."

Tübingen has been crowded with students and professors ever since Eberhard in the Beard founded the university there in 1477. Both have been the butt of *Gogen* jokes. Just as the simple Yankee farmer takes extreme pleasure in deflating windbags from the big city, or leading out-of-town tourists astray, so did the winegrowers delight in ridiculing the academic world. It was usually done with a snappy punchline illustrating that even if a *Gog* lacked education, he at least had a ready wit.

For example: a *Gog* asked a student if he read the *Tübinger Chronik*. "Not me," the student replied. "I read the *Frankfurter Allgemeine*. The *Tübinger Chronik* has nothing in it. I use it to wipe my behind." "If that's true," the *Gog* commented dryly, "you better watch out that your ass doesn't get smarter than your head."

Another example: A *Gog* and a professor met at the site where a new clinic was under construction. Looking at the foundation, the *Gog* asked the professor: "What will it be used for, if you don't mind my asking." The professor replied: "A clinic for the insane people of Tübingen." "That's what I thought," the *Gog* said with a quick repartee, "because for students it would be much too small."

But often his ready wit only betrayed his ignorance. A *Gog* had his picture taken together with his pigs. With great pride he passed it around at the *Stammtisch,* emphasizing to his drinking buddies: "I'm the one in the middle." And Sophie couldn't understand why her prescription instructed her to insert the suppositories in the "anus," so she asked the druggist. After his discreet explanation, she commented: "I never would have thought that the ass has a nickname!"

My favorite Swabian joke is also in Schramm's collection. It tells of Hannes and his wife Anna who are caught in a storm while working in their vineyard. They take shelter in an old shed. The thunder, the lightning and the hail in the pitch-black sky frighten them so much that they decide to confess their sins to each other before the world comes to an end. After hemming and hawing, Hannes admits to having cheated on her a few times. Enraged, Anna calls him all kinds of bad names (see chapter one, page 10), but finally concludes: "Since it's our last day on earth, I forgive you." Hannes breathes a sigh of relief and then says: "Now, woman, it's your turn. Tell me about all the sins you have committed since our wedding." But Anna jumps up and points to the sky exclaiming: "Kiss my ass – it's clearing up over there!"

I also like the story about the *Schwob* who has a fatal heart attack while playing *Skat* with his Stammtisch buddies in his *Boizle.*

They toss him into a cart and while wheeling him home they discuss various ways to break the bad news to his wife.

As you have no doubt already discovered, no matter where you are in Germany at any time of day or night, someone is always looking out of the window.

So it was with the widow. "Is that my Fritzle?" she asked, when the men stopped the cart with the corpse in front of the window.

"Yes," they answered.

"Was he playing cards?"

"Yes."

"Was he drinking?"

"Yes."

"Was he drunk?"

"Yes."

"Did he lose money at cards?"

"Yes."

"The Devil take him!"

"He did."

Swabian humor is not solely robust. It can also display charm, sophistication, and subtlety, as in the cabaret, radio, film, stage, and

TV routines of the late Willy Reichert, who was born in Sutttgart in 1896. (He died on 8 December 1973.) A well-known comedian long before World War II, he was loved by non-Swabians for his delightful portrayal of all-that-is-Swabian because it gave them something to laugh at. He was criticized by true *Schwobs* for living in Upper Bavaria and for speaking "stage Swabian."

In 1932 Willy Reichert created the Swabian characters Häberle und Pfleiderer. He played the role of Pfleiderer on the radio, in the movies and on TV. Although fictional, Häberle und Pfleiderer became as famous in Germany as Abbott and Costello in America.

I shall never forget my half hour with him in the TV studios at the Villa Berg in Stuttgart on 17 May 1968. He was filming an entertainment series about the fortunes and misfortunes of several generations of a fictional Swabian family ("The Chronicle of the Nägele Family"). I was coordinating the guest appearance of the 3d Infantry Division's "Marnemen" on a German quiz show.

We met in the foyer between the two studios and drank a *Viertele* together.

He asked me how I liked Stuttgart, and if I got along well with the Swabians.

"The Swabians are not easy to get to know," I said.

"Hano," he said, using that Swabian phrase around which he was capable of building a half hour of humor. "It takes time. But it's time well spent."

"I wish all the Swabians had your sense of humor," I said.

"They do," he answered. "It just doesn't show too often. I get paid to show it constantly. The Swabian can't jump over his shadow, but he's very reliable, When he says he'll do something – and that usually takes some time in itself – he does it."

He sipped his wine and smacked his lips. "Swabian women are faithful to their husbands, and the men wear the pants in the family."

"Why do you live in Bavaria?" I asked him impulsively.

He grinned. "I could say, to get away from Swabians and enjoy some peace and quiet."

"That's not the reason?"

"Only partly." He tilted his glass and set it down. With a twinkle in his eye, he said, "My wife's a Bavarian."

VI Swabian Entertainment + Customs

Dr. Walter Stahl, the Executive Director of the Atlantic Bridge Foundation in Hamburg, which puts on many seminars for the members of the US Forces in Germany and publishes *These Strange German Ways,* is a lawyer and a writer. He is the author of a series of guidebooks to major German cities, such as *Hamburg from Seven to Seven.*

I once asked Walter why he didn't write a guidebook to Stuttgart. His reply was, "Because I'd have to call it *Stuttgart from Seven to Seven–Thirty."*

Is this north-German impression of Swabian entertainment true? Let's face it: it's tough for *any* German city to beat Hamburg, but Stuttgart isn't as dead as some people think.

My friend Wolfgang Hartmann of the Stuttgart Tourist Office recently assembled a 64-page, pocket-size information booklet in *English* with the Swabian title *Info-Päckle* (which means "Little Info Packet"), and subtitle *Stuttgart – What's Where: A Brief Guide.* For a "brief guide," it's very comprehensive, covering (in order of interest) sights and recreation, cultural activities, hospitality and entertainment, and general information "from A to Z." It is color-coded by major section and contains four handy maps.

Under "Night Clubs" he writes: "Although Stuttgart has no exclusive entertainment quarter like Hamburg's *Reeperbahn,* the passionate night-lifer can get his money's worth – in both senses." I'm not quite sure what he means by that, and I'll tell you what little I know about Stuttgart's "exclusive entertainment quarter" in a moment. (In this context the word "exclusive" doesn't mean "fancy," but rather "solely devoted to.")

Herr Hartmann wisely recommends that you spend DM 60 and sample Stuttgart's night life with a guided tour before striking out (I mean just that) on your own. Called "Stuttgart Nights" *(Stuttgarter Nächte),* the tour is conducted every Wednesday, Thursday and Friday from 2000 to 0130. You buy your ticket at the "i-Punkt" of the Tourist Office's outlet in the Klett-Passage and join the tour in front of the Hindenburg building across from the railroad station. You get to see the TV tower, several night clubs (including some strip tease), a drink in all five establishments you visit, and a light supper for your sixty Marks. (The current list of night spots on the tour includes the Königshof, Happy Night, Evergreen, and Four Roses.)

You probably have heard about "The Jungle" in downtown Stuttgart around Nesenbachstraße, Weberstraße, and especially Leonhardstraße. You might also have been warned that you can drop sixty Marks in one of those joints faster than a B-girl can drop a hint that she's thirsty. (Most of the managers will take a credit card as quickly as the girls will take you, by the way.) Long considered a "thorn in the eye" of Lord Mayor Manfred Rommel, these places will be limited in the future to about a dozen on Leonhardsplatz, Leonhardstraße, Richtstraße and Weberstraße, instead of expanding to 40 in the so-called "Old City".

Strip joints are not the Swabian's bag, at least not on his home territory. And to judge by my father-in-law's comments when I showed him a directory of massage parlors I found in a motel in Richmond, I doubt if "erotic" massage parlors do much business with real Swabians in Swabia. ("The real *Schwob,*" he told me, "helps himself through the night. The only thing those girls massage is your wallet.") I hasten to add, however, that a few "sauna clubs" in Stuttgart do advertise "full-service and live-dancing" from midnight to four a.m., in addition to the swimming pool and the solarium.

There is an uncodified custom that the Swabian goes out on Wednesday night. I have no way to account for it except perhaps to note that most establishments are closed on Mondays, several on Sundays, and some on Tuesdays. If he likes to dance, he goes to one or more of Stuttgart's discos, or to the more conservative dance cafés scattered about town.

I think it is indicative of local tastes and habits that there are more *Weinstuben* listed in the bi-monthly *Official Program of Events* published by the Stuttgart Tourist Office than night clubs, bars, cabarets, and places to dance.

Apart from frequenting *Weinstuben* (see chapter three for details), the Swabian will eat out with the family occasionally. This is usually combined with an invigorating, appetite-building walk through the woods of the Swabian Alb, or tramping through the Schönbuch Forest, on a Sunday morning before competing for seats in a Gasthaus or on benches around an authorized fireplace in the great outdoors for a do-it-yourself picnic.

Street festivals and so-called *"Hocketse"* are extremely popular Swabian customs, as well as forms of entertainment. While street festivals usually include a parade of some sort (especially when children's groups are involved), a *"Hocketse"* is a sit-down event with wine and beer. Sometimes the entertainment is a band, sometimes a carnival concession, sometimes even a succession of political speeches (if the host is a local chapter of a political party). The Swabian word *"Hocketse"* is an abbreviated dialect rendition of *"da hocken sie"*, meaning "there they squat." Not only are festivals popular in the environs of Stuttgart (having originated as local village affairs before the villages were incorporated into the Stuttgart city limits). The city itself hosts large open-air events in the summer months, with "long nights" devoted to the folklore of other countries, the annual festival of light with fireworks at Killesberg Park, and the "wine village" of stalls on Schillerplatz and the Market Place in the early fall, where Württemberg white, red, and rosé wines can be sampled.

"Kirbe," orginally a sacred act (the consecration of a church and the annual celebration of the anniversary) became increasingly secular from the 9th century onward. Today it is a *Volksfest* with a fair, dancing, or a *Hocketse,* or various combinations of that kind of public entertainment. The word *"Kirbe"* is a dialect variant of *Kirchmess'* or *Kirchweih',* meaning the consecration of a church.

Although Stuttgart has several large carnival societies to help celebrate the *Fasching* season (from 11 November to the following Ash Wednesday), the true *Schwob* takes a greater interest in the historical Swabian-Alemannic *"Fasnet"* parades of mummers in hand-carved masks of demonic figures in Reutlingen, Rottweil, and cities closer to Lake Constance.

The Stuttgart Tourist Office runs the annual Stuttgart Spring Festival *(Frühjahrsfest)* for local exhibitors on the Cannstatt meadows *(Wasen)* from the end of April until the beginning of May. It also runs the better-known Cannstatt *Volksfest* for 16 days in September and October, which attracts about five million visitors every year. How it all got started can be found on page 75.

The Stuttgart Tourist Office does a superb job of making known what's available for your entertainment, but here are their address and phone number in case you need even further information:

Verkehrsamt der Landeshauptstadt Stuttgart
Lautenschlager Straße 3
7000 Stuttgart 1
Tel.: (0711) 299411

One final word: the guy who coined the phrase that a funeral in Munich is more exciting than *Fasching* in Stuttgart must have gotten embalmed at the wrong wake!

VII Swabian Landlords and Swabian Cleanliness

To a Swabian landlord the word *Hausordnung* or "house rules" has nothing to do with the stakes of the next Pinochle game, but everything to do with what you, as his tenant, must know about taking care of his property.

Kehrwoche or "it's-your-turn-to-clean-the-stairwell-this week" is a Swabian invention. Having examined a typical Swabian rental contract, the last two pages of which contain the "house rules," I now suspect that the so-called *Hausordnung* is also a Swabian invention.

Cleanliness is the very first topic of the copy I have at hand. I borrowed it from a Swabian stairwell. Paragraphs one and two of the bold words printed in boldfaced type read in part:

"Every tenant must keep his apartment, stairs, and landing clean and in order. Impurities arising from maintenance work in rooms, on windows and doors, are to be removed by the tenant."

Let's pause right there for a moment. I mentioned earlier that Swabian house-owners are constantly renovating and remodelling their *Häusle.* In some cases this is an obsession, and in some cases a welcome one. In some cases it is also quite necessary if the tenant who just moved out caused a lot of damage. In any event, the business about the tenant removing "impurities arising from maintenance work" means that *you* are responsible for cleaning up after the landlord makes a mess with wood-shavings, putty, paint, cement, wallpaper paste, etc. He likes to drill the holes and saw the wood, but not swing the broom, mop, or vacuum-cleaner hose.

"The inlaid floor," the *Hausordnung* continues, "just as all hardwood and pitchpine floors and the inlaid steps may neither be washed not oiled without the permission of the landlord, but must be waxed regularly, unless exceptions are granted in writing by the landlord. A thorough cleaning of the window shutters, roller blinds, and louvers must be carried out once a year."

I could quibble with the logic of applying wax to stairs that may not be washed without the landlord's permission. At least that doesn't hurt. Nasty falls on those waxed steps do!

Paragraph two of the *Hausordnung* provides the parameters for

Kehrwoche. It begins with a gargantuan sentence that's a bit long-winded for a Swabian, but it sweeps both sides of the gutter. It reads as follows:

"Cleaning the steps from the top story up to the loft, the landings of the same and of the common toilet, of the steps leading to the lower story and to the basement, the landing thereof, the polishing of the doorbells and of the main door lock, the sweeping of the court-yard, of the driveway and of the street, sufficient spreading /of salt or ice/ in the winter and the removal of snow and of ice in the winter, as well as the cleaning of commonly used equipment and containers alternate from week to week from household to household in continuous order so that on every Sunday morning the successor takes over."

To which I must hastily add that should a tenant, who takes over the *Kehrwoche* chores, actually attempt to carry them out on the holy Swabian Sunday, he's bound to collide head on with the landlord. The only exception I can envision would be a heavy snowfall or sheets of ice on the sidewalks and the driveway. Outside work is simply not tolerated by Swabians on Sundays, not even a silent polishing of the doorbells (they might ring by accident) and of the main dock lock (it might click too loudly).

"The cleaning of the streets and sidewalks will be done daily in accordance with the prevailing police regulations," the text continues. That's actually not as threatening as it sounds because it pertains to snow removal, which is prescribed by law. Failure to do so can result in fines.

The next sentence has a particularly Swabian touch: "The landlord is not obliged to provide cleaning equipment and strewing material."

The final requirement for a well-rounded *Kehrwoche* is a big gamble. Under normal circumstances, seeing the chimney sweep in Germany, or so the superstition goes, is supposed to bring you good luck. But if you're on the duty roster for *Kehrwoche,* he brings you bad luck. Whatever soot he leaves behind after cleaning the chimney of the house or apartment you live in, *you* are obliged to remove.

The third paragraph of my copy of a typical Swabian *Hausordnung* sounds somewhat anachronistic. It permits wood-chopping "only on a chopping block out in the yard or other place provided therefor."

We Americans have been known to do crazy things in German dwellings (in the eyes of our landlords), but chopping wood is a new one on me. However, the general tendency of the Swabian landlord not to heat his apartments at the temperature to which Americans are accustomed might have had some drastic results among those of my countrymen with fireplaces or wood stoves in their apartments. That same paragraph forbids the storing of wood that is suspected of having termites or heating ovens and stoves with fuel not specifically designed for them.

Paragraph four phrases its prohibitions so delightfully that I must give you the benefit of at least the first and the last sentence. It begins with the statement: "In the vestibules, stairwells, corridors, in the yard or in other areas used jointly, in or against the house, it is forbidden to place, lay or hang up anything, including motorcycles and carts." It ends with the remark: "Setting foot on or inspecting the roof is prohibited." If you happen to suffer from vertigo as much as I do, I doubt if the occasion to infringe that rule will ever present itself.

Paragraph four of my sample house rules contains an important message for American animal-lovers. The Swabian landlord, as well as German landlords in general, reserves the right to permit the keeping of pets in his apartments. According to the rules of the house at hand, *any* animal considered to be a pest to other tenants can be prohibited, even if the landlord himself has no objections.

The next paragraph deals with keeping the driveway free of dirt and debris, and especially with the beating of rugs, carpets, mattresses, etc. This is only permitted (should you care to do it at all) at the places prescribed by the landlord. The rules go on to comment: "Rug-beating and the use of electric vacuum-cleaners will be restricted to the hours between 0800–1100 and 1600–1800. Divergent hours established by the police will be respected."

My Swabian wife Margot seems to exceed the German norm when it comes to cleanliness. When we were first married, I used to help her with the dishes. She appreciated the gesture, but my cleanliness standards somehow fell short of hers. Not that I didn't get the dirt and grime and grease off the pots and pans. I just didn't get *the rest of the kitchen* spotless, as well. When it comes to using the vacuum-cleaner, she pays no attention to the house rules limiting the hours. She doesn't hesitate to vacuum the whole house on Sundays and holidays if there is a speck of dust around. And yet she complains when our American neighbors make noise on "days of rest." It's a dilemma, and I don't know how she squares it with her own conscience. All I know is that cleanliness takes priority. (I panic whenever the PX runs out of vacuum-cleaner bags!)

It's not by any philological or etymological error that the word *sauber* (clean) is the Swabian's utmost accolade. Nothing exceeds cleanliness!

Paragraph seven of the typical Swabian house rules pertains to the use of the laundry/dryer rooms in the basement. After a sentence pertaining to the sequence of use, a separate one (underlined in red on my copy) says that the laundry room will not be used on Sundays. A separate paragraph states that after every washing, the tenant will clean the laundry room, its windows, the equipment used for doing the laundry, and remove his or her own equipment.

The next paragraph announces that the apartment house will be closed at 2100 hours during the summer, at 1900 hours during the winter, and at 12 noon on Sundays and holidays. Those who come and go after those hours must "carefully lock the doors again." This is not only a matter of security, I found out in the course of time. It has to do with energy conservation. Leaving the stairwell door open or ajar in the winter creates a substantial loss of heat in the building. This same paragraph also talks about keys to doors and apartments, specifically restricting them to tenants. The Swabian landlord is concerned about his bills for utilities and water, particularly if the rental contract specifies a lump-sum payment *(Pauschale)*. He will not accept "American hospitality" as an excuse for your friends and relatives staying overnight, over the weekend, or for an indefinite period of time (no matter how brief). He worries about how many showers and baths they take, and how often they flush the toilet. (I had this spelled out to me in liters-per-flush by a Swabian landlord.) While on the subject of the toilet, it is customary not to flush it between the hours of nine at night and six the next morning in a Swabian apartment. (Baths or showers during these hours are also discouraged.) There's no meter to register this, so you're on the honor system and must train your kidneys to function accordingly.

Paragraphs 10 and 11 of my sample Swabian house rules explain what *not* to throw into the toilet: broken glass, garbage, wash water, and nonstandard toilet paper. (No corncobs, please!) If you should manage to stop up the toilet, or let the pipes freeze up in the winter, you get the repair bill. According to paragraph 12, if the sewage pipe or canalization gets stopped up, and the exact tenant or tenants at fault cannot be identified, then the repair costs are prorated among all tenants involved. The same goes for damages from freezing or ruptures of the pipeline. Paragraph 12 even holds the tenant responsible for the timely replacement of the rubber cushions on the inside of the toilet lid to prevent it from scratching the bowl with its screws. (I suspect this is also a matter of cleanliness as well as damage prevention.) Paragraph 13 is a warning that if the temperature sinks to four degrees Centigrade (39.2°F), the main waterline can be shut off from at least 1700 hours until 0900 the next morning. If the tenant has the shutoff valve in his apartment, he must perform this task or leave the keys with the landlord. Failure to do so makes him responsible for any damage to the pipeline that might result.

Paragraph 15 addresses noise annoyance. Tenants are permitted to sing or make music only from 0800 to 1200 and from 1400 to 2200 *with the windows shut,* and not at all if someone in the apartments is seriously ill. The same goes for radios and TV sets. Outside antennas can only be put up by technicians with the landlord's permission and must be removed if the landlord installs a house antenna. (Those of you economy dwellers who can get AFN TV only with the help of an extra antenna, please check with your landlord before you try to install it yourself.) Sewing machines must be placed upon soundproof padding in all apartments that have tenants living below them. All irritating noises, especially door-slamming and running up and down the stairwell are to be avoided in the interest of peace and quiet and mutual consideration.

The penultimate paragraph calls for good illumination of the entrance to the apartment and the stairwell from dusk until the main entrance is locked for the night. Unless already provided for by the landlord, this is the tenant's responsibility, including replacing lightbulbs at his own expense. If you think this is a Swabian touch, you're right, but even more so is the next sentence: "Rents will not be reduced" (for replacing lightbulbs).

Now you know what the Swabian means by *cleanliness,* and why the *Schwobs* got kicked out of Scotland.

VIII   (The) Swabian Language

> No matter how his mouth is squirmin'
> With the urge to speak High German;
> You hear it (even if he can)
> For blocks away – the Swabian.
>
> -Sebastian Blau

We Americans are known the world over for practicality, yet we do a lot of things the hard way. Learning (or not learning) foreign languages is one example, and I'm no exception.

I first began to study German back in 1943 at the Hill School in Pottstown, Pennsylvania. One foreign language was mandatory there, or you didn't graduate. Since everyone seemed to be taking Spanish, and since French irregular verbs seemed to defy retention, I signed up for German. (In view of World War II and the nature of the enemy in one theater of operations, I thought it might even come in handy.)

Had I known then that I would be spending half of my adult life in Germany, and more than half of that in Baden-Württemberg, I could have made things easier on myself by enrolling in elementary Swabian – had such a course existed.

It didn't then, it doesn't now, and chances are it never will become a three-credit course, much less an academic discipline.

Language teachers in American schools and colleges either discriminate against dialects in foreign languages, or don't wish to admit that they exist. Instead, they try to perpetuate 18th and 19th century "High" German, so that their students might someday be able to decipher German classics. How much more practical it would be to teach students how to read a menu (especially a Swabian menu)!

Which brings me to my main point: locally organized German-language instruction for Americans should begin with the local language, as it is spoken by the man on the street. Goethe and Schiller can come later.

The first two words you must learn and use whenever you greet a Swabian or enter a Swabian public establishment are: *"Grüß Gott."* The emphasis is on the first word. The expression translates as "Greet God," but just the opposite is intended. The original, much longer phrase expressed the sentiment: "May God greet you."

This Swabian greeting – not to be confused with "The Swabian Greeting" mentioned in chapter one – is the Swabian's way of saying "Good morning" or "Good day." It identifies the Swabian immediately when he is anywhere outside of Swabia. An anonymous non-Swabian made up an irreverent joke about the expression *"Grüß Gott"* by adding a frivolous aside: "In case you see Him."

The standard German suffix to indicate a smaller version of something (called a diminutive) is either *-chen* or *-lein*. The Swabian uses neither of these, but adds *-le* instead. (Thus *"Mädchen"* or "little maid, little girl" is *"Mädle"* and *"Häuschen"* or *"Häuslein"* is *"Häusle."*) The Swabian suffix can be added to any noun, whether the sense of "a smaller version" is intended or not. The great advantage to this for the nonnative speaker, apart from the simplicity, is that every time *-le* is tacked onto a word, that word becomes neuter, so you need only use *das* as the definite article to go with it.

It is even possible to say *"Grüß Gottle"* in Swabia without demeaning Our Savior or offending a Swabian.

When a Swabian says goodbye, he usually prefers the old Latin word *ade* (farewell) to *"Auf Wiedersehen."* You guessed it: he frequently says *"adele."*

One evening I came home from the office to find my wife Margot stooped over in the kitchen. Later on I found out that she was sweeping up with a small broom and a dustpan, but at the moment it wasn't evident because she had her back to me.

"Was machst du, Liebling?" I asked.

"A Häufle," she replied.

Translated literally that bit of dialogue comes out as:

"What are you making (doing), darling?"

"A little pile."

She couldn't understand why I thought that was so funny, and I didn't have the nerve to enlighten her.

So beloved is the addition of the suffix *-le* that it appears on the end of the conjunction *so* (same meaning as in English) and comes out as *"sodele,"* meaning a completed action – or one about to begin – which gives one satisfaction. It is also applied to the adverb *jetzt* (now), as *"jetzetle."*

Thaddäus Troll told the delightful anecdote of the Swabian

bridegroom who gets through his wedding day with only four words. When he accidently steps on the bride's foot, he says: *"Hoppla!"* At the altar he replies *"Jo,"* when asked if he will take this woman in marriage. At the wedding feast he rubs his hands when contemplating the food and drink and says: *"Sodele!"* And as he slips his suspenders off that night he says to his bride: *"Jetzetle!"*

As do all languages, Swabian, too, has its pitfalls. I recall the time Margot and I were mountain climbing in Austria and the ascent was slippery. *"Hier rutscht man gern,"* she said. To the non-Swabian that means: "Sliding here is fun." To the Swabian it means: "It's easy to slip here," implying a warning to watch your step, or you might break something. There's a world of difference (and a world of hurt) between the two.

And as in all languages, it is possible to carry on a seemingly complete conversation by interjecting pet Swabian words whenever the speaker pauses to catch his or her breath and gives you a chance to comment. As Häberle and Pfleiderer (see chapter five), Oskar Heiler und Willy Reichert could do this with extreme economy in their comedy:

Häberle: *"So, so."*
Pfleiderer: *"Ja, ja."*
Häberle: *"So, so."*
Pfleiderer: *"Ja, ja."*

"Hano" was one of Willy Reichert's favorite conversational space-fillers. Its precise meaning is hard to pin down, but the interjection can mean "oh, well," or "perhaps," or "you see," or express surprise or even anger. It is an offshoot of *"Ha, noi,"* meaning "now just wait a minute!" The Swabian says this excitedly when taking exception. *Noi* is Swabian for "no." During the Vietnam war a popular joke had it that *"Ha, noi"* was the capitol of Swabia, not Stuttgart.

The word "not" in Swabian has many varieties: *net, nidda, et, eta, it* or *ita.* "Nothing" is usually *nix.*

Thaddäus Troll quoted King William I of Württemberg as having said: "The first two words my subjects learn are: *Noi, eta."*

Swabian grammar is simpler than standard or so-called "High" German. The *Schwob* disregards the final *-n* or all infinitives and the *ge-* prefix on past participles. The word for "I" is not the *"Ich"* Americans find so hard to pronounce, but simply *"E."* The word for me is *"mi."* The word for "we" is *"mir"* (which means "me" in High German.) The relative pronoun is not *der, die, das, derjenige, diejenige, dasjenige,* or *welcher, welche, welches,* all of which are used in standard German, but simply *wo* (which normally means "where.") Consequently, you will hear Swabians saying *"die Leute, wo . . ."* ("people, who . . .") and that just drives language purists up the proverbial language barrier. The *Schwob* says *"mo"* for *"wo"* as an interrogative.

The Swabian word for "five" and "my" sound almost the same as English. The old Middle High German from *han* survives as the verb "to have," and the *Schwob* says simply *lo-ah* for *lassen* (to let, allow, permit, or have done by someone else.)

Let me conjugate the verb *gehen* (to go) in High German and in Swabian to illustrate how much Swabian deviates in form and sound from High German and how simpler its forms are, at least in the plural:

High German	English	Swabian
ich gehe	I go	*e gang*
du gehst	you go	*du gaschst*
er geht	he goes	*er gaht*
wir gehen	we go	*mir ganget*
ihr geht	you go	*ihr ganget*
sie gehen	they go	*sie ganget*

The difference in sound between standard German and Swabian is most evident when one asks the question, "where are you going?" in High German: *"Wohin gehst du?"* or *"Wo gehst du hin?"* and then in Swabian: *"Mo gasch noh?"*

The expression *"weißt du"* ("you know") is as overworked in German as it is in English. The Swabian has his own version for this. He says *woischt,* a juicy contraction. If you chance to hear it in a conversation, you now know that the subject is *not* sausage. The Swabian language is known for its economy of expression. Some examples follow below:

High German	Swabian	English
Was ist denn?	*Waschisch'n?*	What's up?
Wo bist du?	*Mo bisch'n?*	Where are you?
Was hast du gesehen?	*Wa hösch gsä?*	What did you see?
Was willst du?	*Wa witt?*	What do you want?

42

A supreme example of economy in the Swabian linguistic formula is shown by what it takes to say "in case they have them in stock" in High German: *"falls sie welche vorrätig haben sollten"* versus the Swabian: *"wenn sie hent."*

Other slight but notable deviations from standard German are the Swabian idiom *es hat* instead of *es gibt* (there is/there are), and *verzähle* for *erzählen* (to say or tell).

If there is an *Umlaut* on a verb in the third person singular, the *Schwob* will ignore it. He says *es lauft* instead of *es läuft* for "it runs." The standard German imperative for "eat!" is *iss!* but the Swabian insists on saying *ess!* I find it amusing when my wife commands our daughter Miriam to *"ess voll leer"* her dinner because it sounds like a contradiction, or at least Pennsylvania Dutch in translation ("eat full empty"). The intended meaning, of course, is "eat completely," i.e. all of it.

And speaking of eating, the *Schwob* has only one verb for both tasting and smelling, *schmegga* (High German: *schmecken).* (He smells with both nose and tongue.) So those foreigners who "tasted" their way into Swabian culture, the *Rei'geschmeckte,* might actually have "sniffed" their way in!

Sometimes a High German word does not have the same meaning in Swabian. The word *bereits* means "already" in High German but to the Swabian it means "almost." High German *wirklich* (really, actually) means "at the moment" in Swabian. So if a Swabian couple assures you that *"mir sen wirklich zfriida" (Wir sind wirklich zufrieden* in High German), they are saying they are content *at the moment,* that is, just temporarily.

Because of the many times French troops swept through Württemberg and due to Swabia's possession of the *Grafschaft* Mömpelgard (Montbéliard) for 400 years, considerable French survives in the Swabian language, although often in a bastardized form. (The Swabians have fractured French, just as the Americans impose their own pronunciation on German). A high frequency Swabian expression for "shut your trap" is *"Halt dei Gosch!"* The word *Gosch* comes from *bouche,* the French word for "mouth." You will never hear a *Schwob* call the sidewalk a *Bürgersteig.* He uses the French *trottoir,* which he pronounces *Troddwar.* He calls his ground floor *Padäär,* from the French *parterre,* his basement the *Sudderai',* from the

French *souterrain,* his garage a *Karrasch,* from the French *garage,* his curtains *Rulloo,* from the French *rouleau,* and his shutters *Schalluu,* from the French *jaloux.* His feather bed is a *Plimoo,* from the French *plumeau,* and his chamber pot a *Botschamberle,* a fancier word for what he also calls a *Häfele.*

A more complete list appears below:

Swabian	French	English
badda/baddera	*battre*	hit, strike
barduu	*partout*	in any case
bassleda	*passe-le-temps*	pastime
Bossè	*botte*	high-lows (boots)
buddl	*bouteille*	bottle
Dääz	*tête*	head
dusma'	*doucement*	quietly, softly
duuschuur	*toujours*	all at once
eschtimiere	*estimer*	regard
Fissaasch	*visage*	derogatory for face, e.g. yap, trap, puss, etc.
fra'schama'sch	*franchement*	frank, outspoken
Güh	*goût*	chimera, bugs
Gugommer	*concombre*	cucumber
Kelleretle	*quelle heure est-il?*	watch
leschär	*léger*	informal, relaxed
Malär	*malheur*	misfortune
Patäterle	*peut-être*	lighter
pressiira	*presser*	to be in a hurry
probber	*propre*	clean, proper
Ragall	*racaille*	an evil woman
schassa	*chasser*	chase away, run off
Schüh	*jus*	juice, sauce
Schwittjeh	*suite, suitier*	windbag
wiif	*vif*	vivacious

Joachim Kannicht, Editor-in-Chief of the *Fellbacher Zeitung* and a close friend of many years standing, recently sent me a delightful article he published on 20 February 1980. In it he describes many words with English cognates found exclusively in the Swabian dialect: *afterle* (after), *Dubbel* (dub), *Ruschler* (a rusher), *natappe* (tap), *drivellieren* (drivel), *stiere* (stir), *Wette* = (a damp meadow) (wet), *Gog* (gag, gawk). *Gog* (see page 20) is pronounced "gawk," to which it may be related.

IX   Swabian Characteristics

The Swabian, like the Yankee, has a mind of his own and, like the Yankee, can often be stubborn about it.

You will often hear the *Schwob* render a dissenting opinion by saying: *"Dò sen mir oiga,"* meaning "we have our own way of looking at things." The German word *eigen,* which the Swabian pronounces as *oiga,* has many meanings, including "own" (with respect to ownership or possession), "individual" or "special," "delicate" or "ticklish" (with respect to questions), but also "fastidious," "particular," "squeamish," "choosey," and "finicky" (pertaining to taste), but "queer," "strange," "funny" (peculiar), and "odd" (with respect to persons and things). *All* of these definitions could well apply when the Swabian says *oiga,* depending entirely upon the circumstances and the occasion.

Now, if you take the German word for "mind" or "sense" *(Sinn),* or for "contemplative" or "thoughtful" *(sinnig),* and combine them with *eigen,* you have a characteristic for which the Swabians are very famous:

Eigensinn is a noun meaning obstinacy, stubbornness, or wilfulness.

eigensinnig is an adjective or an adverb meaning headstrong, bullheaded, stubborn, or unreasonable.

Just think of all the Swabians who spent time in prison for their stubborn opposition to Dukes, Kings, and Nazis!

The true *Schwob* is also well known for the firmness of his will *(Zähigkeit des Willens),* which is sometimes a nicer way of expressing stubbornness. But he is equally noted for his dogged persistence, his steadfast stick-to-it-tiveness *(Beharrlichkeit),* especially in saving money to build *Häusle.* And just think of Arnulf Klett rolling up his sleeves to rebuild Stuttgart after World War II, and Manfred Rommel forging ahead with the rapid transit system!

The Swabian is noted for his explosive temper and rash anger *(Jähzorn),* but he is quick to forgive *(versöhnlich)* and does not bear a grudge *(nicht nachtragend).* Some Swabians have been accused of lacking any sense of proportion in either being good or evil, but those are exceptional cases. Perhaps Duke Eberhard Ludwig, the builder of Ludwigsburg castle, and Duke Karl Eugen might have qualified for those doubtful honors.

The Swabian is physically courageous and not afraid to speak his own mind *(sei Sach' uffrichtig und gradraus sage)*. The names of Bolz, Elser, Scholl, Stauffenberg, and Rommel come readily to mind.

The Swabian has been called *"knitz und derb, aber immer voll menschlicher Wärme."* The word *knitz* literally means "of no use" or "worthless." But the *Schwob* uses it in the sense of "cunning," "sly," or "subtle," which is why Hermann Freudenberger chose it as both his title and by-line for his satirical column in the daily newspaper *Stuttgarter Nachrichten. Derb* means "coarse," as I have fully amplified in chapters one and five. "But always full of human warmth" is self-explanatory.

Although the Swabian has often been called light-hearted and cheerful by nature *(Heiterkeit des Wesens),* he can also lapse occasionally into deep introspection, like Schelling, Hegel, and Hermann Hesse, or profound melancholy, like Friedrich Hölderlin.

I have mentioned often enough the Swabian's reticent reserve, his tight-lipped (and tight-fisted) closeness. For this reason he is frequently accused of being *bhäb,* which means hanging on to your valuables to the point of avarice, and also having a closed mind. These characteristics go hand-in-hand, but enough said on that subject!

I remembered having seen a postcard in a Stuttgart souvenir shop with a poem on it called *The Song of the Swabians,* when I started to write this book. Not having one handy, I asked my father-in-law if he had a copy. Eager to oblige (which is also a fine Swabian characteristic), he lent me a song book arranged for the harmonica. It contains a dozen traditional Swabian folksongs, such as *"Muß i denn zum Städtele naus"* (later made famous by Elvis Presley), *"Auf de schwäbsche Eisebahne," "jetzt gang i ans Brünnele," "Hopsa, Schwabenliesel," "Wo e kleins Hüttle steht,"* and Friedrich Silcher's *"Morgen muß ich fort von hier."* But no *Das Lied der Schwaben.* I suspect that this anonymous "Song of the Swabians" is strictly for tourists and *Rei'geschmeckte,* but since it kind of sums up all the attributes for which the *Schwobs* are allegedly famous, I have translated it for you to the best of my ability in verse. (I finally bought it on a postcard at the Stuttgart railroad station.)

LIED DER SCHWABEN
Kennst Du das Land wo jeder lacht,
wo man aus Leber Spätzle macht,
wo jeder zweite Fritzle heißt,
wo man noch über Balken scheißt,
wo jede Bank ein Bänkle ist
und jeder Zug ein Zügle,
wo man den Zwiebelkuchen frißt
und Moscht sauft aus dem Krügle,
wo „daube Sau", „Leck mich am Arsch"
in keinem Satz darf fehlen,
wo sich die Menschen pausenlos
mit ihrer Arbeit quälen,
wo jeder auf sein Häusle spart
hat er auch nichts zu kauen
und wenn er 40, 50 ist,
dann fängt er an zu bauen!
Doch wenn er endlich fertig ist
schnappt ihm das Arschloch zu!
O Schwabenland, gelobtes Land
wie wunderbar bist Du.

THE SONG OF THE SWABIANS
Do you know the land where laughter reigns
Where *Spätzle* are made of liver and no one complains
Where Fritzle is the name for kids that fits
Where logs are still used for taking shits
Where *Bänkle* is the word for bench
And every train a *Zügle*
Where onion cake gives off a stench
And cider comes in *Krügle*
Where "stupid sow" and "kiss my ass"
Are said with every breath
Where every single soul, alas,
Just works himself to death.
The *Schwob* will pinch the Pfennigs hard
And starve just to be thrifty
To build a small house in his yard

But break the ground at fifty.
The job once done, he rests his hand
His asshole closes tight
O Swabia, the Promised Land
You're really out of sight.

In a speech about Swabian characteristics, Lord Mayor Manfred Rommel told an American audience in the Nellingen Officers' Club about the tight-fisted *Schwob* who died without having made any arrangements for his funeral. He was automatically cremated and the ashes given to the widow. She took them home in a Mason jar, and there was a gathering of the clan to decide how best to dispose of them.

In the middle of the lively discussion, the widow suddenly spoke up: "I've got it! I'll put his ashes in the egg-timer and keep him working."

I have a similar story that proves that Swabian economy and the Swabian work ethic are matched by American Yankees.

An old Yankee fisherman was informed by the Coast Guard that the body of his mother-in-law had been found floating in the bay with a five-pound lobster firmly attached to each of her big toes.

"What shall we do with the body?" the caller from the Coast Guard inquired.

The thrifty old Down Easter replied, "Put the lobsters in my trap, and set the old girl out again."

Photo on the right:
The Schiller monument by Bertel Thorwaldsen on Schiller Square in Stuttgart. In the background the tower of the Stiftskirche.

X Highlights of Swabian History (I)

In the sacristy of the Stiftskirche on Schiller Platz in downtown Stuttgart, you can buy a beautiful chart of the rulers of Württemberg for DM 1.50. Sixteen of them, starting with Ulrich I, who died in 1265, lie in the vault of that church. When Duke Eberhard Ludwig died in 1677, he was the first of several sovereigns to be entombed at Ludwigsburg Castle, which he originally planned as a modest hunting lodge.

Swabian history is a lot older than the first of the Württemberg rulers. One could start with the jaw of the Heidelberg man, but that would take us back 600,000 years or more. Let's skip over the stone age and the bronze age, and pause just for a moment in the iron age, when the Celts were living in this area.

Quite recently the grave of a Celtic prince was found at Hochdorf, which is about ten kilometers southwest of Ludwigsburg. When I visited the site – a large circular mound – Dr. Biel and his team of archeologists were sorting the artifacts they had unearthed, including parts of a bronze bier on which the prince had lain. When he handed me a small, decorative figurine with raised arms and a wheel between her feet, I asked him how old it was.

"About 550 BC," he replied.

For me, holding that small piece of metal for a few moments was a greater thrill than being catapulted off an aircraft carrier.

Around 500 BC Germanic tribes began to push the Celts into the foothills of the Alps. Julius Caesar (100-44 BC) fought against Ariovistus and his powerful Suevians for possession of Gaul. The Suevians were absorbed by the Alemanni, but the name "Swabian" survived.

In 496 Clovis, the king of the Franks, defeated the Alemanni and absorbed the northern half of their territory. The southern half was ruled by Theoderic the Great (493-526).

In 751 Pepin became king of the Franks. Only five years earlier his brother Carloman had marched into Cannstatt and slaughtered the best of the Alemannic leaders. Pepin's son Charlemagne, who was crowned by Pope Leo III on Christmas Day of the year 800, united the greater part of western Europe into the Carolingian Empire. As this empire gradually disintegrated during the latter half of the 9th century, the dukes of Swabia began to assert their independence.

The German emperors of the Saxonian dynasty (919–1024) continued the attempt to form a Christian-Germanic empire. They permitted the Swabian dukes to rule that duchy with little interference.

But under the first of the Salic-Frankish emperors, Conrad II, ambitious Duke Ernst II of Swabia tried to lay claim to Burgandy. In the year 1030 he lost both his duchy and his life in a battle with Conrad.

Emperor Heinrich IV gave the duchy of Swabia to his son-in-law, Friedrich I of Hohenstaufen, in 1079. The German nobles elected Duke Philipp of Swabia, the younger son of Friedrich Barbarossa, their emperor in 1198, but he was assassinated in 1208. In 1209 Esslingen became an "Imperial City" *(Reichsstadt)*.

Count Ulrich – whose fortified castle "Wirtemberg" was located near Cannstatt – and most of the Swabian knights opposed the Hohenstaufen rule. Called "Ulrich with the Thumb" (no one knows why), he was the founder of the Württemberg dynasty. He was probably the one who fortified Stuttgart in 1238. (The name Stuttgart has been traced to the stud farm or *"Stutengarten,"* which was started by Duke Liudolf of Swabia during his reign from 948 to 954. Stuttgart is first mentioned in a document from the year 1229.)

When Conradin, the last of the Hohenstaufens, was executed in Naples in 1268, the duchy of Swabia ceased to exist under that name. Its territory was divided up among other nobles. The most influential was Count Rudolf of Hapsburg, who became king of the "Holy Roman Empire of the German Nation" in 1273. He tried to increase his power and wealth by peaceful means and came often to the Swabian imperial cities of Ulm, Heilbronn, and Esslingen.

King Rudolf ran into stubborn resistance from Count Eberhard I of Württemberg and his brother, Count Ulrich II. Open warfare broke out in 1285 between the followers of the king and those of the Württemberg counts. In the fall of 1286 the king's forces attacked Stuttgart, which was Eberhard's main garrison. The siege lasted seven weeks and ended in a draw. In an attempt to restore the duchy of Swabia, King Rudolf went to war once more against Count Eberhard and won, but he was unable to force his will upon the stubborn Swabian. Eberhard outlived the king. When he died at age 60 in 1325, his *Grafschaft* (county) of Württemberg within the former duchy of Swabia was twice the size of what he had inherited from his father, Ulrich I.

Emperor Maximilian I elevated the *Grafschaft* of Württemberg to a duchy in 1495 and its Count Eberhard to a duke. Eberhard V is not only remembered for his funny nickname "In the Beard," but as the founder of the University of Tübingen in 1477. Johannes Reuchlin, the Swabian humanist and opponent of Martin Luther's Reformation, was a professor of Greek and Hebrew at Tübingen University from 1521 to 1522. He was an adviser to Duke Eberhard V and to Duke Ulrich, whose adventurous life would make a great movie.

Emperor Maximilian gave Ulrich permission to rule Württemberg at age 12. Engaged at that tender age to Maximilian's niece Sabine, he enjoyed the Emperor's favor. On 8 February 1511, at age 25, he married Sabine of Bavaria. The festivities lasted a full week.

Four years later Sabine fled in fear of her life to her brothers Wilhelm and Ludwig, the dukes of Bavaria. Her brief marriage had been an unhappy one. Ulrich had fallen in love with the wife of his friend and stallmaster, Hans von Hutten, whom he murdered in the Schönbuch forest near Tübingen. His controversy with the Swabian League, an alliance of independent cities founded in 1331 for mutual protection, led to his expulsion from his duchy in 1519.

For the next 14 years Württemberg was ruled by Hapsburgs. In 1534, with the help of Count Philipp of Hesse, Duke Ulrich regained his territory, but on Austrian terms.

Ulrich died on 6 November 1550 and was interred in the vault of the Stiftskirche in Tübingen. His son Christoph brought his mother back to Württemberg. She lived out her life in Nürtingen.

At age 18 Duke Christoph had demanded in writing the return of his inheritance from the Hapsburgs. King Ferdinand, brother of Emperor Karl V, offered him some land far from Swabia, but he refused. The case was referred to the Imperial High Court of Justice in Speyer.

Emperor Karl V wanted to make his son, Prince Philipp of Spain, the ruler in Germany, but Ferdinand and the German lords put up stiff opposition to this plan. By siding with the Emperor, whom he feared less than Ferdinand, Duke Christoph got back Mömpelgard county and had Spanish soldiers removed from Asperg fortress. A shrewd diplomat and a good administrator, Christoph was successful in the expansion of the Protestant Church, the development of the school system, and the promotion of craftsmanship (for which Swabia is still famous). He was a man of peace who went to war only twice to defend his rights in an age when swords hung loose in scabbards. He died in 1568. His statue is on the Schloß Platz of downtown Stuttgart. (He also remodeled the old Stuttgart Castle in 1558.)

Christoph died from too much food and drink. He was so fat in his last years that he could no longer ride a horse. He had eight daughters and two sons, the elder of whom also died in 1568 of dissolute living. The second son Ludwig succeeded Christoph but took little interest in government. While his advisers conducted the affairs of state, he devoted his time to art and architecture.

Count Friedrich of Württemberg-Mömpelgard succeeded Duke Ludwig in 1593. An absolute monarch ahead of his time, he was determined to strengthen the position of German prices against all internal and external enemies. His chief adviser was Privy Councillor Matthäus Enzlin, a brilliant lawyer who held the chair for Roman Law at Tübingen University. But in his eagerness to consolidate his power, expand his realm, and make the economy sounder, many of Friedrich's plans aborted. But he did succeed in establishing Württemberg's first industry: linen weaving in Urach.

Friedrich died on 29 January 1608. His son and successor, Duke Johann Friedrich, was a weak man with excellent advisers whose advice he did not put to good use. What his father had tried to accomplish with ruthlessness, Johann Friedrich tried to achieve through goodness. His father's old enemies, whom Friedrich had dismissed from parliament, returned and sought revenge. Privy Councillor Enzlin was accused of treason, brought to trial, and finally beheaded in Urach.

At the outbreak of the Thirty Years' War in 1618, Duke Johann Friedrich tried to keep Württemberg in a state of armed neutrality. When his unpaid mercenaries saw troops of other nations plundering, they did the same. The Duke's advisors insisted that the soldiers be discharged. He did so, and they sarcastically dubbed him the "Peaceable."

When Duke Johann Friedrich of Württemberg died in 1628, his eldest son Eberhard was only fourteen years old. Duke Ludwig Friedrich, brother of Duke Johann Friedrich, served as regent until his own death in January 1631. His younger brother Julius Friedrich reluctantly succeeded him. While spending most of his time hunting in the Black Forest, he tried to steer a middle course between the warring factions: King Gustavus Adolphus of Sweden and Emperor Ferdinand. He finally decided to side with the Swedes. Thousands of Württemberg peasants lost their lives when the soldiers of the Emperor and the Bavarians defeated the Swedes at Nördlingen on 6 September 1634, a black day for the German Protestant cause.

Duke Eberhard III succeeded Julius Friedrich in May 1633. The first year of his rule was full of promise. After the defeat at Nördlingen, however, he fled to Straßburg with his mother and spent the next four years there. Upon his return he found devastation in his cities and extreme privation among the people. Of the 450,000 residents of Württemberg at the start of the war, only 60,000 survived.

Four years of peace negotiations were held separately in the Westphalian cities of Münster and Osnabrück. The Emperor met with the French delegation in Münster, where Privy Councillor Johann Konrad Varnbüler represented Württemberg, and with the Swedish delegation in Osnabrück, where Chancellor Andreas Burkard sat in for Duke Eberhard. At the Westphalian peace conference, each of the almost 300 petty principalities of the German "empire" *(Reich)* was represented.It was the task of the Württemberg delegation to guarantee the "restitution" of the duchy and to preserve the Protestant religion. On paper they were successful, but the "restitution" meant accepting the old boundaries of 1624.

On October 24, 1648, the Thirty Years' War ended with the signing of the treaty of Westphalia, the last to be written in Latin. Historians have called that war completely senseless. Fifty percent of the German population lost their lives. Calw, Giengen and Waiblingen were burned down. As late as 1652 one-third of Württemberg's farmland and vineyards were still destroyed. Despite severe human and material losses, the Swabians went right back to work in 1648 – just as they were to do again in 1945 – to rebuild out of the ruins.

Duke Eberhard III steered the political course of Württemberg for forty years. Although not a great ruler, he did have some noteworthy leadership qualities. In his will of 1653 he asserted once more the indivisiblity of his duchy. He had sired 25 children in two marriages. Eight sons and six daughters survived him when he died in 1674.

Eberhard's son and successor, Wilhelm Ludwig, managed to stay out of the conflict between King Louis XIV of France and William III of Orange, but his reign was short-lived. He died of a stroke at age 30 in 1677.

Friedrich Karl ruled from 1677 to 1693 as a guardian Duke-Administrator for Eberhard Ludwig, son of Wilhelm Ludwig, who was not yet of age when his father died. Well-educated and with a sense of responsibility, he set about his tasks. He was the founder of Stuttgart's first secondary school (although it was named after Duke Eberhard Ludwig in 1881).

King Louis XIV of France occupied Straßburg in 1681, then Holland, Luxembourg, and Trier two years later. Although the defenseless German empire signed a twenty-year armistice with France, Louis XIV had his General Mélac occupy the Rhineland. By the fall of 1688 his soldiers reached Württemberg.

When General Mélac's troops marched into the Rems valley, the brave women of Schorndorf threatened to beat up Commandant Peter Krumherr if he dared to open the gates of the fortified city. He didn't. The French bypassed Schorndorf and headed for Stuttgart, where they encountered the troops of Prince Ludwig of Württemberg, Friedrich Karl's younger brother. The French retreated through the Black Forest.

In February 1689 the German Empire finally declared war on France. Württemberg was in danger when the French devastated the Palatinate in the spring of that year and burned down the Heidelberg Castle. Relief finally came when the Imperial Army *(Reichsheer)* stopped the French at Mainz.

In the years that followed, with the help of the Emperor, Friedrich Karl mobilized a standing army and joined the so-called "Grande Alliance" with Austria, England, Holland, Savoy and Brandenburg. He had a cavalry command in the Imperial Army in the campaign against France in 1692. Underestimating the strength of the enemy, he was taken prisoner on 27 September. Released a few months later, he was promoted to Field Marshal by the Emperor. He died in 1698 at the age of 46 and was the *last* of the Württemberg dukes to be interred in the Stiftskirche in Stuttgart.

But Friedrich Karl was the *first* of the Württemberg dukes to have his portrait painted as a "grand seigneur" in the new, more worldly Baroque style. As an art form, Baroque had its origins in Rome, but it soon reflected the elegance, the "I am the State" absolutism, and the frivolity of "Sun King" Louis XIV (1643-1715) and his French court.

The time has come to pause in this outline of Swabian history for a look at Swabian Baroque art and architecture, which you can enjoy today in your explorations of beautiful Baden-Württemberg.

XI   Swabian Baroque

Ludwigsburg Castle, the brainchild of Duke Eberhard Ludwig of Württemberg, gave birth to an entire city.

It all began as a plan to reconstruct a small hunting lodge called the Erlachhof, which French soldiers had destroyed in 1693. Around 1697 Duke Eberhard sent his official builder, Philipp Joseph Jenisch, around the countryside to learn more about architecture. When Jenisch returned in 1703, the Duke ordered him to design a new hunting lodge to replace the Erlachhof. On 7 May 1704 Duke Eberhard Ludwig laid the cornerstone of the so-called *Fürstenbau* ("edifice of the sovereign prince") and went off to do battle as a cavalry general against the French and the Bavarians at Höchstädt.

When the Duke returned, he found a palace emerging in the style of the Renaissance. Having seen Baroque architecture in Austria and the Baroque buildings of his arch-enemy, King Louis XIV, in France – such as befitted an absolute monarch – he replaced Jenisch with a captain of the engineers named Johann Friedrich Nette, who specialized in Baroque design.

It is hard to tell whether Nette or the Duke himself decided to expand those plans into what ultimately became the largest Baroque castle in Germany, but that's what happened. When Nette died in 1714, his work was continued by Donato Giuseppe Frisoni and Paolo Retti. Those imaginative Italians quadrupled the dimensions of the castle complex.

In order to encourage the development of a town around the castle, which the Duke had been calling "Ludwigsburg" since 11 May 1705, he issued a decree in August 1709 offering free land, free building material, and freedom from taxes for 15 years to new settlers. By March of the following year only 21 people had taken him up on the offer. But after he promised to move from the old castle in Stuttgart and take up permanent residence at Ludwigsburg, the settlers began to arrive. By 1717 Ludwigsburg had 18 houses and 260 residents; by 1732 the population had reached 5,000.

Ludwigsburg castle was finished in 1733, the year of the Duke's death. Almost 30 years in the making, it finally consisted of an architecturally integrated complex of 18 buildings grouped around three courtyards, for a total of 452 rooms.

Schloß Ludwigsburg

On the tour in English or in German you don't get to see *all* those rooms (most of which are furnished, by the way). Rest and be thankful. After two hours of examining about 50, you just can't absorb any more Baroque splendor. Save some of your gazing power for the amazing illusion – for which Baroque art is famous – created by Pietro Scotti and Giuseppe Baroffino on the ceiling of the festival hall *(Ordensaal)*. This room is used today for state occasions and for the annual Ludwigsburg music festival. It was here that Württemberg's first constitution was adopted in 1819. The little theater in the castle, redecorated in 1810, contains the world's first revolving stage. The original machinery that turns it still works.

The annual garden show, called "Blooming Baroque," was begun in 1954 to mark the 250th anniversary of the castle. From April through October thousands of flowers are in bloom. Glorious fireworks crown the annual lantern festival as the high point of the floral exhibition. A special treat for young and old alike is the fairy tale garden with sound effects. Kids can shout at fairy tale figures and get replies and watch the dance of the red shoes. An expensive treat is surrendering to the overwhelming impulse to buy Ludwigsburg porcelain manufactured, hand-painted from original designs, and sold at the castle. (Duke Karl Eugen started the business on 5 April 1758.)

As if the Ludwigsburg castle weren't quite enough to gratify and mirror his sense of absolutism, Duke Eberhard Ludwig had Nette, Frisoni and Retti design and build a pleasure palace called "Favorite" between 1715 and 1723. It lies within a forest due north of the castle's main axis. The Duke spent several summers there.

Today it houses the State Office for Nature Protection and Landscape Cultivation.

The city hall *(Rathaus)* in Schwäbisch Hall is a fine example of secular, late Baroque architecture. After a disastrous fire in 1728, the city council had Johann Ulrich Heim, a master builder from Stuttgart, design a new city. Together with his nephew, Eberhard Friedrich Heim, he planned and built the city hall between 1732 and 1735. It burned out during World War II in 1945 but was restored to its original condition.

When Duke Eberhard Ludwig moved his court from Stuttgart to Ludwigsburg, he promised to make the latter his permanent residence. (He was the first of the Württemberg dukes to be interred there.) But Duke Karl Alexander, his successor for less than four years, moved the court right back to Stuttgart and reconditioned the old castle – which was fortunate for Stuttgart. When his eldest son, Karl Eugen, although not quite 16 years old, was declared of age by the Emperor in 1744 and capable of ruling, the people of Stuttgart were worried that he might move back to Ludwigsburg. He promised not to, but only in exchange for a new residence in the style to which he was accustomed. In plain German that meant: "Build me a new one!" He hoped to erect a palace larger than the Ludwigsburg castle, but agreed in the end to the dimensions that the so-called *Neues Schloß* (new castle) has today. Leopold Retti developed the initial plans and construction began in 1746. Philippe de la Guêpière, a French architect, added the finishing touches. The castle is a wonderful example of the transition from the architectural style of late Rococo to early Classicism. Only its external walls survived the air raids of World War II. It was rebuilt and houses today the State Ministry of Finance in the north wing and the State Ministry for Culture and Sport in the south wing. The central portion is used for official state receptions and dinners. (That's where Queen Elisabeth II of England consumed "Mouth Pockets" while the rest of the guests ate "Snout Pockets," if you recall my anecdote from chapter four.)

One of Duke Karl Eugen's final Baroque thoughts (before turning to the classical style of Hohenheim castle) was the "Solitude" pleasure palace between Botnang and Gerlingen, due west of Stuttgart. Its magnificent view of the surrounding countryside is still unbroken by other buildings. It was built between 1764 and 1767 with the Duke's own plans. Philippe de la Guêpière designed the interior.

The term Baroque originally had a derogatory meaning. The Italian word *baroco* meant an obstacle to logical thought for medieval philosophers and was eventually used to describe any contorted idea. The Spanish word *barrueco* (Portuguese *barroco)* means an imperfectly shaped pearl. As a term pertaining to art Baroque means that the artist, sculptor, or architect did his own thing without any restraints on the imagination. Since Baroque is used loosely to describe the art and architecture of the 17th and 18th centuries, art historians distinguish between Early, High, and Late Baroque (or Rococo) for greater precision.

The progress of the Baroque style differed in tempo and form in Italy, Austria, Switzerland, Bohemia, and in southern Germany's Bavaria, Swabia, and Franconia. Most active in Swabia were the artistic members of the Beer, Thumb and Moosbrugger families who worked so closely together that it is often difficult to determine who did precisely what in carrying out the commissions they received from the Benedictine and Premonstratensian abbots. The architects in these families developed a church design with a longitudinal axis or nave with a narrower choir housing the main altar. The main arches of the nave usually reached up to the vault and were often divided halfway up by deep galleries. Twin towers usually decorated the exterior.

In 1684 Caspar Moosbrugger was consulted on the reconstruction of the abbey church at Weingarten. Many other architects, such as Michael Thumb, Enrico Zucalli, Franz Beer, Johann Jakob Herkommer, Donato Giuseppe Frisoni, and Andreas Schreck, eventually had a hand in the planning. Its simplicity and grandeur is the hallmark of Swabian High Baroque. Built between 1715 and 1724, it has the external dimensions of a cathedral (over 100 meters in length) and is the largest church in southern Germany. The interior is completely white up to the beginning of the arcades and arches, then comes the stucco work of Franz Schmuzer of Wessobrunn, crowned by the illusionistic frescoes of the young Cosmas Damian Asam. Frisoni did the monumental main altar, Johann Anton Feuchtmayer the choir stalls, and Fidelis Sporer the pulpit (in 1765 as a late addition). The altar in the transept under the main dome houses the relic of the Holy Blood donated around 1090 by Judith of Flanders, when the abbey was founded by the Guelphs. Every year in honor of the Holy Blood, a procession on horseback, called the "Blood Ride," is held at the Weingarten cathedral.

The pilgrimage church of Our Lady of Sorrows at Steinhausen (southwest of Biberach) has been called "the most beautiful village church in the world." It was built from 1727 to 1735 by Dominikus Zimmermann for the Premonstratensian Brothers of the abbey of Schussenried. The stucco work was done by Dominikus and his brother Johann Baptist, who painted the fresco over the nave depicting the Four Corners of the Earth paying homage to the Virgin Mary as Queen of Heaven. She is surrounded by saints and angels in the clouds. Groups of figures symbolizing the Four Corners of the Earth stand on the bottom edge of the fresco in a landscape that extends around the vault. Adam and Eve in the Garden of Eden and the Fountain of Life are at opposite ends of the painting. This was one of the first of Johann Baptist Zimmermann's major frescoes after he had taken up painting at age fifty. His brother deliberately put windows in the vaulting over the choir to permit more light into the church. (Baroque churches have plain, not stained-glass windows.)

The Zimmermann brothers were great believers in a maximum use of bright light. The interior of the church is finished in white with some touches of orange, pink, and green. Nicolas Powell writes in his *From Baroque to Rococo:* "This delicate and tender church is the first full manisfestation of Rococo, a building in which the elements of design and decoration, fresco and stucco are indivisible."

The design of the church is deceptive. The outside is squared off with a tower on the western end and a gabled roof. Once inside the pilgrim discovers an oval interior with two side altars flanking the main altar inside the choir. The gables serve no structural purpose at all, except to admit light through their windows. The dark green and red side altars, the main altar, and the pulpit - all by Joachim Früholzer – strike a somber note in this otherwise bright and cheerful church.

The Zimmermanns express great joy in nature and life itself with the abundance of flowers and little animals of all kinds in the stucco work of the upper windows. They are best known to Americans, perhaps, for their magnificent church of Die Wies (where Dominikus Zimmermann died in 1766) in Bavaria northeast of Neuschwanstein off route 17.

Between 1736 and 1741 Dominikus Zimmermann built the Church of Our Lady in Günzburg (northeast of Ulm on route 16, Autobahn exit Günzburg). The vault is considerably higher than at Steinhausen and the Wies. The narrow choir at the eastern end is similar to the Wies and has a balustraded gallery with its own altar. The nave forms a simple rectangle with round, flowing lines interrupted by altars at the east corners and the bow of the west gallery. Brightly colored crowns embellish the capitals. Rococo decoration covers the vault and frames the fresco depicting the crowning of the Virgin Mary.

From 1754 to 1761 Dominikus Zimmermann built the library of the Premonstratensian monastery at Schussenried, which is well worth visiting after you have seen the pilgrimage church at Steinhausen. It lies a few miles to the south of it. The decor of the library is white and pink with false vellum book spines on the shelves. The room is low with a curving gallery in the upper part of it. The fresco of the ceiling was painted by Franz Hermann from Kempten. The theme is heavenly and earthly wisdom.

The Benedictine monastery of Zwiefalten lies in a valley between Reutlingen and Riedlingen on route 312. It was founded in 1089. A Romanesque church was consecrated there in 1109. In 1738 the abbot decided to build a new church. The nave of the old one was torn down in 1740 and a new foundation stone laid, but the designs of the masons of the abbey, Josef and Martin Schneider, did not suit the abbot. He summoned Johann Michael Fischer in 1741, who found the choir already completed. A new foundation stone was laid in 1744 and the vaulting finished by 1747. The consecration did not take place until 1765, when the decoration was almost complete.

The church is extremely long with a tunnel-like effect inside. (It seems likely that Fischer was obliged to use the old Romanesque foundation to save money.) A door leads into a large vestibule. There are four bays, with wall columns in pairs of gray, red and blue marble stucco, divided by convex galleries. The central crossing with its saucer dome is as wide as the nave. Franz Josef Spiegler was the principal fresco painter. His work blends into the marvellous stucco decorations of Johann Michael Feichtmayr. The huge mystical fresco painted on the vault of the nave by Spiegler in 1751 is a complex allegory depicting the divine inspiration of Saint Benedict and how the Benedictine Order passes it on to the rest of the world. In their *Baroque Churches,* P. and C. Cannon-Brookes call the statue of Ezekiel by J. M. Feichtmayr, based on a model by Johann Joseph Christian, "one of the most outstanding pieces of sculpture in the German churches of the 18th century," and the pulpit the artists did together at Zwiefalten "one of the triumphs of German Rococo art."

In contrast to the ornate interior, the exterior of Zwiefalten is austere. The central doorway is flanked by massive twin columns on either side. A staute of Saint Benedict is above the entrance and a statue of the Virgin and Child occupies a niche in the facade. Both were carved by Johann Joseph Christian.

The most famous name in German Baroque architecture is Balthasar Neumann (1687–1753). His works include the cathedrals of Bamberg, Speyer and Worms, castles in Brühl, Karlsruhe, Seehof (near Bamberg), Veitshöchheim (near Würzburg), and Werneck, and more than 20 churches, including the world-famous pilgrimage church of *Vierzehnheiligen* (Fourteen Saints) on the Main river between Lichtenfels and Staffelstein. He was also largely responsible for the equally famous *Residenz der Fürstbischöfe* (residence of the princely bishops) in Würzburg. He is buried in the crypt of the *Marienkapelle* (chapel of Mary) that overlooks Würzburg.

Neumann's last creation was the majestic Benedictine abbey church of Neresheim (between Heidenheim and Nördlingen on route 466). Neresheim was begun in 1745 but not consecrated until 1792. It is a compromise between the long and the central-plan church. The nave has a huge rotunda in the middle with four freestanding double columns and altars facing inward. The sections of the nave to the left and the right of the central rotunda have two rotundas each, making five in all. There are also oval vaults at the north and south sides of the central rotunda. The Tyrolean Baroque painter Martin Knoller did the bright cupola frescoes of the life of Christ (including the Last Supper over the main altar). They were his most important work. After Neumann's death in 1753 Domenikus and Johann Baptist Wiedemann continued the construction work, simplifying the plans somewhat. The original central cupola was made of wood, together with its supporting columns. They have been restored in the meantime. The stucco work and the orange alabaster pulpit were done by Thomas Scheithauf.

Compared to Zwiefalten and Neresheim, the Cistercian pilgrimage church of Birnau (on the road along Lake Constance between Überlingen and Meersburg) is almost rural in character. The west front faces the lake. The twin sections of the clergy house flank the entrance through an elegant tower, making the building look more like a city hall than a church, when viewed from the front. (Its total shape is that of a T.)

Birnau is the masterpiece of the architect Peter Thumb (1681-1766), the son of Michael Thumb, who did the Church of the Holy Blood at Weingarten. In the 18th century the monks of Salem wanted to build a new church to house a miraculous statue of the Virgin, which had been kept in a shrine near Überlingen since the 13th century. (It was replaced by a Virgin and Child group in the 15th century.) They chose a site overlooking Lake Constance for their new church. Johann Georg Stahl's plans were submitted in 1741 but rejected in favor of Peter Thumb's design. Work began in 1745. The church was consecrated in 1750 and finally completed in 1758.

Instead of using wall pillars, Thumb built an almost flat vault of plaster and lath on a frame of timber. The absence of external and internal supports enabled him to construct an open and light interior. P. and C. Cannon-Brookes describe the overall effect thus achieved: ". . . at Birnau there is no sense of solid structure whatsoever. Architectural elements and decorative elements have become one and the same thing, and the observer ceases to look for a rational construction where the structural elements are precisely defined. Fantasy reigns supreme and the pilgrim passes into an irrational fairy-tale intended as a foretaste of Heaven."

A gallery around the entire interior divides the church into two storeys, with the windows at both levels allowing plenty of light to enter. The choir is narrower than the nave, and the sanctuary narrower still. Two pairs of side altars by Joseph Anton Feuchtmayer, who also did the pulpit, prepare the way to the main altar. All five can be viewed simultaneously from the nave. Feuchtmayer carved the Stations of the Cross (only eight of them survive in color) from wood in 1753. His most famous (and delightful) contribution, in addition to 18 gilt busts in the gallery, is the charming little angel licking honey from his finger while angry bees swarm out of their hive. This is a humorous allusion to Saint Bernard of Clairvaux, whose rhetorical talent enabled the words to flow like honey from his lips.

Gottfried Bernhard Göz did the frescoes in the vault depicting the Virgin Mary as Queen of Heaven and Comforter of the Distressed. The fresco in the choir has the Christ Child connected by a ray of light to a flaming heart held by the figure of Piety. A second ray of light connects the heart to a real mirror in the plaster, where the visitor can see his own face if properly positioned. The Virgin and Child group from the 15th century, on a pedastal above the main altar, is the focal point of the church. The alabaster relief behind the staute was added in 1790 by Johann Georg Wieland.

Cardinal Eugenio Pacelli (later Pope Pius XII) prayed at Birnau on 30 August 1929. Cardinal Angelo Giuseppe Roncalli (later Pope John XXIII) prayed there on 23 August 1949. Pope Paul VI elevated Birnau to a *basilica minor* in 1971.

With good reason Nicolas Powell calls Birnau "the most completely Rococo church" in Swabia, and thus it is fitting to end our architectural excursion with this late Baroque masterpiece.

XII   Swabian History (II)

Duke Eberhard Ludwig of Württemberg began his 40-year reign at age 17. He spent the first half of it fighting external enemies, particularly the French. He was a courageous soldier and an expert horseman, who was willing to risk his life for the Emperor and for his own subjects. Although his troops fought well at Schellenberg and Höchstädt in 1704 during the War of the Spanish Succession (1701-1714), the great powers involved in that struggle, such as England and Austria, paid little attention to the concerns of the Duchy of Württemberg. As a reward for his courage and his contributions, however, Duke Eberhard Ludwig was named a Field Marshal of the Empire by the Emperor and allowed to maintain a standing army in peacetime.

Duke Eberhard Ludwig spent the second half of his reign doing battle with his wife, his ministers, his advisers, and the clergy. In 1709 he had moved into the new castle at Ludwigsburg (permanently after 1714). There he maintained a court in the splendid style of his arch-enemy, King Louis XIV of France. His marriage to Countess Johanna Elisabeth of Baden-Durlach, celebrated with great pomp and splendor in 1697, did not turn out to be a happy one.

Beautiful, ambitious, ruthless Christiane Wilhelmine von Grävenitz (1686-1744) from Mecklenburg came into his life when she joined her brother in Stuttgart in 1706. Duke Eberhard Ludwig fell in love with her and made her his mistress. He defied the wishes of his Emperor, his councillors, his theologians, and his mother by going through a second marriage ceremony. Performed by a Tübingen theology student, it caused a great stir throughout the realm. Duke Eberhard Ludwig renounced it, however, in 1708 when some crafty advisers figured out a scheme to "legitimatize" Christiane Wilhelmine's position in court. Count von Würben, who was deeply in debt, agreed to go through a marriage ceremony with her in exchange for the title of State Court Master *(Landhofmeister)* and immediate banishment from Württemberg. *"Frau Landhofmeisterin"* Christiane Wilhelmine virtually ruled the court at Ludwigsburg, where she lived for the next 20 years. But stubborn Duchess Johanna Elisabeth did not give up so easily. Refusing to budge and waiting her husband out, she had the belated satisfaction of seeing him dismiss his mistress of two decades and her own marriage restored in 1731.

Nevertheless, Christiane Wilhelmine departed Württemberg a very rich woman. Having cleverly obtained the legal title to all of her properties, including a castle in Stetten in the Rems valley, she forced the Duke into buying them back at a price of 200,000 florins. No wonder he had a special court formally condemn her to death! But instead of escorting her to the gallows, the Duke's hussars guided her to the border.

Prodigal or prince, scoundrel or sovereign, Duke Eberhard Ludwig's monument is the Ludwigsburg castle, where he is interred. Its construction gave birth to a city, provided jobs for thousands, and gave artists a chance to use their talent and earn a living during hard times. Considered a reprobate in his own time, he has the belated gratitude of the tourist office in Ludwigsburg today.

Duke Karl Alexander, a cousin of Duke Eberhard Ludwig, succeeded him as the ruler of Württemberg after the death of the latter in 1733. Karl Alexander had served as a general in the service of Austria. He was wounded twice during the War of the Spanish Succession and also fought in the Turkish wars of 1716-1718. As did many other soldiers in Austrian service, he became a Catholic in 1712. According to the Treaty of Westphalia, however, he was not permitted to change the prevailing Protestant religion in Württemberg to Catholic.

Duke Karl Alexander moved his court from Ludwigsburg back into the old, neglected Stuttgart castle and had it renovated. He did not turn his back entirely on Ludwigsburg, but made it into a garrison city for the first time. (It has been that ever since.) Out of loyalty to Emperor Karl VI, he agreed to provide him an army, but his dealings with a scrupulous Heidelberg financier named Süss Oppenheimer, in order to obtain the necessary funds, turned into a major scandal involving the manipulation of coinage, bribery, and the sale of government offices.

The 52-year-old Duke died of a heart attack on 12 March 1737. A year later Oppenheimer was caught, tried by "the will of the people," and hanged in Stuttgart in the presence of thousands of spectators.

Karl Eugen, the eldest son of Duke Karl Alexander, was nine years old when his father died. He was born a Catholic in Brussels in the palace of his grandparents and first came to Stuttgart in 1736. His regent, Duke-Administrator Karl Rudolf, sent him to Berlin where King Frederick the Great of Prussia looked after his education. In 1744, at age 16, he became the ruling Duke of Württemberg. Four years later he married Elisabeth Friederike von Brandenburg-Bayreuth, the daughter of Frederick the Great's favorite sister. The young couple were great opera and theater lovers. Duke Karl Eugen brought the Italian composer and conductor Niccolo Jomelli to Stuttgart in 1753 as the leading musician at court.

Unhappy with the grim solidity of the old Stuttgart castle as a place of residence, Karl Eugen ordered his architect and builder, Leopoldo Retti, to design a new castle (see also chapter eleven).

Karl Eugen was a sybarite with an enormous lust for life which his cold bride could not satiate. She left him for good and never returned, giving him free rein to pursue a life of excess and extravagance. His government had difficulty keeping up with the costs of his manifold pleasures – the theater, hunting, building, and maintaining an army.

Louis XV of France offered sizeable subsidies to Karl Eugen in exchange for 6,000 troops in case of war. When the Seven Years' War broke out in 1756, pitting France against Prussia and England, Karl Eugen had to live up to his contract with France and provide the 6,000 soldiers. Since conscription was unconstitutional, finding sufficient "volunteers" was not easy. His military advisers, Colonel Friedrich Philipp Rieger and Count Friedrich Samuel von Montmartin, rivals for the Duke's favor, used unscrupulous methods to satisfy his will. Both were hungry for power.

When all else failed, Rieger "recruited volunteers" by surrounding villages with his soldiers at night, yanking young farmers out of their beds and forcing them to sign the enlistment contract. In this fashion the Duke met his quota, but the soldiers deserted at the first opportunity. With such troops under his command, it is not surprising that the Duke did not win any battles.

The competition between Rieger and Montmartin lasted five years. The latter proved to be such a master of intrigue that the Duke lost faith in Rieger and had him imprisoned. Later on, however, Rieger managed to regain the Duke's graces and became the commandant of the Asperg fortress with the rank of a general. (Schiller wrote a poem commemorating his death in 1782!)

Karl Eugen's domestic policy was not much better than his foreign policy. Constantly in need of funds to pay for his extravagance, the Duke tried to introduce a new tax system. He ran into stubborn opposition from the members of the *Landtag* (parliament). The Duke sent two of his best advisers to prison and tried to use force to collect taxes. When a delegation from Tübingen asked the Duke to consider the interests of his country *(Vaterland),* he allegedly shouted in the true spirit of the absolute monarch he was, "What do you mean by *Vaterland?* I am the *Vaterland!"*

At the peak of the conflict with parliament, Karl Eugen made a trip to Venice as a "money-saving gesture," he let it be known. There carnival was in full swing. He took 140 members of his court with him. When he ran out of money, he fired most of them and cancelled the payment of pensions to retired army officers.

Finally, the members of parliament sought help from the Protestant kings of Prussia, Denmark, and England, who had signed an accord with his father to protect the rights of the Protestant Church in Württemberg. After six years of negotiations, Duke Karl Eugen signed a so-called inheritance agreement in 1770 which severely limited his privileges.

In his last years Duke Karl Eugen calmed down, largely due to the influence of his mistress Franziska von Hohenheim, whom he married in 1785. In 1791 she was recognized as the Duchess of Württemberg. It was entirely her doing that Karl Eugen, after a life of extravagance, was ultimately revered by his subjects as "the father of his people."

Two of his pet architectural projects deserve mention here: the Hohenheim castle, where he lived with Franziska, and Castle Solitude, the Baroque pleasure palace near Stuttgart. The former became an agricultural university in 1818 and still is today. The latter was designed by the Duke himself and built between 1764 and 1767. It was the initial location of the Duke's famous military academy, the *Hohe Karlsschule,* in 1770. He selected the teachers and designed the curriculum personally. The purpose of the academy was to give officers a broad liberal education so that they could also become civil servants after completing their active military service.

The academy was moved to Stuttgart in 1775 and located behind the new castle. (The building was destroyed during an air raid in 1944. A small bronze model in the Schloßgarten points to its exact location.) The Duke neglected the University of Tübingen in favor of his brainchild, which was raised to university level by Emperor Joseph II in 1781. Its reputation for strict discipline was well known far beyond the borders of Württemberg. Imbued with the spirit of the French Revolution, Friedrich Schiller, its most famous cadet, spent seven years there from 1773–1780 before escaping to Mannheim in 1782 (see chapter nineteen).

Duke Karl Eugen died on 24 October 1793. His brother and successor, Duke Ludwig Eugen (1731–1795), who did not share his brother's interest in education, dissolved the *Hohe Karlsschule* in 1794. (For financial reasons parliament went along with this decision.) He had served as a lieutenant general in the French army and in the service of Austria during the Seven Years' War (1756–1763). He lived with his wife and three daughters at Lake Geneva for several years. A staunch Catholic, he had refused to recognize his brother's second marriage and did not get along with him. Nevertheless, he was generous toward the widowed Duchess Franziska, granting her a large pension for the rest of her life.

Duke Ludwig Eugen had the best of intentions as a ruler. He tried to abolish the corruption in the sale of government offices, but was unsuccessful because of the universal storm of protest he encountered from his "unicivil" servants. The investigation he had initiated was never completed.

Three of the members of the steering committee of parliament, Johann Georg Kerner (the mayor of Ludwigsburg), a lawyer and former teacher at the *Karlsschule* named Johann Heinrich Hochstetter, and Konradin Abel, a former attaché from Württemberg to the French court, tried to wrest the political leadership from the Duke. But Ludwig Eugen's death from a stroke on 20 May 1795 temporarily ended the power struggle.

Friedrich Eugen, the youngest of Karl Alexander's sons, became the 14th reigning Duke of Württemberg in 1795. A soldier in the service of Prussia, he was happily married to a niece of Frederick the Great. They had three daughters and eight sons, all of whom were raised in the Protestant faith. They lived in the Hohenheim castle. In 1776 the eldest daughter had married Prince Paul, who later became the Czar of Russia. Much to the regret of the people of Württemberg, the French occupied Mömpelgard in 1792 and annexed it the following year.

As a result of a war between the Austrian Emperor and Prussia against France, which came to a brief halt with the Treaty of Basel in 1795, Germany was divided into a neutral zone under Prussia and a combat zone under France. Caught in the combat zone, Württemberg troops put up a token resistance along a defensive position near Roßbühl, but French forces overran them and marched to Freudenstadt. After a defeat of the Austrian forces at Malsch near Raststatt in July 1796, Duke Friedrich Eugen sent an emissary to Paris to begin peace talks. The representatives of the agricultural estate in parliament, now very strong, sent their own emissary to Paris for the same purpose. An armistice resulted, and finally a peace treaty, whereby Mömpelgard and the Alsatian territories on the right bank of the Rhine were to be given up in exchange for war reparations.

Weakened by a stroke, Duke Friedrich Eugen couldn't make up his mind. Finally, parliament accepted the conditions. The Duke gave his negotiators the authority to sign for him. Crown Prince Friedrich II signed the treaty in Vienna and then travelled to London to marry the daughter of King George III of England, whom he brought back to Stuttgart in 1797.

When Duke Friedrich Eugen died on 23 December 1797, a new epoch began for Württemberg. Crown Prince Friedrich II, who loved France as a child and learned the art of absolutism in the courts of Berlin and St. Petersburg, ascended the throne of Württemberg at age 44. Having served as a soldier for Prussia and then Russia, he was an outsider to Württemberg's politics and needs. But he did recognize the need to strengthen his army and his alliance with Austria. In 1800 he concluded a subsidy agreement with his father-in-law, King George III of England. He placed his troops at the disposal of the Emperor.

Deserted by Austria in the peace of Lunéville of 1801, Duke Friedrich negotiated a new treaty with France in May 1802. He was promised a substantial compensation for lost territories on the left bank of the Rhine. In December he was given control over the imperial cities of Esslingen, Reutlingen, Rottweil, Weil der Stadt, Heilbronn, Schwäbisch Hall, Schwäbisch Gmünd, Aalen, and

Giengen, as well as nine cloisters and several other religious institutions. To preclude parliament from exercising an influence over these possessions, Friedrich did not annex them but declared them the state of "New Württemberg" with their own ministries and parliament and the seat of government in Ellwangen. In an edict of tolerance of February 1803, he promised freedom of religion to his new subjects. That same month the Emperor confirmed Friedrich's new possessions and proclaimed him Prince Elector *(Kurfürst)*.

In 1805 Bavaria and Baden concluded alliances with France. Stuttgart and many other cities in Württemberg were occupied by French troops. Friedrich decided it was time to make an arrangement with Napoleon Bonaparte. In exchange for 10,000 troops, Napoleon promised him a share of future conquests. Accordingly, after the battle of Austerlitz during the third coalition war, Württemberg gained additional territory. With the peace treaty of Pressburg in December 1805, Friedrich received full sovereignty and the royal title of King, thus finally dissolving once and for all the old Holy Roman Empire of the German Nation.

With his new title, and assured of his power, King Friedrich put down all resistance in parliament to his rule, arrested the outspoken opponents, and confiscated the treasury. The old constitution was abandoned. Old and New Württemberg were consolidated into one absolute kingdom on 1 January 1806. (King Friedrich officially changed the spelling from *Wirtemberg* to *Württemberg.)*

Napoleon's dream of surrounding France with independent puppet states seemed to be fulfilled, at least with respect to Germany. The Emperor of the French proclaimed himself the protector of these German states and united them in the Confederation of the Rhine *(Rheinbund)*. He tried to anchor them in a constitution in 1808 but gave up the idea. It remained a military alliance only.

Compulsory military service was introduced in Württemberg in 1806. Soldiers from that kingdom fought in 1806–1807 against Prussia, in 1809 against Austria, in 1812 against Russia, and in 1813 against Prussia, Russia and Austria. Casualties were heavy in the campaigns of 1812 and 1813. Friedrich not only developed an excellent officers' corps and increased the combat capability of his troops. He introduced welfare programs for disabled veterans and made civil service jobs available to ex-soldiers.

Napoleon divorced his first wife, Josephine, and married Marie Louise, the daughter of the Austrian Emperor, in 1810. In 1812 he forced Austria into a military alliance with France. That year he went to war against Russia with his "Grand Army" of 600,000 men, including Bavarian, Württemberg, Saxonian, Prussian, and Austrian troops. They marched through northern Germany and Poland to Moscow, but found the city deserted and on fire. Napoleon ordered a retreat. The march homeward was one of horror and privation. Less than one-fifth of the "Grand Army" survived the cruel Russian winter and the attacks of the Cossacks. Of the 15,800 Württemberg soldiers who marched in those ranks, only 500 returned home.

Thus began the so-called War of Liberation of the European states against Napoleon Bonaparte from 1813 to 1815. Russia and Prussia signed an alliance in March 1813. The decoration of the "Iron Cross" was created by Prussia on March 10 and war declared on France on March 16, 1813. Anxious to preserve the old order and the European balance of power, Prince Metternich, the Austrian chancellor and minister of foreign affairs (1809–1848), withdrew from the alliance with France to join Prussia and Russia.

Surrounded on three sides by the forces of these powers, Napoleon was deprived of the initiative for the first time in his military career. In the first two weeks of fighting, Bavarian, Saxonian, and Swabian troops went over to the side of the allies. Napoleon lost the battle of Leipzig. The headquarters of the allies moved to Frankfurt and the Confederation of the Rhine was dissolved. The war ended with the allies entering Paris on 31 March 1814 and the abdication of Napoleon as the Emperor of France. The terms of the Peace of Paris were very lenient. Napoleon was granted a pension and exiled to the island of Elba in the Mediterranean, while France was allowed to keep all of the territories owned in 1792.

The map of Europe was redrawn at the Congress of Vienna in 1815. Although forced to surrender its Polish possessions to the czar, Prussia came away from the Congress as one of the most powerful states in Europe. A committee of representatives from Prussia, Austria, Bavaria, Hanover, and Württemberg created a German Confederation, with Austria as the presiding power, and stipulated the creation of a Federal Diet *(Bundestag)* that was to meet in Frankfurt on the Main. The Confederation consisted of 39 sovereign states.

Due to the reactionary influence of Metternich, however, it turned out to be a kind of life insurance for existing monarchies instead of reflecting the new spirit of liberalism that had emerged from the French Revolution. King Friedrich and Crown Prince Wilhelm of Württemberg personally attended the Congress of Vienna, but when the king saw no opportunity to increase the size of his kingdom, he returned to Stuttgart. He was opposed to the German Confederation, but Württemberg joined it nonetheless. The member states of the Confederation were required to adopt new constitutions. King Friedrich tried to force his own draft on his parliament, but they opposed it, deliberating and debating its provisions until his death on 30 October 1816.

Friedrich's son, Wilhelm I, was quite a different personality from his father, whose politics he had opposed. Sober, well-educated, cultured, and conservative, he eliminated a lot of his father's Baroque pomp on state occasions. He even designed a simpler coat of arms for Württemberg with the antlers, the Hohenstaufen lions, and the motto "fearless and loyal." And yet he lacked a closer relationship to the intellectual currents of his time.

King Wilhelm I conducted foreign affairs himself. He promoted the expansion of agriculture and Württemberg's infant industry. In 1836 he did away with the feudal laws that suppressed the peasantry, thereby emancipating the farmers. After a first marriage that was dissolved by Papal dispensation, King Wilhelm married Catherine of Russia, the widow of Prince George of Oldenburg, in 1816. Two daughters were born of the marriage. After the early death of Catherine in 1819, the king married Princess Pauline von Württemberg, who bore him a son, Karl, in 1823.

At the beginning of the reign of King Wilhelm I, Württemberg was a poor and densely populated country. Crop failures in 1816 and 1817 caused much hunger and privation, which Queen Catherine personally helped to alleviate. She organized help for the needy, founded local charities for the poor, and got her husband to spend 100,000 florins for the *Katharinenhospital* (Catherine's Hospital), designed by Nicolaus Friedrich Thouret (1767–1845). To this day it is one of Stuttgart's leading medical facilities. Queen Catherine also founded the *Katharinenstift,* a boarding school for girls with six classes, where Eduard Mörike taught during the last years of his life (see chapter nineteen).

King Wilhelm's encouragement of agriculture also gave birth to the annual *Volksfest* in Bad Cannstatt. After the years of privation due to bad harvests, the king decreed that a festival be held the day after his birthday every year to encourage the improvement of cattle raising. The occasion was to consist of an agricultural fair side-by-side with athletic competitions, such as horse racing. (The king was an avid rider and horse-breeder himself.) Munich had started its famous 18-day *Octoberfest* in 1812. The thrifty Swabians had only one day to celebrate when their *Volksfest* began on 28 September 1818. Beer and wine tents didn't make an appearance until much later.

Following the principle of the division of power, King Wilhelm reorganized the administration of his kingdom. He gave the initiatives for legislation. The representatives of the people in parliament's chamber of deputies were responsible for passing laws, and justice was administered by independent judges in local courts. The king created four counties, or governmental districts, which lasted until 1924. He did much to grant self-governing powers to the communities.

King Wilhelm reorganized the army and created a military academy in Ludwigsburg in 1820. Built at Mömpelgardstraße 24, it was an officers' candidate school until torn down in 1874. In those days a soldier served six months on active duty and had a reserve obligation of six years. If drafted and able to defray the costs of recruitment, however, he could elect to send a substitute to serve in his place.

A German friend of mine, who knows that I love old books, gave me a bound copy of the *Government Bulletin of the Kingdom of Württemberg for 1837*. On pages 34/35 I found the draft and recruiting quotas for Württemberg for that year by county:

County	Draftees	Recruits
Neckar	3,996	1,009
Schwarzwald	3,665	925
Jaxt (spelled Jagst today)	3,100	781
Donau	3,116	785
Totals:	13,877	3,500

The *Bulletin* also revealed that the king's First Infantry Division was stationed in Stuttgart and the Second Infantry Division in Ludwigsburg.

In 1841 King Wilhelm celebrated the 25th anniversary of his reign. A statue on the Schloßplatz in Stuttgart was erected in his honor with the legend: "dedicated to the true friend of his people, King Wilhelm the much-beloved."

Crop failures in 1846 and 1847 again brought Württemberg privation and starvation. News of the uprisings in Paris, Vienna, and Munich in February 1848 created unrest in Württemberg. King Wilhelm tried to defuse the potential revolution by agreeing to compromise when a large gathering in Stuttgart demanded freedom of the press, the right of assembly, and the right to bear arms, among other reforms. Anxious to maintain his sovereignty, King Wilhelm adopted a watch-and-wait policy. His concessions on press freedom and his quick formation of a liberal parliamentary ministry in Stuttgart kept the revolution at a low boil in Württemberg. By the fall of 1849 it had simmered down completely.

At the National Assembly in the Paul's Church in Frankfurt in April 1848, 586 delegates from the German states deliberated on ways and means to give Germany national unity and a national constitution. Age-old rivalries between north and south, Catholic and Protestant, Prussia and Austria, plus a war in Schleswig-Holstein with Denmark, complicated their work. Nevertheless, by March 1849 they had drawn up a constitution which King Wilhelm of Württemberg was quick to recognize in order to prevent civil war in his own kingdom.

After 13 months of deliberation, the Frankfurt Parliament was finally dissolved. It was a setback for liberalism. In August 1851 the Württemberg constitution of 1819 was restored. While it provided for religious freedom and the foundation of modern political parties, it failed to guarantee democracy.

King Friedrich Wilhelm IV of Prussia had been elected the Emperor of Germany in 1849, but King Wilhelm I of Württemberg was reluctant to recognize him. In 1850 the principalities of Hohenzollern-Hechingen and Hohenzollern-Sigmaringen, which were almost completely surrounded geographically by Württemberg, became a part of Prussia.

Not at all happy with Prussia, yet anxious to remain neutral during the Crimean War (1854-56), King Wilhelm I of Württemberg made an alignment with the Prussian monarch. King Friedrich Wilhelm

IV of Prussia visited Stuttgart during the summer of 1856. King Wilhelm visited him, in turn, at the Hohenzollern Castle in Hechingen that autumn.

In the last years of his reign, King Wilhelm opposed the formation of a national union of Germany under Prussian leadership (without Austria). He died at age 83 on 25 June 1864 in the Rosenstein castle he had built in 1829. It was the site of many a festivity, but never the residence of the royal family.

The king's first overnight stay there was his last.

Schloß Rosenstein

XIII   Swabian Philosophers

Germany has often been called "the land of poets and thinkers." As is evident in chapter eighteen, Swabia produced several notable poets. Two of Germany's greatest philosophers of the 19th century were also Swabians.

FRIEDRICH WILHELM JOSEPH VON SCHELLING was born in Leonberg (near Stuttgart) on 27 January 1775. His father, Joseph Friedrich, was a Lutheran minister there. In 1777 Pastor Schelling was appointed a professor of Oriental languages at the cloister school of Bebenhausen, where his son received his early education. A gifted child, he learned the classical languages at age eight and was admitted to the theological seminary at Tübingen at age 15. His closest associates at Tübingen were Georg Wilhelm Friedrich Hegel and Friedrich Hölderlin (see page 170). All three young men were inspired by the French Revolution. Schelling was influenced by the rational philosophy of Immanuel Kant, the philosophical idealism of Fichte, and the pantheism of Spinoza.

At age 19 Schelling wrote his first philosophical treatise, "On the Possibility and Form of Philosophy in General," which earned Fichte's critical approval. His next works were "Of the Ego as Principle of Philosophy" and the article "Philosophical Letters on Dogmatism and Criticism," both of which were published in 1796 while Schelling was a private tutor to the sons of a noble family in Leipzig. Intellectually, at this time, Schelling was slowly freeing himself of the influence of Fichte. He postulated the absolute ego in each person as the supreme, unconditional element in human knowledge – timeless and eternal. In Leipzig he had the opportunity to attend lectures in physics, chemistry, and medicine. He became critical of Fichte's neglect of nature, to which Schelling now devoted his attention, viewing it as an infinite self-activity, never fully complete. His philosophy of nature and his transcendental idealism made him known in the circle of the German Romanticists and even won the attention of Johann Wolfgang von Goethe.

In 1798, at age 23, Schelling was called to a professorship at the University of Jena, the mecca of German intelligentsia at that time. There he became a close friend of Fichte, the idol of his youth, and associated with Goethe and Schiller, the Romanticists and trans-

Schelling

Hegel

lators of Shakespeare's plays Friedrich and August Wilhelm von Schlegel, the writer and critic Ludwig Tieck, the poet Novalis, and his old school friend Hegel. Between 1797 and 1800 Schelling published in rapid succession several works on his philosophy of nature: "Ideas toward a Philosophy of Nature" (1797), "On the World Soul, a Hypothesis of Advanced Physics for the Interpretation of the General Organism" (1798), and "System of Transcendental Idealism" (1800). Around 1800 his break with Fichte was complete. For the next two years the two philosophers attacked each other in a correspondence that led nowhere and ended in 1802. They could not agree on the importance of the ego (Fichte's thesis), and the role of the Absolute (Schelling's thesis) as the keystone of philosophy.

Schelling became particularly attracted to Caroline Schlegel, the wife of August Wilhelm von Schlegel, one of the leaders of Romantic criticism. The daughter of a professor at Göttingen University, she had married a doctor at age 21. After his death she lived in Mainz and bore a child to a French officer. In 1796 she met and married Schlegel, who brought her to Jena. Schelling and Caroline became attracted to one another. When her 16-year-old daughter Auguste became fatally ill, Schelling treated her. His ministrations brought him ever closer to Caroline, but he was blamed by many for Auguste's death in 1800. Goethe helped Caroline to obtain a divorce from Schlegel in May 1803. That same year she married Schelling. All three remained good friends, but Schelling's dispute with Fichte and the rumors about his part in Auguste's death caused him to leave Jena to accept an appointment at the new University of Würzburg in 1803.

Between 1802 and 1803 Schelling and Hegel were co-editors of the "Critical Journal of Philosophy." Although five years older than Schelling, Hegel was considered to be the younger philosopher's disciple. Hegel's first book, published in 1801, was a comparison of the philosophical systems of Fichte and Schelling. At that time Hegel sided with Schelling in his disagreement with Fichte. By 1807, however, he attacked Schelling's system in his book, *The Phenomenology of Mind,* without mentioning Schelling's name. Hegel compared Schelling's definition of the Absolute as an indiscriminate unity of the subjective and the objective to the night "in which all cows are black." It was the end of their friendship. As Hegel's book gradually gained recognition, Schelling's popularity as the leading philosopher of the time began to wane.

In 1860 Schelling moved to Munich to become the secretary general of the Academy of Arts. Later on he was appointed the secretary of the philosophical section of the Academy of Sciences. These government posts gave him time to lecture at Erlangen and Stuttgart. In 1827 he became a professor at the University of Munich, in 1841 a privy councilor in Prussia, a lecturer at the University of Berlin, and a member of the Berlin Academy.

Caroline's death in Maulbronn on 7 September 1809 was a severe blow to Schelling. He married a friend of hers, Pauline Gotter, in 1812. At this time, and for the remainder of his life, he became interested in existentialism. His writings on that subject were published after his death at Bad Ragaz, Switzerland, on 20 August 1854. As a forerunner of modern existentialism, Schelling is more popular in the English-speaking world today than Hegel. Not far from the *Liederhalle* in Stuttgart a Schelling Straße commemorates the name of this philosopher, who was a key figure in the intellectual world of 19th-century Germany. King Maximilian II of Bavaria erected a gravestone for Schelling at Bad Ragaz in recognition of "the foremost thinker of Germany."

A square and a street in Stuttgart are named after one of Germany's best-known philosophers: GEORG WILHELM FRIEDRICH HEGEL, who was born in Stuttgart on 27 August 1770. He studied at the theological seminary in Tübingen (the so-called *Tübinger Stift)* from 1788 to 1793, where he became close friends with Hölderlin and Schelling. It has been said somewhere by someone that the *Tübinger Stift,* with its rigid and demanding intellectual regimen, produced more poets and philosophers than it did Protestant pastors, perhaps because its curriculum induced them to question theology rather than profess it. As did Schelling and Hölderlin, after deciding not to become a minister, Hegel, too, was a private tutor, at first in Bern, and then in Frankfurt. In 1800 he went to Jena, where Schelling had succeeded Fichte as professor of philosophy. On the basis of his dissertation, *De Orbitis Planetarum,* Hegel was awarded a teaching position at the University of Jena.

Hegel's first book and his collaboration with Schelling as co-editor of the "Critical Journal of Philosophy" have already been mentioned in the previous pages about Schelling. Two articles of Hegel's worth mention in the "Critical Journal" were "Belief and Knowledge" of 1802 and "Methods of Scientific Treatment of the Law of Nature" of 1803. At Jena Hegel wrote his famous *The Phenomenology of Mind.* He finished it just about the time of Napoleon's victory over the Prussians at Jena. It was not published until after Hegel had left Jena to become the editor of the *Bamberger Zeitung* in 1807. From 1808 to 1816 he was the director of a secondary school *(Gymnasium)* in Nürnberg. While there he published his two-volume *Science of Logic.* In 1816 he became a professor of philosophy at Heidelberg University, where he wrote his *Encyclopedia of the Philosophical Sciences in Outline,* published in 1817. The following year he was called to a professorship at the University of Berlin, where he died during a cholera epidemic on 14 November 1831.

Several of Hegel's important works were not published until after his death. Between 1832 and 1840 a group of his friends assembled his lectures and other unpublished writings for publication in what ultimately became an 18-volume edition of his collected works.

For Hegel, philosophy is the science of the development of absolute mind (*Geist,* in German) in all its manifestations, past and present. According to Hegel, it is the function of the philosopher to make men conscious of what art and politics, commerce and religion are so that mind can exert itself to its utmost capability and thus become absolute. Hegel's philosophical system encompasses parts of logic, of the philosophy of nature, and of the philosophy of the mind, with logic supreme. Another feature is the philosophy of history, which Hegel viewed as man's intellectual development as well as external events.

Anyone who has studied philosophy, intellectual history, or literature even, will recall that Hegel was the philosopher who developed the dialectical method of thesis–antithesis–and synthesis. His followers split into the so-called "left Hegelians" and "right Hegelians." Three of the best-known "left Hegelians" were the Ludwigsburg theologian David Friedrich Strauss (1808-1874), the philosopher Ludwig Feuerbach (1804-1872), and Karl Marx (1818-1883), the spiritual father of Communism. All three ultimately rejected Hegel's teachings to do their own thing.

XIV   Swabian History (III)

The crop failures in Württemberg in 1846 and 1847, and especially the political failure of liberalism after the collapse of the revolution of 1848 (and the dissolution of the Frankfurt Parliament), gave rise to a large exodus of Swabians. Between 1849 and 1855 alone, more than 70,000 people from Württemberg – in excess of five percent of the entire population – emigrated either to southern Russia (especially Bessarabia) or to the American West and Middle West.

In the second half of the 19th century Prussia became the dominant German power. Part of Prussia's power resulted from its position as the leading state in the Customs Union of 18 German states created in 1834, which included Württemberg. When the contract expired in 1865, Prussia demanded the creation of a customs parliament to solidify its political power. The man in the driver's seat was Count Otto von Bismarck (1815-1898), the "Iron Chancellor" who directed the domestic and foreign policy of Prussia and later of the Second German Empire until his dismissal in 1890.

Karl I (1823-1891) succeeded his father as the King of Württemberg in 1864, when Bismarck was still wrangling with the opposition in the Prussian government concerning the Schleswig-Holstein question. In 1848 the duchies of Schleswig and Holstein in northern Germany, which had been united with Denmark, rose in revolt to obtain their independence of the Danish crown. The German Confederation had sided with the insurgents and Prussian troops joined the war. It ended with a Danish victory. The Treaty of London (1852) decreed that the duchies remain part of Denmark with the crown prince as the reigning duke of Schleswig-Holstein. The treaty also prescribed that the rights of the Germans living in those duchies must be respected. When the king of Denmark issued a new constitution for all Danish territories that abrogated the Treaty of London, Bismarck used the opportunity to provoke a war in 1864, not to help the Danish and German populace of Schleswig-Holstein, but to incorporate those duchies into the Prussian state. That year Prussian and Austrian troops fought the Danes successfully in a nine-month campaign, occupied Jutland, and offered conditions for peace which Denmark ultimately accepted. In the Peace of Vienna, Denmark agreed to surrender the two disputed duchies. Austria gained administrative control over Holstein and Prussia over Schleswig in accordance with the Treaty of Gastein (1865).

Shortly thereafter, Bismarck took advantage of a dispute with Austria to provoke a war with Prussia's former ally. Württemberg joined several other German states in siding with Austria. The war lasted seven weeks, ending with Austria's complete defeat at Königgrätz on 3 July 1866. Only a few days before the armistice, Swabian troops were routed by the Prussians in a battle at Tauberbischofsheim (24 July). Württemberg concluded a separate armistice with Prussia on 2 August. Under its terms the Swabians had to pay war reparations amounting to eight million florins and to recognize the North German Confederation, but did not have to give up any territory. (The Bavarians did.)

King Karl I was quite unlike his father and his grandfather. Soft and reserved by nature, he let his senior minister, Baron Karl von Varnbüler (1809-1889), handle the foreign affairs of his kingdom. During the seven weeks' war with Prussia, after the Austrian defeat at Königgrätz, Varnbüler made a personal trip to the Prussian headquarters in Nikolsburg, but Bismarck gave him the cold shoulder initially. Nevertheless, the Württemberg foreign minister ultimately managed to conclude a secret alliance with Prussia, placing the Württemberg army under Prussian command. The treaty was approved by the Württemberg parliament by a 53 to 37 vote and made public in 1867. Most of the support had come from the members of the German Party. Karl Mayer and the members of the Württemberg People's Party, which he had founded in 1864, wanted to form a "Southern Confederation" of south-German states, but neither Württemberg nor Baden wanted to accept Bavarian leadership. In 1868 the Social Democratic Party was organized in Württemberg. Although it quickly found support among the growing number of industrial workers, it was not immediately represented in the State Parliament.

Emperor Napoleon III of France demanded part of the left bank of the Rhine and the city of Mainz in 1866, but Bismarck refused to give up an inch of German territory. Instead, he used the occasion to arouse the southern German states against France. Napoleon had no better luck when he tried to purchase Luxembourg from the Netherlands in 1867.

Using a political disagreement between Napoleon III and King Wilhelm of Prussia as an excuse to edit the famous "Ems Dispatch," Bismarck managed to get France to declare war on Germany on 19 July 1870. The German states quickly rallied behind the flag of Prussia. Even Karl Mayer approved of Württemberg's soldiers fighting side-by-side with the Prussians. With strategic plans prepared in advance and armed forces in a high state of readiness, the Germans defeated the French within six weeks. France was overrun and Paris besieged. Württemberg soldiers, under the command of the Prussian General Obernitz, prevented a breakout of the encircled French army at Champigny on 30 November 1870.

On 25 November 1870 Württemberg had signed the agreements making the kingdom a part of the North German Confederation. They were approved by the *Landtag* in Stuttgart by a vote of 74 to 14 on 5 December 1870. On 1 January 1871 the Kingdom of Württemberg was officially proclaimed a federal state of the German Empire. At Versailles on 18 January, King Wilhelm I of Prussia became the German Kaiser. The peace treaty with France, ending the Franco-Prussian War, was signed in Frankfurt on 10 May 1871.

King Karl had replaced Karl von Varnbüler as foreign minister on 30 August 1870, naming Hermann Mittnacht (1825-1909), a seasoned statesman, as Varnbüler's successor. (A street in Stuttgart perpetuates Varnbüler's name.) Mittnacht's political views were more in accord with King Karl's than Varnbüler's had been.

A Catholic lawyer, Mittnacht had served as Minister of Justice since 1867. He is given the lion's share of the credit for overcoming objections against Württemberg joining the German Empire. He served as Minister President until 1900. The *Mittnachtbau,* a large building in downtown Stuttgart beween Kronprinzstraße and Königsstraße, was named in his honor.

King Karl died on 6 October 1891 and his wife a year later. (He was interred in the crypt under the old castle in Stuttgart.) In 1846 he had married Grand Duchess Olga, the daughter of Czar Nikolaus I of Russia. Queen Olga was not only beautiful, but bright and ambitious. She overshadowed her colorless, hesitant husband and made many of Württemberg's political decisions for him. She saw eye-to-eye with Karl von Varnbüler and was a great supporter of special charities for the offspring of deceased military and civil servants.

Olgastraße, a main traffic artery in Stuttgart, keeps her name alive. Two blocks away from the intersection of Charlottenstraße (B-27) with Olgastraße, my office is located in a neo-classic private villa built during the so-called "founding years" *(Gründerjahre)* or "founding period" *(Gründerzeit)*. These were the years between 1871 and 1873 when the money that flowed into the German Empire as war reparations from a defeated France led to the "founding" of countless speculative enterprises, many of which went broke. Some historians identify the period with economic expansion, some with the "founding" of the Second German Empire, and still others with a remarkable and memorable period of private architecture, when wealthy people built fabulous dwellings.

As the US Forces Liaison Officer for Baden-Württemberg, I have the good fortune to have such a former private home as my office. Designed in 1871 by Karl Beissbarth, a prominent Stuttgart architect, it was built in 1872 as the home of Artur Bohnenberger, an affluent landowner. In those days the city limits of Stuttgart ended on the slope behind the building. Since 1908 the house at Olgastraße 11 has been in para-military hands. It was the Stuttgart headquarters of American military government after both world wars. Today it is a protected monument.

When he ascended the throne of Württemberg on 22 October 1891, King Wilhelm II promised a timely revision of the constitution of the kingdom, the safeguarding and enhancement of economic interests, the further development of public transportation, and the promotion of commerce and agriculture.

As the heir presumptive to the throne he had studied at Göttingen and Tübingen. He had served in the seven week's war against Prussia in 1866 and in the Franco-Prussian War on the staff of Crown Prince Friedrich Wilhelm of Prussia. In 1882 he ended his active military service as the commander of a Württemberg cavalry brigade with the rank of major general. He had two children by his first marriage with Princess Marie von Waldeck und Pyrmont, who died in 1882. In 1886 he married Princess Charlotte zu Schaumburg-Lippe, who bore him no children.

The reign of King Wilhelm II began when the Second German Empire was at the peak of its power. It ended with his abdication on 9 November 1918. (He lived until 1918 in the Wilhelmspalais on the corner of Konrad Adenauer Straße and Charlottenstraße, which presently houses the city library and archive.) He had reigned for 27 years, earning not only the respect, but the love of his people. He lived out his life after 1918 at the cloister in Bebenhausen until his death in 1921. The last of the regents of Württemberg, he is buried in the old cemetery in Ludwigsburg.

On 10 November 1918, yielding to the pressure and advice of his generals Groener und Hindenburg, Kaiser Wilhelm II abdicated his throne and departed Germany for 23 years of exile in Holland. With this decision some 500 years of uninterrupted rule by the Hohenzollern dynasty had come to an end in Germany.

That same day the political leadership of Württemberg passed from royal hands to those of a Social Democrat named Wilhelm Blos (1849-1927), whose title was "State President" *(Staatspräsident)*. A rift in his own ranks made it hard for him to govern effectively. Nevertheless, a new constitution for Württemberg was one of the achievements of his provisional government.

The Social Democrats lost out in the parliamentary elections of 1920. Dr. Johannes Hieber (1862-1951), a liberal democrat, succeeded Blos as State President. The baptism of fire for his government was the implementation of a controversial wage tax deduction, which the unions opposed. Minister of Justice Dr. Eugen Bolz (1881-1945) successfully intervened and brought about a compromise, after Württemberg's leading industries – Bosch, Daimler, and the Esslingen Machine Factory – had gone on strike.

In June 1924 Wilhelm Bazille (1874-1934), the former leader of the opposition in parliament, was elected State President. His Minister of the Interior was Eugen Bolz. The strongest opponent of both of them in the state parliament was Dr. Kurt Schumacher (1895-1952), the editor of a Stuttgart newspaper, who became the chairman of the Social Democratic Party in Germany after World War II.

The voters of 1928 for the members of the state parliament chose Eugen Bolz as their State President. He picked Reinhold Maier (1889-1971) as his Minister of Economics. In an official report of the *Reich* (federal government), Württemberg was cited as a model state for all of Germany because of its excellent administration. Nevertheless, Bolz was pessimistic about Germany's immediate future. He introduced an austerity program for his budget, as did

Chancellor Heinrich Brüning for all of Germany in 1930, in view of rampant inflation and unemployment. "Black Friday," the collapse of the New York Stock Exchange on 25 October 1929, had global re-precussions, especially in Germany, where unemployment affected three million people by the winter of 1929/30 and more than six million by January 1933. With 133,604 out of work that month, Württemberg was better off than the rest of Germany. This was due to this state's many consumer goods industries, such as food and textiles, which were able to keep most of their employees on the job.

The first photograph in Paul Sauer's *Württemberg During the Time of National Socialism,* published in 1975, shows Adolf Hitler in uniform on a visit to Stuttgart on 7 December 1930. In the elections of 4 April 1932 for the state parliament of Württemberg, the National Socialists got 29 percent of the votes and 23 seats. The Nazi professor Christian Mergenthaler became the president of the parliament, but Bolz and his ministers remained in office as a "caretaker cabinet" without a parliamentary majority.

On 30 January 1933 President Paul von Hindenburg of the German *Reich* dismissed General Kurt von Schleicher as the German Chancellor and named Adolf Hitler as his successor. Hitler's appointment brought such a flush of victory to the 23 Nazi deputies to the Württemberg parliament that they appeared in uniform for the proceedings on the following day. State President Eugen Bolz of Württemberg, Minister of Justice Joseph Beyerle, and Minister of Finance Reinhold Maier were noted opponents of National Socialism in southwestern Germany. Bolz's anti-Nazi speeches during the national election campaign of 1933 prompted Hitler to come to Stuttgart on 15 February and attack the State President in a speech. Gauleiter Wilhelm Murr (1888–1945) set the stage in his introductory remarks with an inflammatory tirade against Bolz.

Scheduled to speak in the courtyard of the New Castle, but shifted to the Stadthalle at Neckarstraße 230, Adolf Hitler was in a foul mood. He intensified Murr's invective against Bolz. The South German Radio carried the speech live, but the broadcast was interrupted when Communist agitators cut the main transmission cable. Hitler and his propaganda chief Dr. Paul Josef Goebbels placed all of the blame on Bolz and his government. Nevertheless, Bolz continued to criticize the Nazis in his public speeches in Württemberg.

Hitler demanded that all State Presidents cease their criticism of the government of the *Reich*. But Bolz and his ministers, such as Reinhold Maier, were not impressed. Their criticial remarks in public during the national election campaign were probably the reason why the National Socialist Party in Württemberg received almost two percent less than the national percentage of 43.9 when the polls were closed on 5 March 1933.

At a mass meeting of National Socialists in Stuttgart on the evening of 6 March, Gauleiter Murr stated in his speech: "Bolz must go. Order must also be brought to Southern Germany . . . Stuttgart is National Socialist, Württemberg is National Socialist, and now the Württemberg government must also become National Socialist." The meeting ended with a stirring rendition of the *Horst-Wessel Lied,* the Nazi "national anthem."

That afternoon SA-Group Leader Dietrich von Jagow from Esslingen had coerced State President Bolz into granting permission to fly the Swastika flag over public buildings in Stuttgart. Recognizing the weakness of the Württemberg government, Hitler made use of emergency legislation and appointed von Jagow the police commissioner for that state. On 8 March the latter took control of the entire Württemberg police force and assigned deputy police functions to members of the SA, SS, and *Stahlhelm*. The reign of terror began in Württemberg, as elsewhere in Germany. Jewish-owned stores were boycotted, Communists arrested (200 alone on 11 March), Social Democratic newspapers put to bed for good. Bolz and his government had to witness helplessly how police commissioner von Jagow solidified the power of the Nazis in Württemberg.

On 15 March, following considerable political in-fighting between President of the Landtag Mergenthaler and Gauleiter Murr, the latter was elected State President. Dr. Jonathan Schmid, also a member of the Nazi Party, succeeded Mergenthaler as President of the Landtag (state parliament). Murr chose Mergenthaler to be the Minister of Justice and the Minister of Culture in his new government. On 5 May State President Murr received the new title of *Reichsstatthalter* (viceroy). He appointed Mergenthaler Minister President and Chairman of the State Ministry of Württemberg. Mergenthaler also remained the Minister of Culture. The Ministry of Justice was virtually abolished. Württemberg had now become a satellite of the National Socialist regime in Berlin.

On 9 May 1933 Dr. Karl Strölin succeeded Carl Lautenschlager as Lord Mayor of Stuttgart. Former State President Dr. Eugen Bolz gave up his seat in parliament on 3 June. Sixteen days later he was placed under arrest in the Hohenasperg prison for having attended a meeting of the Austrian Christian-Social Party. Fanatics threw rotten eggs and tomatoes at him on his way to jail. He was released on 12 July 1933. An unrelenting opponent of the Nazis, Bolz took part in the 20 July 1944 plot to kill Hitler. He was executed by guillotine in Berlin-Plötzensee on 23 January 1945. Two plaques and a street in Stuttgart, three blocks south of the main railroad station, bear his name.

Hitler and Goebbels were VIP guests at the German gymnastics competitions in Stuttgart on 30 July 1933. In February 1938 Hitler visited the Daimler-Benz plant and made a later visit to Stuttgart on 1 April 1938. Thousands of people gathered on the market place and later in the *Schwabenhalle* to see and hear the Führer, who was greeted by Gauleiter Murr and Lord Mayor Dr. Strölin. During the infamous *Reichskristallnacht* throughout Germany on 9 November 1938, 18 synagogues in Württemberg were burned down and 12 demolished. At least 13 Jews lost their lives and 878 were sent to concentration camps.

Shortly after the start of World War II in September 1939, the first hostile aircraft flew over Württemberg for leaflet drops. That same month the first bombs were dropped in an air raid on Klingenstein, near Ulm, and five people were killed. That April Stuttgart airport opened to replace Böblingen airport (now the US Army Maintenance Plant), which the Luftwaffe had taken over for tactical use and training of ME-109 fighter pilots.

The bomb that might have killed Hitler in the *Bürgerbräukeller* in Munich on 8 November 1939 – had the Führer not decided to begin his speech to his old cronies a half-hour earlier – was built and planted by a Swabian *Tüftler* named Johann Georg Elser. A carpenter and loner from Hermaringen (Heidenheim county), Elser was arrested in Konstanz while trying to escape to Switzerland. The Gestapo refused to believe that he had done the job all by himself. Without a trial, Elser was sent to a concentration camp. He died in Dachau in April 1945.

One of Hitler's domestic orders for September 1939 was the killing of "those not fit to live." In the following year in Württemberg some 10,000 mentally ill people were put to death in Grafeneck near the present-day Münsingen training area. (The name of the place has been changed.) The first major air raid on Stuttgart took place on 25 August when 20 bombers attacked Untertürkheim and took four lives. A second raid on 8 November 1940 caused only slight damage.

In May 1941 the last of the free press, the 156-year-old *Schwäbische Merkur* and the *Cannstatter Zeitung* went out of business. That year Minister President Mergenthaler continued his persecution of the church by confiscating the theological seminaries at Blaubeuren, Maulbronn, Schöntal, and Urach.

Air raids increased in intensity as of 1942. Stuttgart was hit on 5/6 May, 29 August and 22 November, resulting in 41 casualties and 108 wounded. Due to the lack of coal, schools were closed down partially or completely for weeks at a time from January to March. In Stuttgart gas was available only during mealtimes. Robert Bosch died on 9 March 1942. He had been an outspoken opponent of National Socialism from the outset. On 22 September 1933 at an automobile show in Berlin, he said to Hitler: "You must feel uncomfortable sitting in Bismarck's chair." He supported theology students after they lost their scholarships from the state, helped Jews to escape, and gave money to anti-Nazi organizations. He worked for French-German relations and even invited a delegation of French veterans of World War I to Stuttgart in 1935.

The capitulation of the surviving 100,000 men of the German Sixth Army at Stalingrad in February 1943 was the turning point of the war for Germany. As students at the University of Munich in 1943, Hans Scholl and his sister Sophie from Ingersheim (near Ulm), together with their friend Christoph Probst, prepared and distributed leaflets in Munich denouncing "World War Private" Hitler for having sent 330,000 German men to their deaths at Stalingrad with his "ingenious strategy." Betrayed by a university employee, they were arrested on 18 February and executed four days later. Goebbels propaganda attempts to take the sting out of Stalingrad failed miserably. Only 30 people attended the special showings of his newsreels at the Ufa-Palast movie theater in Stuttgart on 1/2 March 1943.

Stuttgart was the target of six air raids (the first one in daylight was on 6 September) that year. A total of 971 people lost their lives and 1,768 were wounded. Württemberg's smaller communities began to accept evacuees from the larger cities of Germany as well as from Stuttgart. In 1943 a total of 222,500 tons of bombs was dropped on Germany and German-occupied territory. Early in 1944 Stuttgart was hit on 21 February and again on 2 March. Deaths from those raids totaled 280 people. Concerned about the increasing air raids on Stuttgart and Hitler's eccentric fanaticism, Lord Mayor Dr. Strölin began to lose his initial enthusiasm for National Socialism as the German way of life. Through Carl Goerdeler, the former Lord Mayor of Leipzig who was working as a financial consultant to Robert Bosch and Company, Dr. Strölin came into contact with the people in the resistance movement against Hitler. He met frequently with Goerdeler in the Rathaus, in hotels, and in his own home to discuss ways to avert a total catastrophy for Germany.

Since 1941 Strölin had been on the outs with Gauleiter Murr. In 1943 he wanted to discuss protective measures for the civilian populace with the International Red Cross in Geneva, but Hitler would not allow him to leave the country. In an attempt to convince Hitler of the futility of continuing the war, Strölin and Goerdeler met with Erwin Rommel in the Field Marshal's home in Herrlingen in February 1944. According to historians Paul Sauer and Desmond Young, Strölin was able to enlist Rommels's aid, but the popular Field Marshal was unable to change Hitler's mind and make him draw the political consequences. On 17 July 1944 Rommel was severely wounded when a British fighter pilot strafed his staff car.

Colonel Count Claus Schenk von Stauffenberg, a Swabian from Jettingen, placed the bomb in the command bunker in East Prussia that failed to kill Hitler on 20 July 1944 and brought devastating consequences for all those involved in the plot. Field Marshal Rommel was forced to take his own life on 14 October 1944. (Hitler's wreath for his state funeral arrived at the railroad station in Ulm while Rommel was still alive.) The people were told that the Field Marshal had died of the wounds he received in France.

On 24 July 1944 the Stuttgart Opera gave its final performance during the Second World War. In the air raids on Stuttgart of 25, 26, 28, and 29 July, 12 September and 19 October 2,750 people died. On

Downtown Stuttgart in 1946

4 December Heilbronn suffered the worst of all Württemberg cities, with 6,530 people killed in a single air raid. The year ended with Gauleiter Murr's calling upon the people of Württemberg to fight on to victory in loyalty to the Führer, in an editorial published in the Stuttgart Nazi newspaper *NS-Kurier* for 30 December 1944.

Minister President Mergenthaler's New Year's greeting to Hitler expressed his confidence that Germany would never capitulate. Less than five months later it was all over.

Up to 19 April 1945 Stuttgart was bombed 15 times and 281 people killed in those raids. American Forces captured Heilbronn on 13 April, Schwäbisch Hall on the 17th, Freudenstadt on the 19th, Tübingen and Crailsheim (for the second time) on the 20th. Lord Mayor Dr. Strölin, who had escaped detection for his part in the 20th of July assassination attempt on Hitler, managed to save Stuttgart from total destruction. He offered the city's capitulation through an agent on 10 April and surrendered it to the French on 21 April 1945 in the *Gasthof zum Ritter* in Degerloch, the temporary headquarters of the First French Army. Gauleiter Murr and Minister President Mergenthaler had left the city a day earlier. Murr committed suicide on 14 May 1945. (His house in Stuttgart at Richard Wagner Straße 8 is the residence of the American Consul General today.) Mergenthaler was a POW of the French in Balingen for many years before his release. Dr. Strölin died in Stuttgart on 21 January 1963.

The French named Dr. Arnulf Klett (1905–1974), an anti-Nazi lawyer, the provisional Lord Mayor of Stuttgart at the end of hostilities. On 8 July 1945 the American Regional Military Government moved its headquarters from Schwäbisch Gmünd to Olgastraße 11 (my present office) in Stuttgart. The headquarters of the French Military Government moved from Karlsruhe to Freiburg on 10 July. The boundaries of the American and French Zones of Occupation were established on that date.

General Dwight D. Eisenhower announced the foundation of the state of Württemberg-Baden on 19 September 1945. Five days later Reinhold Maier was sworn in as Minister President of the new state, which consisted of North Baden and North Württemberg in the American Zone of Occupation. In their occupation zone to the south, the French established State Secretaries in South Baden and South Württemberg-Hohenzollern.

OCCUPIED AREAS OF GERMANY

MAP

DENMARK

SCHLESWIG-HOLSTEIN

U.S. ENCLAVE

HAMBURG

MECKLENBURG

BREMEN

BRITISH ZONE

LOWER SAXONY

HANOVER

BRANDENBURG

BERLIN

NETHERLANDS

ESSEN

NORTH RHINE WESTPHALIA

KASSEL

SACHSEN - ANHALT

SOVIET ZONE

COLOGNE

U.S. ZONE

THURINGIA

SAXONY

DRESDEN

COBLENZ

HESSE

FRANKFURT

RHINELAND-PALATINATE

FRENCH ZONE

CZECHOSLOVAKIA

HEIDELBERG

NUERNBERG

WUERTTEMBERG-BADEN

BAVARIA

FRANCE

ZONE

WUERTTEM-BERG

SOUTH BADEN

MUNICH

AUSTRIA

SWITZERLAND

ITALY

The *Stuttgarter Zeitung* was the first German newspaper to be licensed by the American Military Government. Its first issue appeared on 18 September 1945, followed by the first issue of the *Schwäbisches Tageblatt* in Tübingen three days later. The schools reopened on 1 October.

On 30 June 1946 the constitutional assembly for Württemberg-Baden was elected. The first Landtag convened on 24 November and 90 percent of the populace accepted the state's new constitution on that date in a plebiscite. In the French Zone the first consultative state assembly did not convene until November 1946. Beginning on 22 November its 65 members met in Bebenhausen to draft a constitution for South Württemberg-Hohenzollern, which was accepted on 20 May 1947. Lorenz Bock became State President. After his death in 1948 he was succeeded by Dr. Gebhard Müller.

Stuttgart will never forget the "speech of hope" delivered by U.S. Secretary of State James F. Byrnes in the State Theater on 6 September 1946. It marked a major change in American foreign policy toward a just-defeated Germany, offering the readiness of "the American people to help the German people to win their way back to an honorable place among the free and peace-loving nations of the world." The Byrnes' speech set the stage for the Marshall Plan, which made possible post-war economic recovery in Germany and elsewhere in Europe.

The Basic Law of the Federal Republic of Germany came into being on 23 May 1949. Article 29 permitted the restructuring of German internal boundaries based on cultural, historical, economic, and demographic considerations. In a plebiscite on 9 December 1951 in North Württemberg 93.5 percent, in South Württemberg-Hohenzollern 91.4 percent, in North Baden 57.1 percent, and in South Baden 37.8 percent of the populace voted for the formation of a southwest state. On 25 April 1952 the new state of Baden-Württemberg was created and Reinhold Maier elected its first Minister President. (The name Swabia was deliberately not chosen in order not to offend the sensibilities of the people from Baden.) Although 52.2 percent of the residents of Baden were against becoming a part of Württemberg in 1951, a new vote on 7 June 1970 showed that 81.9 percent wanted to stick with Baden-Württemberg after 18 years of a happy political marriage.

Reinhold Maier stepped down as Minister President in the fall of 1953. He was succeeded by Dr. Gebhard Müller. The constitution of Baden-Württemberg was adopted on 1 November 1953. Following Dr. Müller's appointment as President of the Federal Constitutional Court in 1958, Dr. Kurt Georg Kiesinger was elected Minister President. Dr. Hans Filbinger became the Minister of the Interior in his cabinet.

In December 1966 Minister President Kiesinger became the Chancellor of the Federal Republic of Germany. His successor as Minister President was the Freiburg lawyer Dr. Hans Filbinger, who was born in Mannheim in 1913. In the 1968 elections Dr. Filbinger's party, the Christian Democratic Union, won an absolute majority in Baden-Württemberg, and again in the elections of 1972 and 1976. In the summer of 1978 playwright Rolf Hochhuth, author of "The Deputy," "Soldiers," and "The Death of a Hunter," made a public statement about Dr. Filbinger having condemned a German sailor to death while serving as a judge advocate in the German Navy in World War II. A court case ensued. Further investigation by the German newspaper *Die Zeit* brought to light additional questionable actions by Dr. Filbinger which the Minister President denied. Under pressure from his own party, he finally resigned as Minister President on 7 August 1978. Professors Heinz Hürten, Wolfgang Jäger and Hugo Ott published a study of "The Filbinger Case" in 1980, but it came out too late to save his political career.

On 30 August 1978 Dr. Filbinger was succeeded by Lothar Späth, who had been the chairman of the CDU faction in the Landtag for six years until becoming Minister of the Interior in February 1978. Born in Sigmaringen on 16 November 1937, he is the youngest Minister President in the Federal Republic. In the *Land* (state) elections on 15 March 1980, the CDU again won an absolute majority and Lothar Späth was confirmed in office by popular vote.

Dr. Arnulf Klett died on 14 August 1974, having served as Lord Mayor of Stuttgart longer than any other Lord Mayor of any other post-war German city. He was succeeded by State Secretary Manfred Rommel of the Ministry of Finance. The son of Field Marshal Erwin Rommel got 58.9 percent of the votes in the election held on 1 December. You can read more about both of these Swabian politicians in the next chapter.

XV Swabian Statesmen and Politicians

Present and future generations of Germans can be grateful that the tender infancy of the Federal Republic was entrusted to such capable statesmen as its first Chancellor, Konrad Adenauer (1876–1967), a Rhinelander, and its first President, Theodor Heuss, a Swabian.

The grandfather of Theodor Heuss was a business man from Heilbronn, where his son Louis was born. Louis (1853–1903) attended the royal *Karlsgymnasium* in Heilbronn. After completing his studies at the Stuttgart Polytechnic, he built roads, waterways, and streetcars as a civil servant in Brackenheim. He married Elisabeth Gümbel in 1880. Their three sons Ludwig, Hermann, and Theodor were born in Brackenheim, the latter on 31 January 1884.

In 1890 the Heuss family moved to Heilbronn, where Theodor attended primary school and then earned his *Abitur* at the *Karlsgymnasium* in 1902. He read literature with a voracious appetite, wrote poetry, sketched people and landscapes, and took an avid interest in politics while at the *Gymnasium,* which was renamed in his honor after he had become the President of the Federal Republic. In his speech at the dedication of the school on 16 September 1950, he said he hoped the city council would not regret the new name. Although he had enjoyed his days there and was a good student, he admitted to having spent some time in the school's lockup – twice within three weeks – as a student. The first time he had boxed another student's ear, shattering the drum. The second time he had insulted a policeman. Heuss was fond of telling this anecdote throughout his life.

From his earliest years Heuss wrote articles about literature and politics, as well as poetry. His first published effort appeared in Friedrich Naumann's magazine *Die Hilfe* on 20 April 1902. The subject was Wilhelm Busch, the creator of "Max and Moritz" (and probably the world's first comic strip), in whom Heuss recognized the serious satirist and first-rate artist at a time when few were willing to agree with him. Shortly thereafter, Heuss' byline appeared frequently under poems, articles, and book reviews in the Heilbronn *Neckar-Zeitung* while he was still a student in Munich.

At the University of Munich (and for two semesters in Berlin), Heuss studied national economy. He completed his doctorate at

Theodor Heuss

Munich in 1905 with a dissertation on "Winegrowing and the Status of Winegrowers in Heilbronn on the Neckar."

In 1905 Friedrich Naumann asked Heuss to take over the duties of political editor of his weekly magazine, *Die Hilfe,* which first appeared in December 1884 and went out of business under Hitler. Heuss moved to Berlin to accept the position and continued to furnish articles to the *Neckar-Zeitung* in Heilbronn.

Friedrich Naumann (1860-1919) was a Protestant pastor turned politician and publisher. He had a life-long influence on Heuss, who wrote his biography in 1937 (republished in 1949). With the help of Heuss and other friends who campaigned for him in his electoral district in Heilbronn, Naumann was elected to the federal parliament *(Reichstag)* in 1907 and again in 1913. In 1919 he represented the German Democratic Party, which he had helped to found, in the National Assembly in Weimar, and became the party's first chairman. He died suddenly on 24 August 1919.

Elisabeth Eleonore ("Elly") Knapp was a student at the University of Freiburg when she first met Theodor Heuss while visiting Berlin in 1903. Her father was a well-known professor of national economy at the University of Strassbourg. She was a follower of Friedrich Naumann, in whose home she saw her future husband for the first time. They were married on 11 April 1908 in Strassbourg.

The pastor who performed the marriage was Albert Schweitzer, who later became one of the world's most revered humanists.

Elly was not too enthusiastic about her husband's dedicated involvement in politics. Instead, she wanted him to write a historical novel based on the life of his grandfather.

In 1912 Heuss moved from Berlin back to Heilbronn to help Naumann get reelected to the *Reichstag*. His financial future was assured by his becoming the editor-in-chief of the *Neckar-Zeitung*, but his attempt to win a seat in the Württemberg parliament *(Landtag)* at the end of that year was a failure. At that time he helped to save the magazine *März (March)*, which almost went under, by becoming a part-time editor and changing its business methods. The weekly magazine had been founded by Albert Langen and Ludwig Thoma, the Bavarian writer, in 1907. (They had founded the famous satirical magazine *Simplicissimus* in Munich.) The magazine carried articles about politics and literature. Hermann Hesse was its first literary editor. Under Heuss the political side received increased attention, despite Hesse's objections. In addition to Hermann Hesse, many of Germany's leading writers were contributors to the pages of *März* including Thomas and Heinrich Mann, Franz Werfel, and Stefan Zweig.

Theodor Heuss was not called up for military service in World War I for reasons of health. In 1917 the publisher of *März*, Conrad Haußmann, and his partners, had to cease publication for financial reasons and the paper shortage caused by the war. Furthermore, most of the editors of the magazine, including Theodor Heuss, were considering employment with other magazines. In the spring of 1918 Heuss moved back to Berlin to become the editor of *Deutsche Politik (German Politics)*. The death of Friedrich Naumann in August 1919 was a great personal loss.

In 1920 Heuss was elected to the district assembly of Berlin-Schöneberg. On 24 October of that year the German Political Academy *(Deutsche Hochschule für Politik)* was formally opened in Berlin in the presence of Friedrich Ebert, the first President of the Weimar Republic. The academy had top-flight professors and guest lecturers from government officials and active politicians. Its purpose was to develop political awareness, independent of partisan politics and political parties, among people from all walks of life, and to promote understanding between peoples while supporting the Weimar Republic. Theodor Heuss was the director of studies at the academy from 1920 until 1924, when it became the Otto-Suhr Institute at the Free University of Berlin. He gave lectures there on history and politics until 1933.

Elected to the *Reichstag* on the Württemberg list in 1924, Heuss represented the German Democratic Party until 1928. (He lost in the elections of 1928, but was reelected to serve from 1930 to 1932. His party was renamed the *Staatspartei* in July 1930.) In their congratulatory letters, his friends said that his sense of humor and Swabian thick-headedness would serve him well in wading through the swamp of German politics. In his speeches and writings he advocated the strengthening of democratic ideals while stridently speaking out against the Nazis. In 1923 he had become the editor of the political magazine *Die Deutsche Nation (The German Nation)*. In a speech before the Reichstag on 19 March 1927 he called the attention of the delegates to the need to support independent cultural institutions, such as the Swabian Schiller Museum in Marbach, which had run into financial difficulties. He called it "the Pantheon of Swabian Intellect" and continued: "Were I to provide statistics about the contribution of the Swabian intellect to German cultural history, I would need a half an hour . . . The contribution of Swabia to German history, I believe, is substantial enough so that a certain repayment, not in an intellectual sense – which we don't need very much—but in a financial form is not asking too much." The 43-year-old deputy to Parliament received loud applause, and the Schiller National Museum in Marbach is still alive and well today.

After delivering a lecture to his students on National Socialism in 1931, Heuss was urged by them to expand the material into a book. His *Hitler's Way* was published in 1932. Heuss had read *Mein Kampf* and was one of the first journalists to examine National Socialism with care before 1933. In parliament he debated with Göring, Frick, Goebbels, Strasser, and other Nazi bigwigs. On 11 May 1932 he remarked during a speech: "I have had to put up with so much stupid and also evil nonsense from National Socialists during my life that they no longer get on my nerves. I have developed an immunity in this area." By the end of July he was one of only four from his own party to be reelected. The *Reichstag* was dissolved on 12 September

1932. In the new elections that followed, Heuss did not regain his seat.

In an article published in the *Frankfurter Zeitung* on 25 July 1932, Heuss was critical of Hitler's twisting the truth around. With keen foresight he observed: ". . . it is not the first time that the National Socialist ideology, taken seriously, delivers weapons to the arsenal of non-Germans for use against Germany or Germans." Heuss managed to get reelected to the *Reichstag* on 5 March 1933 by appearing on the Social Democratic list, but his mandate was revoked on 12 July.

Shortly after Hitler came to power on 23 March 1933, the German Political Academy in Berlin was "aligned" by the Nazis and Heuss dismissed from the faculty. (His name on the list of those to be fired came before Socialist and Jewish colleagues.) His Hitler book, which had been translated into Dutch, Swedish, and Italian, was now burned in public.

Stripped of his political and professorial offices, Heuss worked hard to build up the circulation of *Hilfe,* but he had to leave the magazine for political reasons in 1936 after constant conflicts with the Nazi Propaganda Ministry concerning censorship and his political views. His wife Elly got into advertising, writing copy and recording it on records and radio spots to keep the family solvent. Over the years she turned it into a profitable business. In 1941 Heuss received a two-year contract with the *Frankfurter Zeitung.* Martin Bormann, Secretary of the Nazi Party, tried to prohibit Heuss from writing, but Heuss got around it by using the penname Thomas Brackheim (from Brackenheim where he was born) and writing anonymously. Always just a step ahead of the Gestapo, he managed to avoid serious trouble with the Nazi government because of his close friends in editorial offices and in the Propaganda Ministry itself.

The *Frankfurter Zeitung* ceased publication on 31 August 1944. Between 1937 and 1945 Heuss devoted a great deal of his time to writing the biographies of his old mentor Friedrich Naumann (1937), the architect Hans Poelzig (1939), the zoologist Anton Dohrn (1940), the natural scientist Justus von Liebig (1942), and Robert Bosch (published in 1946). The heavy air raids on Berlin prompted Heuss and his wife to move to Heidelberg in the fall of 1943, where he worked on his biography of Robert Bosch. They lived in the attic in the house of Elly's sister in the suburb of Handschuhsheim. In January 1945 Heuss visited and described the bombed-out city of Heilbronn, which had been destroyed on 4 December 1944 in a half-hour air raid.

On 30 March 1945 American troops occupied Heidelberg. Even before the war ended on 8 May, Heuss had been ear-marked for a role in the provincial government of Heidelberg-Mannheim. At first he was put in charge of the schools. In September he became one of those licensed by military government to publish the newspaper *Rhein-Neckar-Zeitung*. When the state governments were formed in September 1945, Heuss was named Minister of Culture as an American condition for approving the cabinet of Reinhold Maier in Würt-temberg-Baden. Between 1946 and 1949 Heuss and his wife were delegates to the state parliament *(Landtag)* from the Democratic People's Party/Free Democratic Party (which Heuss had led since December 1948). When Colonel William W. Dawson, the first American military governor for the state, died suddenly in 1947, Heuss wrote a touching obituary praising his humanity and humor and thanking the American officer for having converted his head-quarters into a source of help rather than just orders.

In January 1948 Heuss was named a professor at Stuttgart Poly-technic, but he was able to teach only during the summer semester. Elected a delegate to the federal parliamentary council in Bonn for Württemberg-Baden, he worked on the shaping of the constitution of the Federal Republic, its so-called "Basic Law," between 1 September 1948 and 23 May 1949.

On 12 September 1949 Professor Dr. Theodor Heuss was elected the first President of the Federal Republic of Germany. Accused by some reporters of not having sufficient "elbow power" to be a successful politician, Heuss responded in his first speech as President: "I think we have really had enough of 'elbow politics' . . . What is the office of President of the Federal Republic of Germany? Thus far it has been a tangle of paragraphs. From this hour on it is an office re-plete with humaneness."

Frau Elly Heuss died in July 1952. Theodor Heuss was reelected on 17 July 1954 (he had turned 70 in January that year) for a second term of office from 1954 to 1959.

President Dwight D. Eisenhower invited Theodor Heuss to visit the United States during the summer of 1958. On 5 June of that year he spoke before a joint meeting of the two Houses of Congress. At that time he said in his speech:

"We shall never, never forget how President Truman by means of the so-called airlift in 1948-49, with the approval of the entire American people, saved Germany's old capital of Berlin – literally saved it – and thus decided the fate of Europe at a crucial point. The Germans, too, have perceived it as their duty to participate as free and active partners in the potentialities of peace and freedom implicit in this concept of the fate of Europe. Hence, the Federal Republic's loyal cooperation in the overall defense planning of NATO. *Never again in the future shall German and American soldiers fight each other.* And we realize that the sacrifice made by American mothers in having their sons in German garrisons – not, indeed, for the purpose of preparing wars but to prevent them by their presence and thereby to secure the democratic way of life for the future – we realize that this sacrifice corresponds to the great sense of duty which marks your tradition of liberty."

"Believe me that our Germany will never again depart from the path of democracy and freedom. It is our sincere resolve to be good and dependable allies. . . . It is my firm conviction that the peoples of the Free World – deeply rooted as they are in the Christian faith-- possess the moral strength to maintain their position and uphold their ideals. All that is required is to set in motion some of the all-pervasive forces inherent in human nature: reason, a sense of proportion, and perhaps a little love."

By law President Heuss was not allowed to serve a third term. He stepped down on 12 September 1959. In June 1961 Oxford University awarded him an honorary doctorate of civil law. He visited Israel and India in 1960, making important contacts for post-war Germany. He began to write his memoirs, completing the first volume, describing the years from 1905 to 1933, in 1963. As he set to work on the second volume in May of that year, his health began to fail. He died on 12 December 1963 and was buried after a state funeral in Stuttgart's *Waldfriedhof.*

Eduard Adorno, then a deputy to the *Bundestag,* said of Theodor Heuss in April 1964: "With Heuss, as hardly before in the German political sphere, humaneness became a power which found resonance among the masses. It is not just a phrase to say that he will never be forgotten."

On the morning of 26 April 1969 (then) Major General Edward Leon Rowny, the Deputy Chief of Staff of the United States European Command, asked me to kidnap Lord Mayor ARNULF KLETT of Stuttgart and bring him to Patch Barracks.

I borrowed the General's staff car and driver and headed for the woods near the Solitude Ring, where I knew that Dr. Klett would be leading a volunteer clean-up action of discarded trash and litter. When I spotted him tugging on an old spare tire, I flashed my ID card and asked him to follow me to the car.

Once inside, I explained that Major General Rowny wanted to see him right away in his office.

"And just who are you?" he asked, the flashy bow tie bobbing on his Adam's apple.

"The Special Assistant to the Director of Public Affairs at European Command Headquarters in Patch Barracks," I replied.

"And just what kind of a 'public affair' do you have in store for me?"

"General Rowny heard that you were cleaning up out in the woods this morning. He wants to show you the American Boy Scouts and Cub Scouts doing the same thing at Patch."

"In his office?" he asked skeptically, a grin playing about the edges of his thin lips.

"Not quite, sir," I said. The Scouts are cleaning up outside, of course, and you'll see them in action. But before you do, General Rowny would like to offer you a cup of coffee and talk a little business."

"Such as?"

"The lack of lighting on Katzenbachstraße. A man was killed there not too long ago."

"Have you told the authorities?"

"A letter was sent to the Rathaus quite some time ago."

Dr. Klett pulled a black notebook out of his pocket. "I haven't seen it," he said, as he wrote a note to himself, "but I most certainly will."

"I really shouldn't help you Americans at all," he said, "not after the way you treated me."

"You mean this little 'kidnapping'?"

He smiled broadly. He shook his silver head, with the hair combed straight back. "You know, Herr Larson, I've been the Lord Mayor of Stuttgart for almost exactly 24 years now, but the Americans didn't want me to have the job at first."

"How so?" I asked, as we drove through Stuttgart-Vaihingen.

"The day after the French occupied Stuttgart in April 1945, they appointed me Lord Mayor of Stuttgart. The Americans investigated me for eight months before they agreed to let me keep the job."

He broke out laughing. "Don't look so serious," he said. "It's a true story, but I was only pulling your leg. I love the Americans, and I don't bear any grudges. But it's true that I wasn't administered the official oath of office until 8 October 1945 by Lieutenant Colonel Charles L. Jackson, the American Military Commandant for Greater Stuttgart."

At Patch Barracks Dr. Klett had a leisurely cup of coffee with Major General Rowny before we went out to see the Boy Scouts and Cub Scouts at work. He shook hands not only with the Scout leaders, but with each one of the Scouts, praising them for their interest in protecting the environment.

A photographer from Patch took pictures, and I sent several to Dr. Klett, with the request that he autograph one of them with the both of us on it. It hangs in my office today with the note in his handwriting: "We Oldies take a well-earned rest while the Scouts are hard at work."

Two weeks later lights were installed along Katzenbachstraße.

That was my first personal encounter with this famous Lord Mayor. He was an optimist who had become a legend in his own lifetime for his boundless energy, his Swabian stubbornness and unswerving determination to get the job done with as little red tape as possible, his love of people, and particularly his Swabian sense of humor.

Arnulf Klett was born in Stuttgart on 8 April 1905. He studied law at the University of Tübingen and was a practicing attorney from 1930 to 1945 in Stuttgart. He defended many a client who had gotten into trouble with the Nazis. He was active in resistance circles. In November 1944 he was obliged to perform mandatory service in the city administration. On his 40th birthday Dr. Klett was working in the war damage office when he was urged to contact Dr. Strölin about saving Stuttgart from further destruction by surrendering it to the advancing Allies. Actually, there wasn't much left to surrender. Of the 63,000 buildings in Stuttgart, 14,370 had been totally demolished in air raids, 9,620 so badly damaged that they couldn't be used until rebuilt, and only

2,000 left intact. Since Stuttgart's bridges over the Neckar were blown up senselessly on 21 April, the French First Army was the first to occupy the city. The American 100th Infantry Division came to a temporary halt on the right bank of the Neckar.

Lord Mayor Dr. Strölin surrendered the city to the French. General Schwarz of the First Division appointed Dr. Arnulf Klett the new Lord Mayor around noon on 23 April 1945. Dr. Klett's first public proclamation appeared on 14 May and stated, in part:

"I am a Swabian by birth and I reached the Swabian age of 40 just a few weeks ago. I have always been a man of action. In my profession as a lawyer I fought against encroachment by the National Socialist system. Just as I was able to justify the trust of my clients in those cases, so do I now ask for the trust of all my fellow citizens. I need it for a task assumed under the most difficult of conditions. People of Stuttgart, think of the time when our efforts made Swabia almost an envied Paradise. We don't want to lose what's left of it, but rather to rebuild it step by step. Our work is no longer destruction, but reconstruction. Do your part!"

He set the example by rolling up his sleeves, taking off that bow tie, and digging up rubble himself. Meeting with his new City Council in an improvised office at 20 Mörikestraße (incendiary bombs had destroyed the old Rathaus, which was not completely rebuilt until 1956), he set to work to restore utilities, provide food, housing and public transportation for a city of 325,000 survivors of the war (which was growing daily with returning evacuees and refugees), while trying to meet the demands first of the French and then of the American military governments. On 8 October 1945 the Americans confirmed Dr. Klett's position by administering to him the formal oath of office.

Dr. Klett's accomplishments as the dynamic Lord Mayor of Stuttgart for the next 29 years were legion. With indefatigable energy and boundless optimism he tackled the immediate and long-term projects that raised Stuttgart from the ashes to the beautiful, modern metropolis it is today. A brief chronology of the most important of these will give you a thumbnail history of post-war Stuttgart:

1946

7 January	Gas works back in operation
14 January	First express train leaves Stuttgart for Munich
19 January	Stuttgart Polytechnic reopened

1947

3 February	Stuttgart public library reopened

1948

27 September	Rebuilt König-Karls Bridge opened to traffic
3 October	First PAA flight lands at Stuttgart Airport

1949

3 September	Kursaal in Bad Cannstatt reopened
17 September	Cannstatt Volksfest reopened
29 October	Rebuilt Wilhelms Bridge opened to traffic

1950

11 January	Gaisburg heating plant in operation
19 March	Dedication of rebuilt Leonhards Church
13 May	Opening of steetcar line between Zuffenhausen and Stammheim
1 June	New signal system at Stuttgart railroad station goes into operation
3 June	Opening of the Federal Horticultural Exhibit at Killesberg Park

1951

In January	Stuttgart Opera performs Hindemith's opera "Matthew the Painter" as first post-war ensemble in Rome
28 June	The 1,000th Porsche comes off the assembly line in Zuffenhausen

16 December 1952	Opening of extended runway at Stuttgart Airport
13 May	Rebuilt synagogue dedicated
19 December 1953	New Mörike library on Silberburgstraße opened
In March	Youth Hostel in Haußmannstraße opened
12 September	Rebuilt choir of Stiftskirche dedicated
25 November 1954	Stuttgart Streetcar Corporation opens Filder Line
22 March	New annex of South-German Radio in Neckar-straße dedicated
23 April	Dedication of rebuilt Gustav-Siegle-Haus
15 June	First camp site opens on the Cannstatt "Wasen"
28 June	Dedication of new building for the Stuttgart Chamber of Commerce and Industry
1955	
9 January	City Council approves trial use of parking meters on Sophienstraße
19 March	Rebuilt St.-Eberhards Church dedicated
21 May	Rebuilt Leutze mineral bath opened to the public
15 October	Dedication of the rebuilt Stuttgart School for Music
1956	
5 February	Dedication of the Stuttgart TV tower, which has become a symbol of the city
4 May	Dedication of the Market Square wing of the re-built Stuttgart Rathaus
29 July	Dedication of the Stuttgart Liederhalle
1957	
7 March	Two Neckar boats begin passenger service between Stuttgart and Besigheim
6 April	The Eberhard-Ludwigs-Gymnasium is the 29th school built in post-war Stuttgart
1 October	City administration goes on a 5-day-week work schedule
1958	
17 March	The Wagenburg Tunnel is opened to traffic
31 March	Dedication of the Stuttgart Neckar harbor

1 June	Dedication of the fully rebuilt Stiftskirche
9 October	Reopening of the Municipal Gallery

1959

20 May	Reconstruction of Bürgerhospital completed
16 October	Rebuilt Königsbau opened to the public

1960

21 February	Dedication of the Hospital Church
30 June	Dedication of the Middle School in Degerloch
12 August	A PAA DC-6 B is christened "Clipper Stuttgart"
27 December	Stuttgart's first ice-skating rink opens

1961

22 April	Dedication of the Amerika Haus on Friedrich-straße
6 June	Dedication of the rebuilt State Parliament *(Landtag)* building

1962

13 March	Dedication of the new Schloßgarten Hotel
5 October	Dedication of the *Kleines Haus* (small house) of the Württemberg State Theaters

1963

15 March	The Wilhelms-Gymnasium in Degerloch is the 75th school built in post-war Stuttgart
16 September	Stammheim prison opens as the most modern confinement facility in the Federal Republic
11 November	The "Salute" high-rise in the Fasanenhof housing area is the highest apartment building in post-war Germany (70 meters tall)

1964

21 March	The mid-section of the rebuilt New Castle is dedicated

1965

26 March	The rebuilt Wilhelms-Palace *(Wilhelmspalais)* is dedicated as a library and historical archive of the city

1966

27 March	More than 72,000 citizens visit the Rathaus during its first "open house"
10 May	The first 750 meters of Stuttgart's new subway

| | system are opened to the public |
| 20 October | Stuttgart's first pre-fabricated school, named after Herbert Hoover, is dedicated |

1967

10 May	Stuttgart's 200th traffic light is switched on
2 October	Germany's first psychotherapeutic clinic is dedicated in Stuttgart-Sonnenberg
24 November	The Charlottenplatz traffic artery is completed

1968

19 February	Rebuilt main building of the Katharinenhospital is dedicated
6 May	Stuttgart "Air Terminal" on the corner of Lautenschlager and Kronenstraße is dedicated
5 December	The *Kleiner Schloßplatz* (little Castle Square) in mid-town Stuttgart is dedicated

1969

23 July	Floodlights go into operation in the Neckar Stadium
19 September	The hotel Stuttgart International, the largest in Baden-Württemberg, opens
In June	The Stuttgart Ballet completes the first of two triumphant tours to America
In November	The Stuttgart Ballet completes its second triumphant tour to America

1970

21 April	The new "Theater der Altstadt" (old city theater) opens beneath Charlottenplatz
12 July	The first Boeing 747 "Jumbo Jet" lands at Stuttgart Airport
18 September	The Stuttgart Chamber Orchestra celebrates its 25th anniversary under the direction of Professor Karl Münchinger
8 November	Dedication of the "Monument of Admonition" (the massive blocks across from the New Castle) for the victims of National Socialist tyranny

On 23 April 1970 Dr. Klett celebrated 25 years in office – longer than any other post-war Lord Mayor in the Federal Republic. In honor of this occasion General David A. Burchinal, then Deputy

Commander in Chief of the United States European Command, asked me to prepare the paperwork and citation for an Outstanding Civilian Service Award for Dr. Klett, which he presented to the Lord Mayor during a special ceremony in the Stuttgart Rathaus on his Silver Anniversary in office. Dr. Klett had already received many international honors – from Sweden, France, Austria, Finland, Greece, Belgium, and Italy – in addition to the Grand Cross of Merit with Star from the Federal Republic of Germany, but I know that the Outstanding Civilian Service Award from the United States of America also meant a great deal to him. It is not only mentioned in a list of his decorations in the memorial booklet prepared after his death, but the full text of the citation appears in a book published in honor of his 25 years as Lord Mayor of Stuttgart.

Dr. Klett's list of directorships and memberships in industrial and private associations is as long as his list of awards and decorations. One wonders how he found the time to attend the board meetings of the German Parliament of Cities, the Baden-Württemberg Parliament of Cities, the Union of Communal Employers' Associations, the Federation of Communal Enterprises, the International Mayors' Union for Franco-German Understanding, the Administrative Union for the State Water Supply, the South German Gas Supply Corporation, the Stuttgart Airport Corporation, the South German Radio Network, the Baden-Württemberg Red Cross Association, the executive council of the Baden-Württemberg State Theaters, the Stuttgart Transportation Corporation, the Stuttgart Power and Light Corporation, and the Stuttgart Streetcar Corporation, to mention only a few.

His deputy for ten years, former First Mayor Dr. Jürgen Hahn, described the Klett "style" in the Rathaus: "No breaks, no slackening of energy, no desire for rest and introspection, no relaxation, no private life, too little time for the family, no leisure time or idleness. He was the motor that drove everything, and its propulsion was felt in the remotest corner of City Hall."

He was everywhere, like an American politician up for reelection, but on a year-round basis. He went from his office to official functions, to banquets, to people's homes to bring them the best wishes of the city on their anniversaries. That grin and bow tie were his trademarks. He took the steps in the Rathaus two at a time on the way up to his office just before eight o'clock every morning. That was his only form of exercise.

His favorite role was tapping the bung at the opening of the annual Volksfest in Bad Cannstatt, which reopened on 17 September 1949. He always began with a speech, full of wit and earthy Swabian humor. And after tapping the bung, he led the band. That was probably his only form of relaxation.

Dr. Klett not only personally guided the restoration and development of Stuttgart's major industries, the construction of the harbor, the expansion of the airport, and the start of the rapid transit system. He promoted the cultural activities for which Stuttgart is now famous: the Stuttgart Ballet, Professor Karl Münchinger's chamber orchestra, the theater and the opera.

In June 1948, just three years after the war, he met with French mayors in Mont Pèlerin, France, to form the International Union of Mayors. In May 1950 he chaired a Franco-German Mayors' Conference in Stuttgart and opened a "French Week" in the city. In May 1958 he was dubbed a Knight of the Legion of Honor in recognition of his efforts to promote better understanding between the peoples of France and Germany. On 26 May 1962 a partnership agreement between Strassbourg and Stuttgart was signed in the Stuttgart Rathaus. (An enlarged photograph of that occasion hangs in the waiting room outside of the Lord Mayor's office.) A second "French Week" in Stuttgart followed and President Charles de Gaulle visited Stuttgart that September. Lord Mayor Pierre Pflimlin of Strassbourg and Dr. Arnulf Klett became close personal friends.

From the start of the occupation by the Americans, the opening of the Headquarters of VII Corps in Kelley Barracks in Stuttgart-Möhringen, the reactivation of Seventh Army at Patch Barracks in Stuttgart-Vaihingen in November 1952, the move of Headquarters Seventh Army to Heidelberg in December 1966 to merge with Headquarters US Army, Europe, and the arrival of Headquarters United States European Command from Paris, Lord Mayor Dr. Klett was a good friend and genial host to the US Forces and their families. One of the first of the German-American Clubs, Stuttgart Men's 1948, was founded by Joseph Hall, a close friend of Dr. Klett. It is alive and well today.

On the afternoon of 14 August 1974, while on a rest cure near

Baden-Baden, Dr. Klett died of a cardiac arrest and embolism of the lung. He was buried in Stuttgart's *Waldfriedhof* after having served 29 years, three months, and 21 days in office. Of all the speeches in the memorial ceremony held in the *Liederhalle* on 21 August 1974, Professor Walter Erich Schäfer, the former Managing Director of the Württemberg State Theaters, came closest to describing the Dr. Klett I knew. In so doing, he also described the nature of the Swabian, so permit me to quote a bit of it here:

"It has been said frequently today, that Arnulf Klett was a Swabian. One couldn't fail to hear that. But I'm not sure that everyone who cited him as a Swabian is aware of the difficulty of defining the nature of the Swabian; for the Swabian is a multi-faceted type, difficult to descry and to see through. Often we don't even know ourselves and that has created many a misunderstanding. For the Swabians are not only the little people who built up an industry in the last quarter of the previous century – far from any raw materials, far from the centers of trade – which has become the best and most dependable in Germany, supported solely by the derring-do of the entrepreneur and the high quality of his employees. This Swabia also has quite a different side: it has produced Friedrich Schiller and Hölderlin, Mörike, Hermann Hesse, and countless others. And Arnulf Klett once said in a conversation with me that one should look somewhere in the world for a small apartment like the room in the Tübingen theological seminary where Hölderlin, Hegel and Schelling lived together. That is completely in keeping with the nature of the Swabian, with the nature of Arnulf Klett. In an extraordinary fashion he felt himself in harmony with this part of the domestic character."

One of the busiest places in Stuttgart is the underground passageway and shopping center between the railroad station and the beginning of Königsstraße, Stuttgart's main shopping artery. It is quite in keeping with the restless, bustling nature of Dr. Arnulf Klett that this passageway bears his name.

MANFRED ROMMEL, the son of Field Marshal Erwin Rommel, won the election as the successor to Dr. Arnulf Klett as Lord Mayor of Stuttgart in 1974. His father's name had something to do with it, but what counted even more were his 18 years of successful service in the Baden-Württemberg government, and especially his Swabian upbringing. (Most of the conservative Swabian electorate remembered the activist, "Juso" background of Peter Conradi, his closest opponent.)

He was born on Christmas Eve in Stuttgart in 1928, the only child of Captain Erwin Rommel (then serving with the 13th Infantry Regiment) and his wife Lucie Maria, nee Molling. He attended elementary school in Goslar, while his father was a battalion commander in Infantry Regiment 17, and then in Potsdam, where his father taught at the officers' school. He continued his education in Wiener Neustadt, after his father assumed command of the War Academy there, and then in Ulm.

From 1 January 1944 until 15 March 1945 Manfred Rommel was a *Luftwaffenhelfer,* helping to load anti-aircraft guns near Ulm. He was called up to perform labor service on 18 March 1945 and taken prisoner by the French on 22 April. He was released six months later. On 8 September a statement he had prepared the previous April about the real circumstances surrounding his father's death was published in the first post-war issue of the *Südkurier.*

After earning his *Abitur* in Biberach in 1947, Manfred Rommel studied law at the University of Tübingen. He passed his first state examination in 1952 and his second one four years later. In 1956 he started his career as a civil servant as an assessor in the Baden-Württemberg government. He refused to go to the Federal Parliament as a young man but he worked his way gradually up through the ranks of the governmental hierarchy, catching the attention of fellow members of the Christian Democratic Union (to which he has belonged since 1953): Minister Presidents Kurt Georg Kiesinger and Hans Filbinger. The latter assigned him to the State Ministry to straighten out the finances of Baden-Württemberg. Having accomplished this task superbly, he became the State Secretary, or number two man, in the Baden-Württemberg Ministry of Finance in 1972.

It was in this capacity that I had my first formal dealings with Manfred Rommel. The planning for the annual NATO exercise, REFORGER '74, was well underway when a group of government geologists came to my office in July 1974 to request that the entire exercise be relocated or cancelled.

"But the march tables have already been printed at Fort Riley,

Kansas," I protested.

"That's too bad," they said. "The entire state of Baden-Württemberg has a limestone subsoil. If any oil is spilled, it will pollute the water supply for nine million people."

They were adamant, and the meeting got nowhere. Afterwards, the Exercise Officer for VII Corps, a Canadian lieutenant colonel named Harry Stein, asked what we

should do. He showed me a bunch of pictures of civilian tank trucks dispensing gasoline in violation of environmental laws which he had taken all around Baden-Württemberg.

It was late in the afternoon on a Friday. I picked up the telephone and got an appointment to see State Secretary Rommel the following Monday morning in the Ministry of Finance, which was responsible for requirements of the US and Allied Forces in the state.

"That's great," Harry Stein said, "but how can *he* help us?"

"I hope you don't have any plans to go golfing or fishing this weekend, Harry," I replied, "because your work's cut out for you. Come back here Monday with a VII Corps Spillage Prevention Plan for Petroleum, Oils, and Lubricants – in English and German – and we'll discuss it with State Secretary Rommel Monday morning."

Somehow, Harry Stein, who was a remarkable person, got the miracle performed. He came to my office with an eight-page plan in English and German that Monday morning, and we went over to the Ministry of Finance.

Manfred Rommel listened attentively as Harry Stein described the dilemma we (and thousands of Allied soldiers) were in. He glanced at the spillage prevention plan and at Harry's photos of civilian tank trucks.

"You can discipline your people to follow these instructions," he said, holding up the plan. "I can't issue orders to civilian firms."

Harry Stein nodded. "Sir, we can put a sergeant next to every soldier who refuels his vehicle or pours a Jerry can of gas into the heater in his tent."

Manfred Rommel grinned. "We Germans have an old saying: 'In case of inclement weather, the battle will be fought indoors.' I know that this exercise is important for realistic training. I'll go tell the boss about it at the cabinet meeting this afternoon. You tell General Blanchard it's a go."

When the exercise was over, and not a drop of oil had been spilled, I thought of the irony of it all. Had it not been for the son of the "Desert Fox," there might not have been a REFORGER exercise in 1974 for the sons of his father's former enemies.

While no one envied Manfred Rommel the task of following in the giant footsteps of Arnulf Klett, everyone had great expectations of the first new Lord Mayor of Stuttgart since World War II. Their first discovery (and one they are still making) was that he has a mind of his own. Dr. Klett had run up the Rathaus stairs to get to work promptly at eight o'clock. Manfred Rommel came at nine.

In a conversation he told me why. "At first I got there at eight, too," he admitted, "but I found all kinds of people waiting with problems, requests, you name it. After several weeks of that I got smart and arrived at work at nine. No one was there. Either the staff had taken care of their problems or they got tired of waiting."

Which is not to say that Manfred Rommel is lazy or takes a lackadaisical attitude toward his job. He inherited all of Dr. Klett's directorships of executive boards and acquired a few more, such as deputy chairman of the administrative council of the Stuttgart Lindenmuseum and membership in the Association of Friends of Stuttgart University, the Society for Beautifying Stuttgart, the Society of Friends of the Stuttgart Museum of Nature, and in the Württemberg Association of Savings and Transfer Banks. He also visits the aged, congratulates the octogenarians on their birthdays and those celebrating Golden Wedding anniversaries, and he opens the annual Volksfest in Bad Cannstatt with a humorous speech before tapping the bung.

Invited to visit St. Louis, the sister city of Stuttgart, early in his new position, he turned the invitation down out of Swabian frugality. "I could never convince the taxpayers that I wasn't spending their money," he told me at a reception. When a rash of incidents with

American GIs and taxi drivers brought the latter to his house in Sonnenberg in the middle of the night with their complaints, he sat down the next day with the Commanding General of Seventh Corps and worked out a solution involving the use of ID cards. He told the soldiers to report cab drivers who refused to accept them as fares. When one GI took him at his word, the offending driver promised never to do that again, to save his license. And when the owner of a night club discriminated against black Americans, Lord Mayor Rommel took her license away and her to court. Although the case was not finally settled, the precedent had been set for other establishment owners – and not just in Stuttgart.

Manfred Rommel is a conservative in his politics, but liberal in his thinking and his actions. He is not afraid to oppose the wishes of his city council, or of the members of his own party, for that matter. When the conservative Swabians wanted the Stuttgart theater director Claus Peymann removed because he planned to produce a play by Ulrike Meinhof, the terrorist, and collected money to have the teeth of her colleague in Stammheim prison, Gudrun Ensslin, fixed, Manfred Rommel stood by Peymann despite a storm of criticism.

And when the key figures of the Bader-Meinhof gang took their own lives in prison, Manfred Rommel saw to it that they were buried decently in the *Dornhalden* cemetery. "In death there is no enmity," he said on that occasion.

When I came to Stuttgart in the fall of 1967, the street in front of the railroad station was all torn up as work "progressed" on the rapid transit system begun under Dr. Klett. That street remained torn up for so many years that it became the subject of a local joke. Whenever strangers in town were looking for the railroad station, they were advised to head for that big hole in the center of town. Before the Federal Horticulture Exhibit opened in Stuttgart's Killesberg Park in 1978, Manfred Rommel had lived up to his promise of cleaning up the mess in front of the *Bahnhof*. Today the rapid transit system is nearing completion.

The citizens of Stuttgart have Manfred Rommel to thank for the pedestrian zone that now leads from Arnulf Klett Square in front of the railroad station to Bolzstraße at the Schloßplatz. He has been cited for his personal efforts to promote city planning with the needs of the human being in mind.

Manfred Rommel is a great believer in the power and importance of grassroot politics and critical of rules and regulations from above that can stifle the initiative and freedom of action of cities and communities. (While attending a conference in Washington, D.C. on city planning, he delighted his American hosts by stating that Germans "just worship" rules and regulations.)

In a speech before an American audience not too long ago, Manfred Rommel observed: "The Swabians are the world's most obedient bureaucrats. What is decreed in Bonn is laughed at in Munich--but duly executed in Stuttgart."

Recently he told the American journalist Neal R. Peirce that unless the communities and their elected officials are given "more freedom and the power to act, democracy itself is in danger. For many people the trustworthiness of the system is proven at the local level, where people believe that they really have influence."

Lord Mayor Manfred Rommel was one of the co-founders of the Stuttgart United Service Organizations (USO) in 1975. One of the standing monthly events sponsored by that organization is the "Meet the Mayor" program. Lord Mayor Rommel invites newly arrived Americans to the Rathaus for champagne, a film about Stuttgart, and a city tour including a visit to the TV tower.

If you want to shake hands with Lord Mayor Rommel, whom Michael Getler of the *Washington Post* recently called "one of the more thoughtful men in West German politics," check with the USO Information Booth in the Robinson Barracks PX building or call Stuttgart Military (2721) 6261 or Stuttgart Civilian (0711–819) 6261.

XVI   Swabian Generals

The British historian J. W. Wheeler-Bennett once wrote of a Swabian general: "Throughout his army career he felt himself to be a lonely man, a Swabian unable to fit in completely with the rigidity of the Prussian military machine."

He was not writing about Field Marshal Erwin Rommel, but General Wilhelm Groener, about whom he also said: "Few men have given more selfless service to their country, both as soldier and statesman, and few have been treated with greater lack of gratitude."

Of the same man German historian Friedrich Meinecke wrote: "He held his own at important turning points in German history and thus has earned a place of honor."

Those "turning points" were the abdication of Kaiser Wilhelm II in November 1918 and Germany's acceptance of the conditions of the Treaty of Versailles in June 1919. Groener's connection with both events didn't add to his popularity, especially among his own comrades.

WILHELM GROENER was born in Ludwigsburg – that garrison city mentioned so often in this book – on 22 November 1867. His father, a non-commissioned officer, was an assistant paymaster in the 4th Cavalry Regiment ("Queen Olga") at the time of his birth. Wilhelm attended elementary and secondary schools in Ulm and Ludwigsburg. In the summer of 1884 he took retired Captain Hanke's cram course at the latter's military preparatory academy in Stuttgart and passed the officer's candidate test that October with honors. He had to wait for his 17th birthday, however, before he was eligible to join the 121st Infantry Regiment ("Old Württemberg") in his home town. On 9 September 1886 he completed officers' candidate school as best in his class and was commissioned a Second Lieutenant. On 1 April 1890 he became the adjutant of the III Battalion of the 121st Infantry Regiment, where he spent all of his free time studying for the entrance exams to the War Academy, to which he was admitted as a First Lieutenant on 1 October 1893.

After finishing the three-year course in Berlin, Groener was assigned to the railroad division of the General Staff. Here he acquired the broad logistical knowledge of mass movement of men, equipment, and horses, which was to serve him well in later years.

He also became a great disciple of General (Count) Alfred von Schlieffen, the Chief of the General Staff and architect of the famous "Schlieffen Plan" for a victorious, simultaneous campaign against France in the West and Russia in the East. On 25 March 1899 he was promoted to Captain in the General Staff.

After commanding a company in an infantry regiment in Metz, Groener was reassigned to the General Staff in Berlin to work once more with the railroad division, this time for four years. Three years of troop duty and a promotion to major followed. In the fall of 1911 he returned once more to the General Staff. On 1 October 1912 he was promoted to lieutenant colonel and made the Chief of the General Staff's field railroad section. In that capacity he set about improving the German railroad network for combat support and increasing the speed of rail traffic in order to save days of mobilization time.

The war proved the wisdom of his planning. His logistical genius and untiring efforts made possible the smooth functioning of the transport of German troops and materiel, the tactical relocation of divisions, and the speedy removal of wounded during the first two years of combat operations. His work did not go unrecognized. Promotions came quickly: to colonel on 5 September 1914, to major general on 26 June 1915, a good three years ahead of his contemporaries. On 11 September 1915 Kaiser Wilhelm II decorated him with the *pour le mérite*. In May of that year Stuttgart Polytechnic awarded him an honorary doctorate of engineering.

From August 1914 to May 1916 Groener had been able to devote his time and energies exclusively to his railroads. On 22 May 1916 the War Food Office was created with leading representatives of unions and industry on its board of directors. Four days later General Groener was placed at the disposal of the new office to assist in balancing strategic and economic, military and civilian needs. The assignment not only gave him direct access to factories, but insights into problems of the "home front."

When the bloody offensive against Verdun bogged down in the summer of 1916, Kaiser Wilhelm replaced General Erich von Falkenhayn as Chief of the General Staff with Field Marshal Paul von Hindenburg on 29 August and named Erich Ludendorff First Quartermaster General. As J. W. Wheeler-Bennett points out, "Together they formed one of the most amazing military combinations in history." These two popular heroes of the Battle of Tannenberg reorganized the General Staff and made civilian industrial production subservient to the needs of the military. That very month the "Hindenburg Program" for war production called for double the amount of mortars and munitions, and triple the amount of cannons and machine guns.

Representatives of the unions, of the Social Democratic Party, and the workers themselves stubbornly opposed the new quotas. In order to make the program (and the workers) work, Groener, a lieutenant general since 1 November, was made the head of the War Office in the War Ministry. His fairness and diplomacy soon won them over. As a deputy delegate for Prussia in the Upper House (Bundesrat) of Parliament, he was able to convert a compulsory working law from one of force (as demanded by Ludendorff) into one that appealed to the patriotic instincts of the workers. Thanks to his persuasive powers, he got the "Hindenburg Program" to work, at least partially, and Hindenburg got the credit.

Wheeler-Bennett claims that Ludendorff, a contemporary of Groener's, was jealous of him and thus brought about his "downfall" in the War Ministry. But a close friend and fellow officer, Lieutenant General Ernst Kabisch, wrote in a monograph published in 1932 that "purely military reasons" accounted for his assignment to command the 33 Infantry Division in August 1917. Helmut Haeussler of the University of Wisconsin comes closest to the mark in his book about Groener (published in 1962). He writes of the bomb that Groener "threw into the Ludendorff ranks" when "he submitted a memorandum to the government which recommended stringent national control of both wages and profits" in order to prevent German industrialists from war-profiteering.

In any event, Groener read about his transfer to the Western front in the newspaper, although he had seen Ludendorff only the day before.

There was little combat action in his division's sector in Lorraine. Just before Christmas Lieutenent General Groener was given command of the XXV Reserve Corps, and then of the I Army Corps on 25 February 1918. Less than a month later he was named Chief of the General Staff of the Army Group commanded by Marshal von

Eichhorn (later called Army Group Kiev) in the Ukranian theater. With the treaties of Brest-Litovsk of February/March 1918, Germany and Austria-Hungary recognized the independence of the Ukraine from Soviet Russia.

As a railroad expert it was Groener's mission to organize the shipment of grain and foodstuffs by rail from the occupied Ukraine to Germany and Austria, where they were badly needed. Haeussler describes the near futility of the task: "The Ukrainian grain bin was empty. Years of war had strained agricultural production; months of revolution disrupted it. German soldiers moved into a land where orderly economic life had ceased. What the peasants needed for themselves, they hid in underground caches. Neither the Germans nor the Bolsehviks could locate these, and for Groener's purposes they were insignificant."

Marshal von Eichhorn was killed by a bomb in an assassination that might have taken Groener's life, too, had he not stayed behind in his office to catch up on his work. The day before, on 29 July, the Marshal had written Groener's efficiency report, earmarking him for the highest positions in the Army and in government. He cited his "profound knowledge in all fields, his critical judgment, his knowledge of people, tact, instant perceptivity, and the valuable gift to be able to handle people and to influence them."

"But not even Groener's persuasive qualities," Wheeler-Bennett notes, "could break down the sullen opposition of the Ukrainian peasant farmer, and the organization, brilliant in conception, had depressingly meagre results. Only 42,000 truck-loads of grain in all were exported from the Ukraine during the whole period of German and Austrian occupation (March-December 1918)."

In late September Groener visited the headquarters of the German High Command in Spa. Ludendorff briefed him on the situation on the Western front, summing it up with the famous comment: "The situation is serious, but not immediately threatening." Groener pressed for the truth, and Ludendorff remarked: "We must have peace by Christmas."

A few days later, Ludendorff asked for an immediate armistice. On 26 October he turned in his resignation, which the Kaiser accepted, and fled to Sweden in civilian clothes and dark glasses. Groener was summoned to Spa to be his successor as First Quartermaster

General. He arrived in Spa on the same day as Kaiser Wilhelm (30 October), who had fled from a restless Berlin to seek the security of the High Command's headquarters.

Prince Max von Baden, known for his humanitarian work on behalf of POWs and his democratic feelings, had become Chancellor on 3 October. He dispatched the Prussian Minister of the Interior, Dr. Drews, to Spa to ask the Kaiser to abdicate so that the Allies might offer better truce terms. The Kaiser received him in the presence of Hindenburg, Groener, and his two adjutants general, von Plessen and von Marschall.

The Kaiser said that he had sworn an oath to Germany and would restore order. Groener accused Dr. Drews and the Prussian government of neglect in tolerating accusations against the Kaiser which were harmful to the morale of the troops, who had sworn their loyalty to Wilhelm II. Heartened by Groener's defense, the Kaiser said to Drews, "Now a Swabian has been forced to tell you what is proper for a Prussian patriot!" And to his aide-de-camp he remarked later: "How splendid to see the solemn Groener so aroused. He told Drews where the main danger to the fatherland lies: not in the superiority of our enemies but in discord and rebellion at home. How gratifying to see a South German general so ready to defend the German Kaiser and King of Prussia. The upright Swabian!"

Although he had berated Dr. Drews, Groener had his own view of how the Kaiser should behave. To both of his adjutants general and to Hindenburg he suggested in private that the Kaiser be persuaded to go to the front, where hundreds of thousands of German soldiers were in the trenches. Groener hoped that such a move would appeal to the sentimentality of the German people and rally them behind the Kaiser, but his proposal fell on deaf ears.

As operational commander of the German Army, General Groener visited the Western front during the first days of November. Upon his return to Berlin he heard a report about the mutiny of the German Navy in Kiel. Prince Max von Baden told General Groener that in the negotiations with President Wilson the chief obstacle to favorable terms for Germany was the Kaiser's stubborn refusal to abdicate.

On 6 November Groener met with leaders of the unions, who were concerned about an internal revolution if the Kaiser did not step down. Convinced by their arguments, Groener tried to persuade Hindenburg that it was his job, as Chief of Staff, to make it clear to the Kaiser that he no longer had the loyalty of his troops, up front or at home. But after 30 years of service to Kaiser Wilhelm II, the old Field Marshal did not have the heart to mention abdication. (He would rather resign than report the army's disloyalty.) Instead, he ordered Groener to present the considered opinion of the High Command.

At the morning briefing at Spa on 9 November Groener outlined objectively the hopeless situation of the army. But Count von Schulenburg, the Chief of Staff of Army Group "Crown Prince," called Groener's analysis too black. Schulenburg urged the Kaiser to give up only the crown of Germany and return home as Prussian King in the safe escort of his loyal troops.

Groener lost his patience at this unrealistic proposal. He told the Kaiser bluntly: "The army will march home in peace and order under its leaders and commanding generals, but not under the command of Your Majesty, for it no longer stands behind Your Majesty." Having just come from the front himself, Groener knew what he was talking about. Colonel Heye, the next briefer, backed Groener up. He reported that the army wanted peace, rest, and an armistice.

A telephone call to army headquarters in Berlin brought confirmation that the army was unable to control the uprising of workers and demonstrators. The Kaiser decided to give up the German, but not the Prussian crown. But before his intentions could be telephoned to Berlin, the government's proclamation of Kaiser and King "renouncing the throne" had already made newspaper headlines. Unable to launch a counter-revolution, Kaiser Wilhelm II, on the recommendation of Hindenburg, went into exile in Holland.

On that eventful 9 November, Friedrich Ebert, the socialist leader, had been persuaded by Prince Max von Baden to become the chancellor of the new German republic. That night, and on many nights thereafter, General Groener and Friedrich Ebert discussed the state of the army and the nation on a secure line. It was the beginning of a long and fruitful association.

General Groener's expertise on rail movement and organizational genius made possible the orderly return of the German army from the Western front, beginning on 12 November 1918. The same man who moved them into battle positions in 1914 now brought them home in defeat. Without him it might not have been accomplished so smoothly.

On 23 June 1919, when Ebert's government had only 24 hours left to accept Marshal Ferdinand Foch's ultimatum to accept the provisions of the Versailles Treaty, the first President of the Weimar Republic was on the phone to Groener to ask his advice. Public sentiment, to a man, was in favor of rejecting the harsh terms of the treaty.

It wasn't the first time that Wilhelm Groener had the courage to swim against the tide of public opinion. Concerned with the future of his country, he advised Ebert to accept the "conditions imposed by the enemy." President Ebert had agreed to sign the treaty only if the army had no chance to put up successful resistance. Again, as in the showdown with the Kaiser, Hindenburg had deferred to Groener. Again, Groener's name was permanently tied to an unpopular decision, but one that saved Germany from further devastation.

In March 1920, after the abortive Putsch of Dr. Wolfgang Kapp (and Ludendorff, fresh from exile) against the government, Ebert appointed Wilhelm Groener, who had resigned from the army the previous September, as his Minister for Transport. For three years he turned his energies and his knowledge to converting Germany's war-torn railroad net into one of the most efficient systems in the world. He retired from his second career on 12 August 1923, but re-entered government service as the Minister of the Interior and of Defense on 8 October 1931.

An ardent foe of the Nazis, Groener suppressed the storm troopers of Adolf Hitler in the early summer of 1932 with the backing of the government of Chancellor Heinrich Brüning. Betrayed by General Kurt von Schleicher (one of his former students), who urged the army to support the Nazis, Groener lost his mandate as Defense Minister and retired on 9 May 1932 after a courageous speech before the Chamber of Deputies *(Reichstag)* in defense of his policies.

Wilhelm Groener died on 5 May 1939. In his will of 1934 he spoke warmly of his "old friend" Schleicher but warned of Adolf Hitler.

If I have devoted a lot of space in this book to General Wilhelm Groener, it is not just because he exemplified the courage of so many Swabian soldiers. He had the courage of his own convictions, in full measure, and that is an attribute of the Swabians that I admire most of all.

On 2 November 1918 the Chief of Staff of the German Seventh Army, a Swabian Colonel named WALTHER REINHARDT, wrote to his wife from the Western front:

"We had heavy fighting on 25, 26, 27, 29 October and on 1 November, which was largely successful, especially yesterday. Of course, that boosts the morale and behavior of the entire Army and that is of the greatest importance. The news from Berlin is gray . . . . Gröner takes over a crushing legacy. I shall see him today. If I had to choose, my choice would be him. He is a man well above average."

The following day Colonel Reinhardt was informed that he was to report to Berlin to the Prussian Ministry of War to work on Army force structure. He said farewell to his comrades of the Seventh Army (with which he had served since 10 February 1917) on 6 November and arrived in Spa the next day. On his way from there to Berlin he had his first encounters with revolutionary elements on the home front. He had hardly arrived at the War Ministry when the announcement came that the Kaiser had abdicated and Friedrich Ebert named the provisional Chancellor of the new Republic. Hindenberg had stated his readiness to bring the field Army home.

Colonel Reinhardt was given the task of heading the demobilization department of the Prussian War Ministry, of paving the way for the adjustment of the German Army from wartime to peacetime conditions. He thought at the time that the task would be finished within six months. But in December 1918 his boss, Prussian Minister of War Scheuch, resigned. Chancellor Ebert, who had taken a liking to Reinhardt, appointed him as Scheuch's successor. Full of misgivings about all of the Prussian officers who could cause him trouble, the Swabian colonel accepted the post only after asking Hindenburg for an endorsement, which he promptly received. Together with Gustav Noske, the Social Democratic deputy to the *Reichstag* who had put down the naval mutiny in Kiel, Walther Reinhardt created the *Reichswehr,* the peacetime German Army after World War I.

A regulation of 19 January 1919, signed by Reinhardt and his Undersecretary for the Ministry of War, by Ebert and Noske for the government, and by von Cohen and Hermann Müller for the "Central Council of Workers and Soldiers Counsellors of the German Socialistic Republic," paved the way for the peacetime Army and established some of its ground rules. But it also made enemies of some of Reinhardt's old comrades-in-arms, who were jealous of him and considered him a traitor to tradition. As Fritz Ernst wrote in his monograph based on Reinhardt's papers:

"Reinhard had an experience here that was similar to Groener's after the Kaiser's abdication, no matter how different the situations and the individuals involved were. In the disappointed and embittered officer corps many looked for a scapegoat. Each had to deal with his own lot, but only a few had the opportunity to understand Reinhardt's situation."

Walther Gustav Reinhardt was born in Stuttgart on 24 March 1872. His father was a captain in a Württemberg division at the time of his birth. He had served as a company commander in the Franco-Prussian War of 1870/71. Later on he served in Ludwigsburg and Heilbronn and retired as a colonel in August 1885. His sixth child, Walter, passed the officers' candidate exam with excellence while still in secondary school in the spring of 1889. Too young for active duty, he completed the last two years of secondary school in the Corps of Cadets and earned his diploma in January 1891. A month later he was commissioned and assigned to the Grenadier Regiment "Queen Olga" (1st Württemberg) No. 119.

On 1 October 1897 Walther Reinhardt entered the War Academy *(Kriegsakademie)* in Berlin, where he rejoined his brother Ernst for the next two years. (Ernst retired from the Army as a lieutenant general.) While still a student at the academy, Walther Reinhardt married Luise Fürbringer, the daughter of a prominent Berlin doctor, on 7 April 1900.

For several years Reinhardt served on the General Staff and was named a Captain of the General Staff on 24 March 1904. A year later he was assigned to the XV Army Corps in Strassbourg. In February 1907 he was named a company commander in the Infantry Regiment "Old Württemberg" No. 121 in Ludwigsburg. Promoted to major in September 1910, he was again assigned to the General Staff until he joined the XIII (Royal Württemberg) Corps in Stuttgart and served on its general staff until January 1915. He fought on the Eastern front at the outbreak of World War I. In June 1915 he was promoted to lieutenant colonel.

In the fall of 1915 Lieutenant Colonel Reinhardt fought in the Argonne and then at Verdun with a Hessian infantry regiment he commanded until June 1916. In November 1916 he was sent to Macedonia as Chief of Staff of the Eleventh Army. On 10 February 1917 he became the Chief of Staff of the Seventh Army, where he soon earned the highest praise of Ludendorff and of General Graf von Schulenburg, the Chief of Staff of Army Group "German Crown Prince."

In the early months of 1919 Prussian Minister of War Walther Reinhardt still hoped to be able to maintain a peacetime Army of 200,000 men or more. But the peace conditions presented to the German delegation at Versailles on 7 May 1919 called for a ceiling of 100,000 at a time when the German Army still had more than half a million men in its ranks. Reinhardt was opposed to the conditions of the treaty, even after a major vote of the National Assembly in Weimar on 22 June 1919 approved the signing. He considered the reduction of the Army to a total strength of 100,000 fully unacceptable. Although not in agreement with General Groener's estimate of the situation of 18/19 June 1919, he defended him against the attacks of his fellow officers of the General Staff. Despite the conflict between the two over the issue of the Versailles Treaty, Reinhardt wrote a warm and laudatory letter to General Groener after the latter resigned from active service on 30 September 1919.

While serving as Prussian Minister of War, Reinhardt had the thankless task of deciding whom to retain in the new *Reichswehr* as he reduced it, increment by increment, from a strength of 400,000 in the summer of 1919 to 100,000. He was severely criticized from all quarters. On 29 August, for example, General Colonel Hans von Seeckt, the Chief of the General Staff, complained that the Army Personnel Office allegedly gave preference to officers who had service at the front over General Staff Officers because the General Staff was supposedly "unpopular and no longer important." Reinhardt did not have an easy time smoothing over such ruffled, high-ranking feathers. (In reality, according to General von Braun, the Chief of the Personnel Office, thousands of officers had been discharged since November 1918, but not a single General Staff Officer had been forced to resign.)

On 1 October 1919 the various war ministries were abolished. Reinhardt resigned as Prussian Minister of War to become the first Chief of Army Operations with the rank of major general. On 16 May 1920 he was named commander of *Wehrkreis V* and promoted to lieutenant general on 16 June. He assumed command of the 5th Division in Stuttgart on 1 October 1920, a post he held until 1924. It was his task to develop an effective combat force of the *Reichswehr* that had the respect of the civilian populace in times of great domestic political turmoil.

Promoted to General of the Infantry on 1 January 1925, Reinhardt became Commander-in-Chief of Group II in Kassel, which consisted of four divisions in western and southern Germany. He retired from active service on 31 December 1927. He went to the University of Berlin as a student, attending the same lectures as his daughter.

In the fall of 1929 General Reinhardt fell seriously ill. In May 1930 his lingering illness prevented him from attending the dedication of the artillery observation tower named after him at the Münsingen Training Area. He died on 8 August 1930 and was buried with full military honors at his wife's side in the Prague Cemetery in Stuttgart (along B 27 between Friedhofstraße and Eckardshaldenweg). She had preceded him to the grave a decade earlier.

In 1977 David Irving's *The Trail of the Fox,* a biography of Field Marshal ERWIN ROMMEL, was published in London. By midsummer of 1978 it had been translated into German and published under the title *Rommel.* The 21 August 1978 issue of the German newsmagazine *Der Spiegel* ran a cover story "Field Marshal Rommel: The End of a Legend" and published the final chapters of the Irving book in somewhat condensed form as a series in the succeeding four issues.

Together with the first in *Der Spiegel,* four columns of commentary on the Irving book by Lord Mayor Manfred Rommel of Stuttgart appeared. In his acknowledgements Irving had been "happy to place on record" his indebtedness to Manfred Rommel's generosity and Frau Lilo Rommel's hospitality. He added that he owed his good fortune in obtaining access to the Rommel correspondence to her.

But the Lord Mayor of Stuttgart and son of the famous soldier wrote in *Der Spiegel:* "At that time upon my advice my mother had allowed David Irving to look at the letters of my parents in the archives. That was probably premature. At the time I thought the time had come to evaluate such documents without preconceived notions."

Having enjoyed the trust and the hospitality of the Rommels, David Irving attempted to "document" that the Field Marshal's Chief of Staff in Normandy, Lieutenant General Hans Speidel, had implicated his commander in the 20 July plot against Hitler to save his own skin and then himself created the Rommel "legend" as a conspirator against Hitler immediately after the war. In his *Spiegel* comments, Manfred Rommel pointed out that documents alone are not the fountain of truth, that his father had never considered himself a member of the Berlin resistance movement but accepted the consequences nevertheless. "Hitler certainly had deeper insight into conditions than David Irving or any other historian has today," he wrote. "Just what he thought of my father's behavior is evident in his having had him killed." Finally, the son of Field Marshal Rommel concluded his remarks with the statement: "The role of General Dr. Speidel, I am firmly convinced, is presented falsely in David Irving's book. My father was firmly convinced up to his death of the loyalty of Dr. Speidel. My mother and I never had any reason to doubt this."

Another historian, Brigadier Desmond Young, enjoyed the trust and hospitality of the Rommels and the Speidels shortly after the war and wrote *Rommel, the Desert Fox,* which was published in 1950. It presents quite a different view of the Rommel-Speidel relationship and the connection of both with the plot against Hitler.

When I went to see Lord Mayor Rommel at his home in Stuttgart-Sonnenberg, on behalf of an American publisher who wanted to publish his father's letters (which Irving had used), Manfred told me unequivocally, "If anyone publishes my father's papers from now on, it will be *me,* after I retire from political life."

Erwin Johannes Eugen Rommel was born in Heidenheim, near Ulm, on 15 November 1891. His father was a schoolteacher, as had been his grandfather. His mother was the eldest daughter of the President of the Landtag of Württemberg. Not at all tough as a child, Erwin was what we call a late-bloomer. At first he wanted to become an engineer, but then he decided to join the army over his father's objections.

On 19 July 1910 he became an officer candidate in the 124th Infantry Regiment "King Wilhelm I" at Weingarten. In March 1911 he entered the War Academy in Danzig, where he received his commission after nine months and returned to his regiment as a second lieutenant. While in Danzig he met Lucie Mollin, the daughter of a Prussian landowner, whom he later married while on leave in 1916.

World War I was hardly underway when Lieutenant Rommel had already displayed the courage and initiative that were to become his style on the battlefield. Twice wounded and holder of the Iron Cross, First Class, by the spring of 1915, he was promoted to first lieutenant and assigned to the Württemberg Mountain Battalion. After special training in Austria and a year in a relatively quiet sector in the Vosges, the battalion went to the Rumanian front to join the Alpine Corps. Rommel's exploits on the eastern front against Rumanian and Italian soldiers were not only legendary, but characteristic of the tactics he was to use as an armor commander in World War II. Desmond Young describes some of that campaign action: "When he took the strongly fortified Rumanian position of Mount Cosna in August 1917, he led four companies in single file through the woods between two enemy posts, 150 yards apart, without being detected, and laid a telephone wire at the same time. By the time he reached the summit he had been virtually without sleep for nearly a week and had also been severely wounded in the arm several days before . . . . When he took the village of Gagesti in January of the same year, he lay out until ten o'clock at night within the Rumanian outpost line in a temperature ten degrees below freezing . . . . The climax of his career in World War I was reached with the capture of Monte Matajur, southwest of Caporetto, on October 26, 1917 . . . . When Rommel eventually scaled Monte Matajur from the rear and fired his success rockets from the summit, he had been continuously on the move for fifty hours, had covered twelve miles as the crow flies in mountainous country, had climbed up to 7,000 feet and with never more than six companies under command, had captured 150 officers, 9,000 men and 81 guns." In recognition of that latter action he received the *pour le mérite* and was promoted to captain.

After World War I Captain Rommel rejoined his original regiment in Weingarten. He was one of the 4,000 chosen officers in General Hans von Seeckt's *Reichswehr* or 100,000-man Army for nine years, training the German Army of the future. From January 1921 until September 1929 he was stationed in Stuttgart with the 13th Infantry Regiment. His son and only child Manfred was born on Christmas Eve in 1928.

From October 1929 to October 1933 Rommel was an instructor at the Infantry School in Dresden. His lectures there were published later on (in 1937) in a book called *Infantry Attacks,* which Lieutenant General George S. Patton, Jr., among others, read on a sleepless night in his tent in France on 8 November 1944.

Promoted to major, Rommel commanded the 3d (Mountain) Battalion of Infantry Regiment 17 in Goslar in the Harz Mountains from 1933 to 1935. He began a three-year tour of duty at the War Academy in Potsdam in the fall of 1935 as a lieutenant colonel, was promoted to full colonel in 1937, and assumed command of the Officer's School at Wiener Neustadt in the mountains south of Vienna in November 1938. But before he left Potsdam for a new assignment, Hitler personally selected Rommel to command the battalion responsible for his safety during the march into the Sudetenland in October 1938, having read *Infantry Attacks* with great admiration. The Führer called on Rommel to command his escort battalion again on 13 March 1939 when he marched into Prague. On 23 August Rommel was promoted to major general and assigned to Hitler's headquarters to look after the Führer's safety.

On 15 February 1940 Rommel was given command of the 7th Panzer Division. On May 10th he crossed the Belgian border at Liége and went into combat for the first time in 22 years. "One might have expected the gulf between a 26-year-old infantry captain and a 48-year-old armored general to be almost unbridgeable in one step," writes Charles Douglas-Home, "but it is remarkable how little Rommel's style changed." His advances in that rapidly moving *Blitzkrieg* were so audacious and so swift that the 7th Panzer was dubbed the "ghost division." The tankers fired while on the move and made deep penetrations behind enemy lines, with Rommel himself leading the forward element of the assault regiment into the fray. In less than six weeks, from 10 May to the capture of Cherbourg on 18 June, Rommel had covered 350 miles and captured 97,458 prisoners, 458 armored vehicles, 5,000 trucks, 800 other wheeled vehicles, and five admirals.

During the summer of 1940 Rommel trained his divison for an invasion of England that was scrubbed by Hitler ("Operation Sea Lion"). When the Italians began to sustain serious losses in North Africa in early 1941, Hitler summoned Rommel (now a lieutenant general) on 6 February and appointed him Commander in Chief of the German Troops in Libya. A week later Rommel landed in North Africa.

Desmond Young sums up Rommel's difficulties there, despite tactical successes that earned him the nickname "the desert fox": "The story of the war in North Africa is the story of an unending battle between Rommel, who saw – and proved – the possibility of a major success there and a High Command which refused to take the North Africa campaign seriously." Hitler had his hands full with the Russian campaign, and the "chairborne" generals of the High Command – Keitel, Jodl, and Halder – were jealous of Rommel's enormous popularity in Germany.

After dazzling victories and some severe defeats, after advances and retreats across Africa, Rommel was finally brought to a halt at the El Alamein line in July 1942. By October the situation had badly deteriorated and Rommel himself was in poor health. Upon his return to Africa prematurely from a brief stint in a German hospital that month he found an impossible military situation for his *Afrika Korps*. Allied landings in North Africa on 8 November and ever-dwindling supplies, especially gasoline, made matters even worse. Rommel retreated to Tripoli in December and lost the city to the British in January 1943. His last battle in North Africa was at Medenine on 5 March. Five days later he was in Hitler's headquarters in the Ukraine. The Führer awarded him the diamonds for his Knight's Cross, reluctantly agreed to shorten the line of defense of the *Afrika Korps,* and sent Rommel on a rest cure instead of back to Africa. But on 7 May the last of the *Afrika Korps* surrendered and its troops went into captivity without their beloved Erwin Rommel.

After seven weeks in the hospital, Rommel served as a military adviser to Hitler in the latter's headquarters. He was chomping at the bit for a new assignment, a chance to overcome the sting of defeat in Africa, which Hitler now agreed was a lost cause. Fearing the surrender of the Italians on their own home front, the Führer decided to relocate eight armor and four infantry divisions under a new Army Group in northern Italy. He appointed Rommel its commander on 15 July, five days after the Allied invasion of Italy. The specter of enemy landings in Greece or Crete prompted Hitler to divert Rommel to Salonika to become "Supreme Commander in Greece," but he recalled him to his headquarters 24 hours later after Mussolini's arrest on 25 July. Suspecting that the new Italian government under Marshal Pietro Badoglio would sell out to the Allies, leaving 70,000 German troops cut off in Sicily, Rommel was ordered to have his troops infiltrate into Italy. They were to avoid friction with the Italians, if possible, but if they met with resitance, they had the authority to use force. Rommel's men met with no resitance; the Italian government proclaimed loyalty to the Axis while planning to swing a deal with the Allies. Rommel went back and forth from his Army Group Headquarters in Munich to Hitler's "wolf's lair" headquarters near Rastenburg in East Prussia. Given command of all German and Italian troops in northern Italy, he began to set up his headquarters near Lake Garda on 17 August. While in Munich on 8 September, he learned of Italy's surrender to the Allies. German troops seized Rome. Troops of Sepp Dietrich's S.S. Corps went about putting down Communist uprisings in Milan and Turin, using brutal methods and indulging in widespread looting. Rommel was indignant, ordering the removal of S.S. troops from Milan.

Near the end of October, Hitler decided to make Field Marshal Albert Kesselring, the Commander in Chief of the German Forces in southern Italy, the Supreme Commander, Italy. Rommel, who had hoped for this distinction, was given a special mission instead: the complete overhaul and strengthening of the Atlantic Wall to withstand an Allied invasion. Rommel's new boss was Field Marshal Gerd von Rundstedt, the Commander in Chief, West. As his naval adviser he selected Vice Admiral Friedrich Ruge, with whom he became fast friends. (He lives and writes in Tübingen today.)

By shoring up the defenses of the Atlantic Wall, and with hopes of full support from Hitler and the High Command, Rommel for a time felt that the Allies could be stopped in the water. He underestimated the devastating effect of naval gunfire. After the Allies had succeeded in establishing beachheads in Normandy, and lacking adequate air and armored forces to push them back into the ocean, Rommel and von Rundstedt contemplated the idea of making overtures to the Western Powers, indeed, of letting them pass swiftly through the low countries and Germany in order to beat the Russians to Berlin.

Since 15 April 1944 Rommel's Chief of Staff at his headquarters in the chateau at La Roche-Guyon had been a fellow Swabian named Hans Speidel, who had just received the Knight's Cross from Hitler in Freudenstadt for his heroic fighting on the Russian front. He had joined the Army in 1914 and served on the Western front. Between the wars he earned his doctorate in philosophy and history *summa cum laude* at Tübingen University in 1925.

Early in July Field Marshal von Rundstedt was relieved and replaced by Field Marshal Günther von Kluge, a hard-bitten veteran of the Russian front who immediately locked horns with Rommel. In due time he discovered how hopeless the situation was. General Speidel inspected the fighting at Saint Lo and concluded that the front line could collapse at any time. His Chief of Staff prepared a report of the situation for von Kluge on 15 July to which Rommel added a paragraph: "Everywhere our troops are fighting heroically, but the unequal struggle is drawing to its close. In my view the consequences of this have just got to be drawn."

Two days later, following a tour of the front, a British Spitfire attacked Rommel's car. The Field Marshal suffered a triple skull fracture, a broken cheek bone, a wound in the left eye, and facial cuts from broken glass. Quick treatment at a French religious hospital and later in an air force hospital saved his life. He was out of action. Von Kluge had forwarded his report to Hitler on 21 July.

After spending several weeks in the hospital of Professor Esch at Vesiner, near St. Germain, Rommel insisted on being taken to his home in Herrlingen. There he was placed in charge of Professors Albrecht and Stock of Tübingen University. Although Professor Albrecht declared that no man could be alive with such wounds, they mended quickly.

In the meantime SS-Obergruppenführer Dr. Ernst Kaltenbrunner and his Gestapo were busy investigating and arresting all those suspected of having been involved in the abortive attempt to kill Hitler in his headquarters on 20 July. On 6 September General Speidel came to Herrlingen to tell Rommel that he had been suspended the previous day as Chief of Staff of Army Group B. That night Speidel was arrested and taken to Berlin for interrogation by the Gestapo about the 20th of July plot. Except for a brief Christmas leave in Freudenstadt, Speidel spent the last months of the war in prison camps until he was able to escape to the advancing French Army on 29 April 1945. An officers' Court of Honor had weighed the evidence of his complicity on 4 October and decided, thanks to the influence of Colonel General Heinz Guderian, not to turn him over to the People's Court for trial, which would have meant death by hanging.

Rommel met a different fate. In order to protect his family from harm, he took the poison brought to him by two German generals on 14 October 1944. The state funeral in Ulm four days later, with full military honors and an oration by Field Marshal von Rundstedt, was orchestrated by Hitler to deceive the German people and not deprive them of one of their last true heroes. He is buried in the small cemetery of the Protestant Church in Herrlingen.

HANS SPEIDEL, who was born in Metzingen on 28 October 1897, was a professor at Tübingen for many years following the war. When the Federal Republic joined the North Atlantic Treaty Organization on 22 October 1954, he conducted the negotiations with Supreme Headquarters, Allied Powers, Europe (SHAPE) in Paris on German military planning on behalf of his government. On 10 November 1955 President Theodor Heuss appointed him as one of the first lieutenant generals in the new German Army.

In April 1957 he was promoted to four stars. While visiting Allied commanders earlier that spring, the Commanding General of the US Seventh Army at Patch Barracks in Stuttgart-Vaihingen, (then) Lieutenant General Bruce C. Clarke, made him the first honorary member of the Seventh Army. In April 1957 General Speidel became the first German commander of Allied Land Forces Central Europe (LANDCENT), with headquarters in Fontainebleau. On 31 March 1964 he retired from active duty in Ulm, where his military career had begun in 1914.

XVII   Swabian Ingenuity

Centuries before four Connecticut Yankees named Thomas Harland, David Burnap, Gideon Roberts, and James Harrison were making interchangeable parts for their grandfather's clocks in 1791 (thus paving the way for mass production), several Swabian *"Tüftler"* were puttering about with clocks.

The word *tüfteln* means to puzzle or mull over a technical problem until a solution is found. The Swabians, just like the Yankees, have a long association with and affinity for this art, which is called "tinkering" or "puttering" down east.

One of the oldest – if not *the* oldest – striking clocks was built by Heinrich von Wick of Württemberg between 1352 and 1370 for King Charles V of France. It is now in the Palais de Justice in Paris, and its parts have been renewed several times over. For a long time it was assumed that the builder was Henri de Vic, a Frenchman from Chateau-Salins in Lorraine, but recent research indicates that it was Heinrich von Wick from the upper reaches of the Rhine.

The Black Forest clock industry, as far as it can be traced with any degree of accuracy, began around 1667, but the first cuckoo-clock was not made until 1730. The *Tüftler* who made it was Anton Ketterer of Schönwald (near Furtwangen). He used the station master's house in Furtwangen for his design. The clock can be seen in the Furtwangen Museum.

Pastor Philipp Matthäus Hahn (1739-1790) of Kornwestheim and Echterdingen loved to tinker as much as he loved to look after souls. In his workshop, in between writing and preaching sermons, he invented and built scales, helio chronometers, and his own calculator which enabled him to build complicated astronomical and calendar clocks. His son Christoph Matthäus Hahn (1765-1833) followed in his father's inventive footsteps. One of his clocks, now in the Bavarian National Museum in Munich, built around 1815, has mechanically driven terrestrial and celestial globes flanking a clock that shows the mean time, hours, minutes and seconds, the date, month, day of the week, length of the month with correction for leap year, sidereal time, and the phases of the moon – all on one base intended for a mantelpiece.

Since 1823 the Kienzle Company has been producing clocks in

Schwenningen in the heart of the Black Forest. The 1,100 employees of the firm today make wrist watches, alarm clocks, period clocks, wall clocks, digital clocks, stop watches, technical clocks, and other time-measuring instruments.

Kienzle's competitor in this field is Junghans in Schramberg, just 23 kilometers south of Schwenningen, Founded in 1861, the company has a working capital fund worth 20 million Marks. Its 2,747 employees make not only clocks of all kinds (including quarz and eight-day clocks), wrist watches, and stop watches, but also milling machines and loud speaker boxes.

Some 30 kilometers southeast of Schwenningen, towards Lake Constance, is Tuttlingen, where the firm of Aesculap manufactures surgical, dental, and veterinary instruments, plus sterilizers and hypodermic needles. The company was established in 1895 by two *Tüftler* named Jetter and Scheerer. Today it employs 1,522 people and has common stock worth eleven million Marks.

Precision instrument making *(Feinmechanik)* and the building of machinery of all kinds *(Maschinenbau)* are old Swabian specialties. Some 340 companies in Baden-Württemberg are in the business of making precision instruments, while no less than 1,134 build machinery.

Württemberg is poor in natural resources. The Swabian craftsman must take these expensive, imported raw materials – iron, coal, oil – and quadruple their value with his indefatigable industriousness if he expects to make a profit. A roving annual exhibition of Swabian commerce and industry bears the proud slogan "Swabian Diligence" *(Schwäbischer Fleiß)*. It's a matter of pride. The true *Schwob* admires quality in the work of others and sets a grat deal of stock in his own. He has no use for junk, for which he has a variety of pejoratives, calling it *Gruscht, Loumpagruscht,* or *Klump.*

Before his retirement my father-in-law was a foreman in the little firm of Dr. Karl F. Nägele in Stuttgart-Hohenheim, just past Kelley Barracks on Plieningerstraße. Its product is one of the longest words in the German language: *Reißverschlußherstellungsmaschinen.* That translates as machines that make zippers. Dr. Nägele was a Swabian engineer who founded his firm in 1932. His widow runs it today with only 70 employees, exporting to an equal number of countries around the globe, or 75 percent of the world market.

A Berliner named C. F. L. Buschmann (1805–1864) gets the credit for having invented both the *Mund-harmonica* (mouth-organ) and the *Hand-harmonica* (accordion), but a Swabian named Matthias Hohner from Trossingen began manufacturing improved harmonicas in 1857. It was the Swabian quest for quality. The one-time watchmaker added the slider stop which switches the instrument to a second diatonic set of reeds tuned a half-tone above the first. His *Melodica* is a chromatic mouth-organ held like a recorder and fingered with a tiny keyboard. The Hohner Company has 1,800 craftsmen in Trossingen today and a sales volume of some 115 million Marks. They make not only harmonicas, but recorders, accordians, electronic instruments, amplifiers and (until 1977) computers.

While those ingenious Yankee tinkers Colonel Samuel Colt (1814–1862) and Dr. Richard Jordan Gatling (1818–1903) were perfecting the weapons that bear their names, the Mauser brothers Paul (1838–1914) and Wilhelm (1834–1882) from Oberndorf on the Neckar invented a rifle in the late 1860s and improved it in 1871 based on experience gained during the Franco-Prussian War (1870–71). Their Model 98 rifle was the basic infantry weapon of the German soldier of World War I. Established in 1884, the Mauser works in Oberndorf (where their biggest competitor, Heckler & Koch, is also located) employs 1,300 craftsmen who not only make hunting, competition, and military firearms, but also machine tools, measuring intruments, and lathes. The capital stock of the company is worth 15.4 million Marks.

The world-famous Luger automatic is manufactured by the Karl Walther Company in Ulm, which was originally founded in Thuringia in 1886. For those of you who might still be skeptical of my Swabian Ingenuity = Yankee Ingenuity theory, keep your Lugers pointed down range. Let me share with you a discovery I made long after I began writing this book.

A Connecticut inventor named Hugo Borchardt designed a self-operating pistol with a toggle-breech mechanism and recoil operation that eventually became the innards of the Luger. I have strong suspicions that Borchardt was a *Schwob* who migrated to Connecticut, but I have no evidence to prove it.

The Walther Company produced the PPK and P-38 pistols used by the *Wehrmacht* and the SS. Today the firm's 430 craftsmen make

PPK automatics for the German police and PP-sport pistols for marksmen and amateur shooters.

Schorndorf, 18 kilometers due east of Stuttgart on Interstate B-29, is famous not only for the brave ladies who forced the town commandant to keep the gates shut to attacking French troops in 1688 (see chapter ten). It is also the birthplace of Gottlieb Daimler (1834–1900). He and Wilhelm Maybach (1846–1929) of Heilbronn were the Swabian *Tüftler* who puttered and puzzled with motors in their experimental workshop until they came up with a workable carburetor and finally an internal combustion engine with hot bulb ignition in 1883.

That invention prompted the following comment by Ernst Jünger in his weird parabolic novel *On the Marble Cliffs,* published in 1939: "In inventing the internal combustion engine, man admired explosion with precision, a sure sign that someday he will blow himself to pieces." Born in Heidelberg on 29 March 1895, Jünger is hopefully outliving his prophecy.

Gottlieb Daimler patented the world's first motorcycle in August 1885 and – thanks to Maybach's ingenuity – an all-steel car in 1889.

Independent of Maybach and Daimler, Karl Friedrich Benz, who was born in Karlsruhe in 1844, developed a car powered by a one-cylinder, four-stroke gasoline engine in his Mannheim workshop. The three-wheel vehicle was first demonstrated in 1886 and is now in the German Museum in Munich. He established his own company, Benz & Cie, in 1883.

In 1890 Gottlieb Daimler founded the Daimler Motor Company in Stuttgart-Untertürkheim with the help of Count Ferdinand von Zeppelin (1838–1917). Maybach started his motor-making company in Friedrichshafen on Lake Constance in 1909. Besides helping Count von Zeppelin to build dirigibles, he also produced automobiles.

As everyone knows, the Daimler Company got together with the Benz Company in 1926 and became world famous for its passenger cars, trucks, and buses. When I took William J. Lederer, author of *The Ugly American* and many other books through the Daimler-Benz Mercedes Museum in Stuttgart-Untertürkheim and the passenger car assembly plant in Sindelfingen, he kept on asking the boss of the export division, "But why are they so expensive?" The answer kept coming back like a broken record: "Quality, Herr Doktor Lederer, quality . . . and quality costs money!" But if you want to just look and not touch, visit the Mercedes Museum.

Born in Albeck near Ulm in 1861, Robert Bosch started out as an electrotechnician. In 1886 he set up a workshop at Rotebühlstraße 75 in Stuttgart. His development of the magneto-ignition for automobiles in 1895 ultimately brought him fame and fortune. Noted for the quality of his products, Bosch once remarked, "I'd rather lose money than trust." He paid high salaries, he was fond of explaining, not to increase his wealth, but because paying high wages had made him rich.

Bosch introduced the eight-hour working day in 1906. He respected his workers as individuals and their right to leisure time. Today the Bosch Company manufactures electrical components for automobiles, hydraulic systems, fuel-injection pumps, brakes, electric tools, refrigerators, and other household appliances.

Speaking of precision instruments, the Märklin brothers established their model train manufacturing company in Göppingen in 1859, only twenty years after the first stretch of the real German railroad network was opened between Nürnberg and Fürth in Bavaria. But it took a Swabian economist from Reutlingen named Friedrich List (1789–1846), a pioneer in the development of the American railroad, to convince his native countrymen of the importance of rail transportation not only for economic and military reasons, but as a means of cultural exchange and of achieving national unity. He was personally responsible for the construction of the railroad connection between Leipzig and Dresden.

In 1817 List was appointed a professor of administration and politics at the University of Tübingen but dismissed two years later for his political views. As a member of the state parliament of Württemberg from 1820 to 1822, he proposed the abolishment of tithes and feudal property taxes, fewer civil servants, and the granting of trial by jury – reforms so radical for the times that he was imprisoned in the Hohenasperg prison northwest of Ludwigsburg for trying to undermine the government. He escaped from prison after eight months, returned two years later in hope of amnesty, but he was deported to the United States instead. He lived in Pennsylvania from 1825 to 1832, where he farmed, edited a German-language newspaper, and lost his money in promoting a coal mine. Unable to support his family, he committed suicide at Kufstein, Austria, on 30 November 1846.

A few years ago, when I was the Special Assistant to the Director of Public Affairs for the United States European Command, with headquarters at Patch Barracks in Stuttgart-Vaihingen, a newly assigned major named Henry C. Rilling reported for duty. Right after our introduction he asked me to draft a letter in German for him to send to the 19 Rillings listed in the Stuttgart phone book.

The response was enormous. It not only led to frequent reunions with Rilling relatives, but got Hank and his wife Carol deeply involved with tracing the family tree back to Konrad Rilling, who lived in Dusslingen (near Tübingen) around 1440. The family history is typically Swabian: farmers in the 16th and 17th centuries, a cooper and mayor of Gomaringen (near Dusslingen) in the early 18th century, then three generations of carpenters, the last of whom started a sawmill. The next generation produced the first manufacturer, Jakob Rilling (1840–1906). His millwright handicraft grew into a family-owned industry, operated by his sons, for the production of motor-driven reapers and other agricultural machinery. That business is called the *"Iruswerke Dusslingen* J. Rilling & Söhne" today.

Ludwig Rilling (1860–1950) walked 12 kilometers to school every day and back to his father's powdermill, where he worked until midnight. After completing a commercial education in Zurich, he worked for a shipping company in Heilbronn, then for a Rotterdam shipbuilder, then for a bank in London, and finally settled down in Cannstatt. In 1888 he married Karoline Pauline Felder. She came from a long line of winegrowers in the Rems valley. She, her husband, and their children grew and pressed their own wine grapes until midnight at the turn of the century. Through hard work, thrift, and saving – those austere Swabian attributes – they started the wine business in Bad Cannstatt known as *Rilling-Sekt.* A family-owned business, it is run today by Frau Ruth Rilling, her son Friedrich and step-son Gerhard. With 100 employees they produce and sell 25 million Marks worth of bubbly giggle juice per year.

My friend Hank Rilling celebrated his promotion to lieutenant colonel in the Rilling Sekt factory in Bad Cannstatt. Today he is the Public Affairs Officer for the 21st Support Command in Kaiserslautern, but he tries to visit his Swabian relatives as often as possible. (No wonder!)

I dwelled at some length on the Rilling family because it is typical of how two Swabian family-owned businesses got started. My last example has to do with Teddy bears.

Perhaps you will recall that the town of Giengen (southeast of Heidenheim) on the Brenz river was destroyed in 1634 during the Thirty Years' War. In the centuries that followed, trades such as weaving, tanning, and stocking-weaving developed there side-by-side with agriculture. In the middle of the 19th century the Württemberg Felt Manufacturing Plant was the first industry to be established in Giengen.

On 24 July 1847 Maria Margarete Steiff, the wife of Master Builder Friedrich Steiff, gave birth in Giengen to a baby girl whom they named Margarete. Two years later Margarete came down with polio and had to spend the rest of her life in a wheelchair. Nevertheless, her ability to tell stories and think up games made her very popular with other children.

She learned how to sew in school. At home she and her sister had one of the first, hand-operated sewing machines. Determined to become financially independent, Margarete Steiff began to make clothes. In 1868 she started her own workshop, making children's coats and dresses using felt from the neighboring factory. Her business did well. Within a few years she trained other seamstresses to work with her. During those years she made a pin-cushion out of felt in the shape of an elefant, using a toy as her model. When she gave it to a child as a present, others came and asked for little elephants. In 1880 she made eight of them, in 1885 production had increased to 596 and in 1886 to 5,066. That year she began to make monkeys, donkeys, horses, pigs, and camels. In 1889 she started her own company with 15 employees.

By 1893 the firm published a catalog and displayed its wares at the Leipzig trade fair. A year later the first travelling salesman was hired. Margarete Steiff's nephew Richard joined the firm after graduating from the School for Industrial Arts in Stuttgart and spending some time in England. The first shipments to that country were made in 1895. Paul Steiff, her eldest nephew, attended the School for Industrial Arts in Stuttgart and then spent two years in the United States.

His tasks as a new member of the company were to develop new products. In 1902 nephew Otto Steiff took over the commercial management of the firm, to include the sales organization and advertising. He had studied at the Academy of Commerce in Cologne. He founded a subsidiary in Paris in 1911 and Margarete Steiff & Co. in New York City the following year. His brother Franz was responsible for the procurement of raw materials. He represented the company at the St. Louis World's Fair in 1904, where a Grand Prize was awarded to the firm.

In 1904 the Steiff trademark "Steiff Button in the Ear" was introduced at the insistance of Franz Steiff, who recognized its value in sales promotion. The trademark was developed from the spiral S of the trunk of an elephant (the firm's first product), representing the first letter of the family's name. It was attached by a rivet to each toy animal.

Margarete Steiff made her five nephews directors of the company three years before her death on 9 May 1909. It is hard to say which of them did the most for the firm, but Richard gets full credit for the famous Teddy Bear (that almost was a loser).

Richard's favorite pastime as a student was sketching bears in the Stuttgart zoo. (Think about that the next time you take your kids to the Wilhelma.) In 1903 he used one of his sketches to have a bear made out of mohair, instead of the customary felt, with moveable arms and legs. It was introduced at the Leipzig trade fair as a new Steiff product, but no one took any interest in it. Then came the *deus ex machina:* a rich American (there seemed to be lots of them back in those days) who liked the fuzzy little toy so much that he ordered 3,000 on the spot.

The caterer responsible for handling the party arrangements at the wedding of President Theodore Roosevelt's daughter used some of those toy bears, which had just arrived from Europe, as table decorations. He knew that the President was a great bear hunter. Someone mentioned the word "Teddy Bear," the press got wind of it, and the Steiff production went from 12,000 toy bears in 1903 to 974,000 within the next four years.

Today the Firma Margarete Steiff GmbH is still entirely in Steiff hands (no pun intended, as the German word *steiff* means "stiff"). It does an annual business amounting to 31.8 million Marks. Of its

2,000 employees, many are home workers. I can't think of any animal a child might take a fancy to that hasn't been reproduced as a Steiff toy. Some are available as hand puppets. Some are lifesize. Some are so ornate, such as the peacock with tail, that you wouldn't want to let your child play with it. (The designer was smart enough to foresee that problem, so the peacock is available without tail, too.) There is a special product line for infants, and some of the animals contain music boxes. The emphasis of the company has always been on quality. Its slogan is: "The best is just good enough for our children."

And, oh, yes, they still make "original" Teddy Bears.

XVIII   Swabian Genius

Swabia produced two scientific geniuses who were three centuries apart, yet remarkably alike: JOHANNES KEPLER and ALBERT EINSTEIN.

Kepler was born in Weil der Stadt, 26 kilometers southwest of Stuttgart, on 27 December 1571. His grandfather Sebald had moved there from Nürnberg in 1520 and became the mayor of the small free city of the Holy Roman Empire, much of which still looks today the way it did in Kepler's time.

Kepler's father Heinrich was a mercenary soldier of unstable character who never returned from his last military campaign. His mother Katharine was an innkeeper's daughter with a mystical streak underneath her bad temper.

Johannes was a sickly child. He barely survived smallpox, and the disease permanently damaged his eyesight. In 1577 his parents moved to Leonberg, where Johannes attended one of the new "Latin Schools" of the dukes of Württemberg. His talent for Latin gained him admission to the convent school at Adelberg and later to the Protestant theological seminary at Maulbronn.

Kepler decided to become a Protestant minister and passed the entrance examinations for the *Tübinger Stift,* the seminary founded by Duke Ulrich of Württemberg as part of the university. In addition to his theological studies, he learned mathematics and astronomy from Michael Maestlin, one of Europe's most respected astronomers. Outwardly, Maestlin taught the Ptolemaic system of astronomy – that the earth was the immovable center of the universe – but surreptitiously he shared with his favorite students, Kepler included, the revolutionary ideas of the Polish astronomer Nicolaus Copernicus (1473-1543), who insisted that the earth was not the center of the universe, but merely a planet of the solar system, revolving about the sun once a year and on its own axis every twenty-four hours.

Had Maestlin taught Copernicus' astronomy in public, he would have lost his job because the Church questioned its validity.

On 11 August 1591, Kepler received his Master's from the University of Tübingen. He continued his studies for the Protestant ministry. In 1594, the year in which he was due to complete them, the mathematics teacher at the Protestant seminary in Graz died, and the faculty senate at Tübingen University recommended Johannes Kepler to fill the vacancy.

Just 23 years old, he arrived in Graz on 11 April 1594. He remained there for six years as a teacher and part-time astrologer (to suit the whims of the nobility and earn some extra money). Still a budding theologian at heart, Kepler was curious about God's grand celestial design. In 1595 he began to puzzle over the divine mathematical laws that regulated the distances of the six known planets of the time – Mercury, Mars, Venus, Jupiter, Saturn, and the Earth – from the sun. Using Euclid's five regular solids, Kepler drew spheres around them to represent the gaps between the orbits of the six known planets. Like Copernicus, he still believed that the orbits of the planets were based on the circle.

In February 1596 Kepler was granted a two-month leave of absence from the Graz seminary to visit his two ailing grandfathers. He saw Maestlin in Tübingen. They discussed the possibility of publishing Kepler's orbital theories. Maestlin was so enthusiastic that he looked after the editing and printing in Tübingen, with the blessing of the university faculty. In 1596 Kepler's *Prodromus dissertationum mathematicarum continens, Mysterium cosmographicum* appeared in print. "The Mystery of the Universe" (its short title in English) ends with a 32-line hymn of praise to God that reflects Kepler's deep-seated religious beliefs. The last two lines read: "Iova sator Mundi, nostrumque aeterna potestas, Quanta tua est omnem terrarum fama per orbem," which translate roughly as: "Lord, you creator of the world, our perpetual ruler, may thy praise ring out through the vastness of the earth."

Kepler sent copies of his *Mysterium Cosmographicum* to Galileo Galilei (1564-1642), who was unresponsive, and to Tycho Brahe (1546-1601), the illustrious Danish astronomer. Although an opponent of the heliocentric planetary system, Tycho recognized Kepler's brilliance and invited him to join his research staff of astronomers. (Tycho had his own orbital system, a peculiar blend of Ptolemy and Copernicus.)

On 27 April 1597 Kepler married Barbara Mueller, the daughter of a wealthy merchant, who had been briefly married twice before. Their first two children, a boy and a girl, died in infancy of spinal meningitis.

148

Despite the dual tragedy, Kepler was preoccupied with finding a way to measure the distance of the stars from the sun and the velocity of the planets in their orbits. Was there a relationship between the time it takes a planet to orbit the sun, and the distance it is away from the sun?

The Counter Reformation in Austria, vigorously supported by Archduke Ferdinand, a staunch Roman Catholic, forced Kepler to leave his Protestant enclave in Graz, at first temporarily, and finally for good.

In January 1600 Tycho Brahe, the imperial mathematician for Emperor Rudolf II of the Holy Roman Empire, reiterated his invitation to Johannes Kepler to join his staff. They met on 4 February at Benatky Castle in Prague. Although Kepler's tenure of employment was vague and uncertain, he was eager to obtain the benefit of Tycho's 20 years of astronomical research. Kepler moved into Brahe's home as his assistant while the Danish astronomer tried to obtain an official position for his protégé at the Emperor's court in Prague.

When Tycho died suddenly on 24 October 1601, Kepler learned that Brahe had appointed him to be his successor, before his death, to complete his planetary tables. As the new imperial mathematician, Kepler was heir to Tycho Brahe's knowledge and equipment, and his jealously guarded scientific secrets.

Kepler's first assignment under the tutelage of Brahe was to pick up the work of Longomontanus, one of Tycho's chief assistants, who had come to a dead end in his investigations of Mars. Later on Kepler wrote: "I consider it a divine decree that I came at exactly the time when Longomontanus was busy with Mars, because assuredly it is either through that planet that we arrive at the secrets of astronomy, or else they remain forever concealed from us."

Kepler's work on Mars had several important byproducts. Before he could make use of the raw data of his observations of that planet, he felt compelled to solve the problem of atmospheric refraction, that is, how is a ray of light, coming from a distant heavenly body located in the less dense regions of outer space, deflected when it enters the denser atmosphere surrounding the earth?

His solution enabled him not only to supplement the work of Witelo, author of the most important medieval treatise on optics, but to advance that science by explaining the nature of vision. People had been wearing eyeglasses for more than three centuries, but Kepler was the first to explain how the refraction of light was related to nearsightedness and farsightedness.

Johannes Kepler possessed what Edward DeBono calls the ability to think laterally. Before Kepler, all of the great astronomers – Aristotle, Ptolemy, Galileo, Copernicus, Maestlin and Brahe – had been hung up on the notion that planets move in perfect circles. But try as he might, Kepler was unable to fit the orbit of Mars to Brahe's observations, regardless of what kinds of circular combinations he could devise. Nor did he have calculus to help him. He had to use geometry and trigonometry, because they were the only mathematical tools known to him. (Newton and Leibniz developed calculus much later.)

Working with radius vectors in 1602, Kepler arrived at his Second Law of Planetary Motion (before he discovered the first): "Motion in the orbit is such that the rate of sweeping out area by the radius vector is constant." In plain English, that means that an imaginary line connecting the sun and a planet sweeps over equal areas of the plane of the planetary orbit in equal intervals of time. This is the so-called Law of Areas, which can be proved in mechanics for all movements controlled by a central force.

Three years later, around Easter 1605, Kepler discovered that Mars revolves in an elliptical orbit with the sun occupying one of its two foci. The perfection of the circle had predominated in the thinking of astronomers before Kepler for so long that the ellipse – the "squashed circle" – had been given short shrift.

Kepler applied his second law to his elliptical orbit for Mars and found that they were fully compatible. Using Mars as the example for all six planets, he was now able to postulate his First Law of Planetary Motion: "Orbits of the planets are ellipses with the sun in one focus."

Due to financial problems, the book containing Kepler's first two planetary laws, his *Astronomia Nova,* did not appear until 1609. It was an apt and prophetic title. Printed in Heidelberg in a small edition, the "New Astronomy" of Johannes Kepler became the first modern textbook of this science – but not over night. It took Sir Isaac Newton (1643-1727) to point out to the scientific world the true signifiance of

Kepler's work.

Kepler's employer and patron, Rudolf II, was more interested in his protégé's talents as an astrologer and kept him busy casting horoscopes for himself and other nobles at court. Because of the emperor's expenditures for wars against the Ottoman Turks, and his investments in his private art collection, Kepler had constant difficulty collecting his salary from the royal treasury, and often it was in the form of a promissory note. But since they were to bear (and perpetuate) his name, Rudolf II was also anxious for Kepler to get on with the enormous task of completing for publication the astronomical *Rudolphine Tables* based on the observations of Tycho Brahe.

In 1609 Kepler applied to Duke Johann Friedrich of Württemberg for permission to work in Swabia. He was thinking of a professorship at Tübingen. Proud of what the Swabian scientist had accomplished thus far at the court of the Emperor, the Duke granted this permission in 1611. It was not a firm job offer, however. In a subsequent letter to Duke Johann Friedrich, Kepler made the mistake of discussing his own liberal religious beliefs, which upset the Duke's theologians. They prevailed upon the Duke to state their objections in a letter, thus blocking Kepler's employment in Württemberg.

The year 1611 brought additional disasters. Kepler's son Friedrich died in February. When he returned from Linz that summer, where he had applied for the post of district mathematician, he found his wife Barbara gravely ill. She died on 3 July. Although he had been accepted for the job in Linz, he did not go there at once. After the death of Emperor Rudolf II in January 1612, his successor, Emperor Matthias, invited Kepler to remain as imperial mathematician with an annual salary and granted him permission to work in Linz.

Leaving his children temporarily with friends in Prague, Kepler moved to Linz. Unfortunately for him, the chief pastor of Linz was his former Tübingen classmate Daniel Hitzler, a strictly orthodox Lutheran. When Kepler applied to him for the sacrament of Communion, they had some heated arguments about Kepler's liberal religious views. When Kepler refused to subscribe to the Lutheran beliefs, as set down in the Formula of Concord, Hitzler excluded him from the Communion service. Kepler's appeal to higher church authorities in Stuttgart was of no avail. He remained excluded from

Communion until 1620, when Hitzler was removed from his post.

On 30 October 1613 Kepler married Susanna Reutinger, an orphan who had grown up at Schloss Starhemberg, the home of Baroness von Starhemberg, one of Kepler's patrons. Emperor Matthias was one of the wedding guests. During their years in Linz she bore him six children, but the first three died of smallpox.

While laying in a supply of wine in 1615, Kepler was amazed and dismayed by the haphazard method his wine merchant used to fill up the casks in his cellar. Noting the lack of uniformity in the shapes of the casks, Kepler decided to take a fresh look at the problem of measuring volume accurately. He picked up where Archimedes (287-212 BC) had left off. His mathematical solution was a book with the title *Nova stereometria doliorum,* "The New Stereometry of Wine Barrels." A second book about "The Art of Measurement of Archimedes" was published a year later. Don't ever let it be said that the mind of an astronomer is constantly on the stars!

In October 1617 Johannes Kepler returned to Leonberg, where he had spent part of his childhood. His reunion with his mother Katharine had nothing to do with sentiment. She had been accused of witchcraft by her neighbors and was about to go on trial. Kepler made the long journey from Linz to defend her.

But her trial was postponed. He returned to Linz to continue working on his *Epitome Astronomiae Copernicanae,* "Handbook of Copernican Astronomy," but put it aside (it did not appear in full until 1621) in favor of a compendium reflecting the universal harmony of astronomy, geometry, metaphysics, esthetics, music, and several other disciplines. Kepler studied in particular the relationships between harmonies of music and the rhythms of planetary movements. That year his daughter Katharina died.

On 15 May 1618, one week before the outbreak of the Thirty Years' War, Kepler discovered his Third Law of Planetary Motion. He stated it in the third chapter of the fifth book of his *Harmonice Mundi* ("World Harmony"), published in 1619:

"The squares of the periods of revolution of any two planets are proportional to the cubes of their mean distances from the sun." Stated another way: "Squares of the periods are proportional to cubes of semi-major axes."

It should be noted here that Kepler's three laws concerning

the movement of the planets around the sun apply not only to the nine planets we know today, but as our astronauts also know, to the motion of any artificial satellite.

From 1617 to 1620 Kepler bombarded the authorities in Württemberg, including Duke Johann Friedrich, with petitions in connection with the charges of witchcraft against his mother. In August 1620 she was arrested and imprisoned.

Kepler again departed for Leonberg. When he arrived, he learned from his younger brother Christoph that the trial had been moved to Güglingen (halfway between Maulbronn and Heilbronn). Kepler prepared a brilliant defense. The evidence for the prosecution and the defense was taken, weighed by the court, and then submitted to a higher authority in Tübingen. The judges then ruled that Frau Kepler was to be shown the instruments of torture in the hope that she would break down and confess.

A year later, on 28 September 1621, Katharine Kepler, 74 years old, was led into the torture chamber after 14 months of imprisonment in chains. She refused to confess; instead she fell to her knees and prayed. In October she was acquitted and set free, but within six months she died.

In 1624, as Kepler was preparing the *Rudolphine Tables* for publication, he happened to read John Napier's treatise on logarithms. The Scottish mathematician, known as Lord of Merchiston (the family castle near Edinburgh where he was born in 1550 and died in 1617), is credited with the invention of this simplified method of multiplication and division. Kepler not only recognized the utility of Napier's invention, but wrote a treatise of his own on the subject called *Chilias Logarithmorum*. At this time he was also corresponding with Wilhelm Schickard (1592-1635), another gifted Swabian *Tüftler,* who had studied under Maestlin and took over his chair for mathematics and astronomy at Tübingen after Maestlin's death.

A philologist, as well, Schickard held the chair for the study of biblical languages at the university. He was a painter, an artist and engraver, and a first-class mathematician. His interests also included geodesy, the science of computing the size and shape of the earth. He developed his own maps for the first geodetic survey of Württemberg. Like Kepler, Schickard was in contact with John Napier.

On 20 September 1623 Wilhelm Schickard sent Johannes Kepler a sketch of his "calculating clock," as he called it. The original of this calculator, which Schickard invented on the side, was lost during the Thirty Years' War.

But Dr. Franz Hammer, a Kepler scholar, found letters and sketches by Schickard in Kepler's papers, dating from 1623/4, pertaining to "a machine which automatically adds, subtracts, multiplies and divides any given numbers." Dr. Hammer reported his findings at a convention on the history of mathematics held on 11 April 1957. Later on, he and Professor Dr. Baron von Freytag-Loeringhoff of the University of Tübingen were able to reconstruct a working model of Schickard's calculator based on the notes and sketches he had sent to Kepler. Working models of Schickard's "calculating clock" can be seen in the German Museum in Munich and in the Kepler Museum in Weil der Stadt.

(Forgive me this digression in praise of yet another Swabian genius who invented the world's first calculator in 1623, almost two decades before Blaise Pascal's machine caught the world's fancy in Paris in 1642 – and it could only add!)

In the fall of 1624 Kepler made a journey to Vienna to discuss the financing of the printing of the *Rudolphine Tables* with Ferdinand II, who had become the Emperor of the Holy Roman Empire in 1519. The Emperor decided that his treasuries in Nürnberg, Memmingen, and Kempten would advance the funds.

For the next three years Kepler traveled from place to place in the effort to collect the money. He paid for the paper, purchased in Kempten, out of his own pocket and had a printing press transported to Linz because the Emperor wanted the *Tables* to be published in Austria. But on 30 June 1626, rebellious peasants set fire to the house of Johannes Plank, who was printing the *Tables*. Fortunately, the manuscript survived, but the printing press was destroyed.

Kepler got the Emperor's permission to have the *Tables* published in Ulm. He took his familiy with him in November 1626, but the Danube froze over while they were visiting Regensburg. The winter was so severe that Kepler left his family there while he continued his journey to Ulm by wagon.

While his 568-page manuscript was being printed by a rather unscrupulous rascal named Jonas Saur, Kepler was asked by the Ulm city magistrate to revise the city's system of weights and measures for use in commercial trade. Kepler devised standards for length, volume and weight and constructed a kettle to show their relationships. The original *"Ulmer Kessel"* is on display in the municipal museum in Ulm. A duplicate can be seen in the Kepler Museum in Weil der Stadt.

The *Rudolphine Tables* were published in 1,000 copies in September 1627. For a full century they were used to make accurate calculations of the solar system and by navigators exploring strange waters.

In November 1627 Kepler rejoined his family in Regensburg and then traveled to Prague to present a copy of the *Rudolphine Tables* to Emperor Ferdinand, to whom they were dedicated. The Emperor was pleased with his work, but he prevailed upon his imperial mathematician to become a Roman Catholic. Kepler refused to do so.

As early as 1608 Kepler had cast a horoscope for Albrecht Eusebius Wenzel von Wallenstein (1583-1634), the Duke of Friedland and Mecklenburg and Prince of Sagan – all territories he had been given by the Emperor in recognition of his military contributions to the Holy Roman Empire and the Hapsburg dynasty, and especially for his victories over Christian IV of Denmark during the Thirty Years' War.

A great believer in astrology, Wallenstein had just been named "General of the Oceanic and the Baltic Seas" by the Emperor when he met Johannes Kepler at court in Prague.

Wallenstein invited Kepler to join him at Sagan in the northern part of Silesia. The Generalissimo of the Imperial Armies became Kepler's patron at 1,000 gulden a year. He provided Kepler with a house and a printing press.

Kepler arrived with his family in Sagan on 20 July 1628. While in Wallenstein's service he completed the second part of his *Ephemerides,* a set of tables showing the positions of celestial bodies on certain dates which were useful to navigators and astronomers.

Johannes Kepler left Sagan for Regensburg on 8 October 1630 to appeal to the Emperor at the Imperial Diet for the 12,000 gulden still owed to him. After brief stops in Leipzig and Nürnberg, he arrived in Regensburg on 2 November. Exhausted in body and in spirit, he contracted a fever and died at noon on 15 November 1630. He was buried in St. Peter's cemetery outside the walls of the city, but the upheavals of the fighting in 1633, during the second decade of the Thirty Years' War, obliterated his grave. Kepler had written his own epitaph several months earlier:

"Mensus eram coelos, nunc terrae metior umbras. Mens coelestis erat, corporis umbra jacet."

"Once I measured the heavens, now I measure the shadows of the earth. Although my soul came from heaven, the shadow of my body lies here."

On 15 November 1980 I was invited to attend a ceremony at Weil der Stadt marking the 350th anniversary of the death of Johannes Kepler. Peter Blauvelt, a brilliant young composer from Harvard University, had told me about it months ahead of time. His father was the head of government relations at HQ USAREUR in Heidelberg and my supervisor. The Kepler society in Weil der Stadt had heard of Peter's string quartet based on Kepler's planetary movement and celestial music. (Kepler had written down the tune of each planet in musical notation). Two years earlier I had brought Peter's composition to the attention of the director of the Stuttgart Planetarium.

The Kepler Society invited Peter to a performance of his composition at the 350th anniversary ceremony. Afterwards, Frau Utta Keppler of Tübingen, the author of a biographical novel about Kepler's mother, read her short story, "Kepler Rides to Regensburg" *(Kepler reitet nach Regensburg),* a piece of prose at once touching and beautiful.

The Kepler Museum in Weil der Stadt occupies two floors of Kepler's birth house right off the market place, to the left of the *Rathaus* as you face it. In addition to fascinating exhibits of Kepler's world and his contemporaries, there is a metal model of the five Euclidian solids he used as the basis for his "The Mystery of the Universe" and an electronically operated, kinematic device demonstrating at the flip of a switch his laws of planetary motion, manufactured by the laboratory of IBM-Germany. The museum is open from

Monday to Friday (9-12 a.m. and 2-4 p.m.), Saturdays (10-12 a.m. and 2-5 p.m.), and Sundays (11-12 a.m. and 2-5 p.m.). The admission fee is one Mark for adults and fifty Pfennigs for children.

On the market square you will find a bigger-than-life bronze statue of Johannes Kepler sitting on a sandstone pedastal. A creation of the sculptor August Kreling, it was unveiled in 1871 to mark the 300th anniversary of Kepler's birth.

The scars of flunking chemistry and economics during my freshman year at Yale – I was sixteen at the time – make me most hesitant to write about ALBERT EINSTEIN.

But Einstein was also sixteen when he flunked the botany, zoology and modern language entrance exams to the Swiss Federal Polytechnic School in Zurich in 1895.

Through bull-headed determination, both of us managed to get back on a solid footing with the schools of our choice, and that is surely the only thing I have in common with that Swabian genius.

It is easy to trace the path of his life, but virtually impossible to reconstruct the workings of the inner man. Einstein deliberately and consistently kept his intellectual life separate from his private life, making it all the more difficult for any would-be biographer to portray his personality. In his autobiography, *Out of My Later Years,* published in 1950, he wrote: "We are hardly aware of whatever is important in our own existence and it certainly should be of no concern to our fellow men. What does a fish know of the water it swims around in for a lifetime?"

Einstein's ancestors were Swabian craftsmen of the Jewish faith. His father , Hermann Einstein, was born in 1847 in Buchau am Federsee (just eight kilometers due north of the Premonstratensian Abbey at Bad Schussenried). He married a Buchau girl, Pauline Koch, in Bad Cannstatt in 1876 and tried to make a living as an electronic technician. The couple moved to Ulm in 1878, where Hermann opened an electrical appliance store that failed to spark. While the Einsteins were living on Bahnhofstrasse, their son Albert was born on 14 March 1879. The people of Ulm were so proud of Einstein in 1922 that they named a street after him, but in 1933 it was changed to Fichte Strasse in honor of a gentile philosopher.

After the failure of their store, the Einsteins moved to Munich, where Hermann went into business with his brother Jakob. They manufactured electrical devices, such as dynamos and measuring instruments, but that business was also doomed to failure.

On 18 November 1881 Einstein's sister Maja was born in Munich. Albert did not talk until age three. His parents worried that he might be retarded. He disliked sports and games, but he began taking violin lessons at age six and enjoyed playing that instrument for the rest of his life. (His mother was an accomplished pianist.)

Dr. Teri Weiss, the Director of the German-American Institute (D.a.I.) in Tübingen, told me two cute anecdotes about Einstein which she heard in graduate school. One of them pertains to his violin playing. While performing a duet with Artur Rubinstein, the famous pianist was overhead to say: "No, no, Albert can't you count?"

Einstein's curiosity about natural phenomena began at an early age. Writing at age 67, he recalled:

"A wonder of such nature I experienced as a child of four or five years, when my father showed me a compass. That this needle behaved in such a determined way did not at all fit into the nature of events... I can still remember – or at least I believe I can remember – that this experience made a deep and lasting impression upon me. Something deeply hidden had to be behind things."

In 1889 Einstein entered the Luitpoldgymnasium in Munich. In 1892 he learned differential and integral calculus and Euclidian geometry. He called the latter "a second wonder of a totally different nature" with a "lucidity and certainty" that made "an indescribable impression" upon him.

After the failure of the Einstein brothers' business, Hermann and Pauline moved to Pavia, and later to nearby Milan, Italy, leaving Albert behind in Munich. Six months later he left school, renounced his German citizenship, and joined his parents in Milan. His father wanted him to become an electrical engineer. He decided to send him to the Swiss Federal Polytechnic School, but, as I mentioned at the outset, Albert failed the entrance exams. Noting his excellence in mathematics, Professor Albin Herzog, the director of the school, suggested that he attend the canton school in Aarau. He went there from the end of October 1895 until his graduation in the spring of 1896. That fall he was admitted to the Polytechnic in Zurich. While there he decided to switch from pure mathematics to the study of physics.

Professor Jean Pernet warned him of the difficulty of this subject, and asked, "Why don't you study medicine, or law, or philology?" Einstein answered: "Because I really don't have the talent, Herr Professor. Why shouldn't I at least give physics a try?"

A loner, Einstein refused to follow the instructions in the textbook and worked out his own solutions. When he injured his hand in an explosion in the lab, Professor Pernet asked his assistant, Dr. Joseph Sauter: "What do you think of Einstein? He is doing just the opposite of what I told him to do."

"Indeed, Herr Professor," Sauter replied, "but his solutions are correct and his methods are always interesting."

Einstein's classroom attendance was irregular. He preferred to read the classic textbooks in theoretical physics by Kirchoff, Helmholtz and Hertz at home. Fortunately, the excellent notes taken in class by his friend Marcel Grossman enabled him to pass the examination for his diploma in the spring of 1900.

On 21 February 1901, a few weeks before his 22d birthday, Einstein obtained his Swiss citizenship. He had been stateless since age fifteen. At a technical high school in Winterthur from 21 May to 14 August, he filled in for a mathematics teacher who was doing his military service. Later on, in response to a want ad, he got a temporary teaching job in a boarding school for boys.

In Volume IV of the *Annalen der Physik* (Annals of Physics) for 1901 he published his first paper on "Deductions from Capillary Phenomena."

Einstein's father died in 1902. In June of that year Albert went to work as a civil servant in the Patent Office in Berne, where he remainded for the next seven years. The position paid well enough for him to establish a household. In January 1903 he married Mileva Maric, a fellow student at the Polytechnic School in Zurich.

Einstein wrote that a practical profession was a blessing for his kind of person. "Most practical professions," he noted, "are such that a person with normal ability can do what is expected of him... If he has deeper scientific interests, then he can pursue his favorite problems as a sideline to his regular work. The fear that his efforts could be fruitless need not trouble him."

Einstein's pursuit of his "favorite problems" was far from fruitless. He published three papers in the *Annalen der Physik* in 1905, a year that was as earthshaking (no pun intended) for modern physics as 1609 was for astronomy, when Kepler's first two laws of planetary movement appeared in print.

In 1949 physicist Max Born, a late discoverer of Einstein's paper on relativity and winner of the Nobel Prize in 1954, wrote: "One of the most remarkable volumes in the whole of scientific literature seems to me Volume 17 (4th Series) of *Annalen der Physik,* 1905. It contains three papers by Einstein... each today acknowledged to be a masterpiece, the source of a new branch of physics."

A fourth paper, entitled "Does the Inertia of a Body Depend upon Its Energy Content?," published in Volume 18 of *Annalen der Physik,* contained Einstein's famous formula $e=mc^2$. It was "probably the only formula ever sent sprawling across the cover of TIME magazine," to quote Michael Polanyi's book *Personal Knowledge.* "The reduction of mass *(m),*" Polanyi writes, "by the loss of energy *(e)* accompanying nuclear transformation has been repeatedly shown to confirm the relation $e=mc^2$, where c is the velocity of light."

Jeremy Bernstein has written a wonderful 230-page book called *Einstein* that makes the latter's theories comprehensible even to a scientific dropout like me. Of Einstein's three-page discourse on "Does the Inertia of a Body Depend upon Its Energy Content?" he writes: "This paper is a perfect model for what the deductive process in physics is at its best. Like the rest of Einstein's early papers it is almost completely non-mathematical, but rests on inventing a 'thought experiment' which when carefully analyzed yields the result. In this case, Einstein imagined an atom, or some other particle, that decayed radioactively by emitting light radiation-gamma rays. We now know many examples of such decays, but in 1905 the study of radioactivity was still in its infancy and decays such as Einstein imagined had not been studied in full detail."

Einstein's paper in the *Annalen der Physik* on "The Electrodynamics of Moving Bodies" was his first essay on his Special Theory of Relativity. He demonstrated that two observers moving at great speed with respect to each other will disagree about measurement of length and time intervals made in each other's systems, that the speed of light is the limiting speed of all bodies having mass, and that energy and mass are equivalent. His paper on the theory of photons explained the photoelectric effect. The one on a molecular kinetic theory of heat, and its effect on the movement of particles suspended in motionless liquids, finally explained the so-called "Brownian motion." This phenomenon had puzzled physicists since 1827, when Robert Brown, a Scottish botanist, observed the erratic movements of pollen grains immersed in water. Jeremy Bernstein describes the importance of this effort:

"It was the experiments suggested by this paper that convinced the skeptics, and there were many even in 1905, of the existence of atoms. The statistical techniques that Einstein developed to cope with this atomic problem he also made use of, at about the same time, to study the quantum aspects of radiation. Hence, the quantum-theory and Brownian-motion papers of 1905 are, in fact, applications of a unified idea, namely, the mathematical description of systems involving enormous numbers of basic units--atoms or light quanta--by statistics."

Einstein earned his doctorate from the University of Zurich in 1905 with his dissertation on "A New Determination of Molecular Dimensions." Max Planck, the physicist who developed the quantum theory around 1900 and won the Nobel Prize for it in 1918, was quick to accept and develop equations for the application of Einstein's Special Theory of Relativity. (Planck was a Professor of Theoretical Physics in Berlin from 1889 to 1926). In Göttingen, the mathematician Hermann Minkowski, who had been one of Einstein's professors at the Polytechnic in Zurich, worked out the "Mathematical Foundations for the Special Theory of Relativity" in 1908.

In February 1908 Einstein succeeded in obtaining an adjunct professorship at the University of Berne, for which he had been turned down the previous year. He had three students for his first lecture on "Theory of Radiation" in the winter semester of 1908/09. In October 1909 he gave up his job at the Patent Office to accept a professorship at the University of Zurich. Since 14 May 1904 he had been the father of Hans-Albert Einstein, who later became a professor of hydraulics at the University of California at Berkeley in 1937. On 28 July 1910 his son Eduard was born.

In March 1911 Einstein was asked to join the faculty of the University of Prague, which had been divided into a German section and a Czech section since 1888. The leaders of society gave a reception for him in one of Prague's best hotels. Einstein showed up in a worker's blue suit. The hotel personnel took him for the electrician whom they had summoned to repair the wiring.

In Prague Einstein came into contact with a Jewish literary circle that included the writer Franz Kafka, his biographer Max Brod, and Hugo Bergmann, who tried unsuccessfully to win over Einstein to the cause of Zionism. He saw Brod frequently. Four years later, in his novel *The Redemption of Tycho Brahe,* Brod based his portrayal of Johannes Kepler on Albert Einstein.

In 1911 Einstein accepted an invitation to a scientific convention in Brussels, hosted by the chemist Ernest Solvay. There he met Madame Curie, Ernest Rutherford, Hendrik Lorentz, and Max Planck. At this time he had begun to work on his General Theory of Relativity. Based on recommendations from Madame Curie and Planck, Einstein was offered the chair for theoretical physics at his *alma mater,* the Federal Polytechnic School in Zurich, in February 1912. He began teaching there on 1 October 1912. But on 30 November of the following year he turned in his resignation. The invitation to come to Berlin as a member of the prestigious Prussian Academy of Science and at the same time as the director of the Research Institute for Physics of the Kaiser-Wilhelm Institute was too tempting to refuse.

In the spring of 1914 Einstein departed Zurich for Berlin, leaving his wife and two sons behind. Max Planck had recommended him for membership in the Academy. In his letter of acceptance Einstein wrote: "What encouraged me to accept the election was the thought that nothing else can be expected of a person than to devote all of his strength to a good cause, and I really feel capable of just that." But his marriage with Mileva was about exhausted after 17 years. (They were legally divorced in 1919.)

A thorough pacifist, Einstein remained untouched by the events of World War I, except to sign a manifesto calling for peace as soon as possible. Between 1915 and 1918 he wrote some thirty papers, including his theory of light deflection by the sun and his book on *Relativity: the Special and the General Theory.* (Published in 1918, it was translated into English in 1920 and reissued in 1947.) Sir Arthur

Stanley Eddington's expeditions, under the aegis of the Royal Society of London, to Sobral, Brazil, and the Isle of Principe in the Gulf of Guinea in 1919 provided photographic evidence of the correctness of Einstein's theory of gravitation which was based on his concept of General Relativity.

In 1919 Einstein met his cousin Elsa in Berlin again. She was living in her uncle's house with her two daughters from a previous marriage. They were married that same year.

The Zionist Chaim Weizmann, one of the creators of the nation of Israel (and its first President from 1948 to 1952), invited Albert Einstein to accompany him on a lecture tour in America to generate funds for the establishment of a university in Jerusalem. During their trip, in May 1921, Einstein delivered four lectures on the theory of relativity at Princeton University. That year he also visited Palestine, but its high point was his receipt of the Nobel Prize for his discovery of the photoelectric effect. He sent the money part of the prize to his ex-wife Mileva.

In 1923 the University of Leyden asked Einstein to follow in the footsteps of Hendrik Lorentz as a professor of physics. Einstein turned it down, but agreed to give a series of lectures. Besides commuting back and forth between Berlin and Leyden that year, he visited England, Spain, Czechoslovakia, Japan und Palestine. In 1925 the University of Leyden gave him an honorary doctorate, one of 25 he was to receive during his lifetime.

The Federal Polytechnic School in Zurich awarded Einstein an honorary doctor's degree in 1930, as did Oxford the following year. Toward the end of 1930 Princeton's faculty asked him to spend each winter semester at the university, and the Academy in Berlin agreed to this arrangement, provided that he spent the summer months there.

In the spring of 1933 Einstein was at the Belgian sea resort of Le Coq-sur-Mer. Having learned that the Nazis had sacked and confiscated his summer home near Berlin and burned some of his writings on relativity in front of the Berlin State Opera House, he severed his connections with Germany. His rights of German citizenship were revoked. He resigned his membership in the Prussian and Bavarian Academies of Science to become the first professor at the newly created Institute for Advanced Studies at Princeton at $16,000 a year.

Jeremy Bernstein describes his life there:

"In 1933 Einstein moved into a rented house in Princeton, three quarters of a mile or so from what is now Fuld Hall at the Institute, where he had his office from 1940. In 1935 he bought a modest white frame house at 112 Mercer Street, where he lived and worked until his death. (The house, which now belongs to Margot Einstein, Einstein's stepdaughter, is shared by Helen Dukas, Einstein's secretary since 1928. Elsa Einstein, Margot's mother and Einstein's second wife, died in 1936.)...When Einstein arrived in Princeton in 1933 he was fifty-four, and while he continued to do extensive work in physics it is fair to say that his great work, the work that created modern physics, was behind him." In 1935 Einstein also bought a summer home in Old Lyme, Connecticut, where he could indulge his love for sailing.

The year 1936 not only marked the death of his second wife, but also of Marcel Grossmann, the industrious student whose notes helped Einstein to earn his diploma from the Polytechnic School in Zurich in 1900 and who worked with him in 1913 on his first draft of a theory of general relativity and a theory of gravitation.

And now for Dr. Teri Weiss' second anecdote about Einstein. At a formal dinner party at Princeton, the guests found a magnolia blossom as a decoration on their plates when they sat down to dinner. Mrs. Einstein ate hers. Her husband took note of that fact, grinned, and then proceeded to eat his. Greater love hath no man...

Despite his deeply rooted pacifism, Einstein listened to the arguments of the American physicists Edward Teller and Leo Szilard, who visited him on 2 August 1939. They convinced him that the Germans were working on the development of an atomic bomb. "I was fully aware of the terrible danger which the success of this experiment would mean for mankind," Einstein noted at the time. He wrote a letter to President Franklin D. Roosevelt, warning of the implications of the discovery of nuclear fission, which Lise Meitner, an Austrian colleague of Otto Hahn and Franz Strassman at the Kaiser-Wilhelm Institute in Berlin, had reported in January of that year. Alexander Sachs, an economist and personal friend and adviser of President Roosevelt, carried Einstein's letter to the White House. Impressed by Einstein's letter and the argumentation of Sachs, Roosevelt appointed an Advisory Committee on Uranium to report to him on the situation.

On 1 October 1941 in Trenton, New Jersey, Albert Einstein swore allegiance to the United States of America and to uphold her Constitution in a ceremony which made him an American citizen. But the atomic air raids on Hiroshima and Nagasaki in August 1945 reinforced his pacificism and turned his thoughts to world government.

Although he was one of the pioneers of the quantum theory of Max Planck, he turned against it in his later years. To Max Born he wrote: "In our scientific expectation we have grown antipodes. You believe in a dice-playing God and I in perfect laws in the world of things existing as real objects, which I try to grasp in a wildly speculative way."

That sounds very much like Johannes Kepler.

"Still there are moments," Einstein had written to Queen Elizabeth of Belgium on 9 January 1939, "when one feels free from one's own identification with human limitations and inadequacies. At such moments, one imagines that one stands on some spot of a small planet, gazing in amazement at the cold yet profoundly moving beauty of the eternal, the unfathomable: life and death flow into one, and there is neither evolution nor destiny: only being."

That also sounds very much like Johannes Kepler.

Albert Einstein died of a malfunction of the liver on 18 April 1955. For almost forty years he had been working on "a favorite problem" - the unified field theory. He was still working on it the night he died, and he put aside an unfinished calculation for the next morning before shutting his eyes forever.

XIX Swabian Men of Letters

Four of Germany's most famous men of letters were Swabians: Friedrich Schiller, Friedrich Hölderlin, Eduard Mörike, and Hermann Hesse.

FRIEDRICH SCHILLER was born at Marbach on the Neckar (18 kilometers northeast of Ludwigsburg) on 10 November 1759. His birthplace, and especially the Schiller National Museum above the Neckar, are well worth a visit.

His father was an army officer, who had served in Bavarian, French, and Swabian regiments. After his military career ended, he became the superintendent of the gardens at the Ludwigsburg Castle.

With considerable reluctance, Schiller's father agreed to send his son Friedrich to the *Hohe Karlsschule* in Stuttgart, which Duke Karl Eugen personally supervised. (You can read more about the *Karlsschule* in chapter XII.) Schiller's parents wanted their son to study for the ministry. The Duke insisted that he prepare for a legal career. Ultimately Schiller switched to medicine.

The rigid discipline of the school, which was a military academy to all intents and purposes, stifled Schiller's craving for free and independent thought. During his eight years in the *Karlsschule* he read the works of Shakespeare and Rousseau and was strongly influenced by them. On 17 December 1779 he saw Johann Wolfgang von Goethe (1749-1832) for the first time during a visit by Germany's greatest poet (then and now) to the *Hohe Karlsschule.*

Disturbed by the despotism of the Duke, Schiller wrote his first play, *The Robbers,* at age 18 and had it printed in 1781 with borrowed money. The play treats the theme of the abuse of power and corruption in high places. Although weakened by improbability and oversimplified characters, it was an immediate success after its initial performance at the National Theater in Mannheim in the neighboring Palatinate on 13 January 1782. (Schiller went to Mannheim without the Duke's permission to attend the opening night.) The enormous success of *The Robbers* made Schiller the leader of the "Storm and Stress" literary movement in Germany, supplanting even the great Goethe.

Schiller completed his medical studies and was posted to a Stuttgart regiment as an assistant medical officer. While he was finishing the first of his politico-historical tragedies, *The Conspiracy of Fiesko in Genoa,* in 1782, he made a second secret trip to Mannheim and was caught. The Duke sentenced him to detention for two weeks and ordered him to stop writing such "comedies."

Determined to pursue a literary career, Schiller fled to Mannheim and then to Sachsenhausen. The mother of a school friend let him live at her estate at Bauerbach (near Meiningen in Thuringia) from December 1782 to July 1783. There he wrote his third play, *Love and Intrigue.* The plot weaves the exploitation of the middle classes, political corruption and social prejudice into an inextricable net of intrigue that drives two socially unequal lovers, a young aristocrat and the daughter of the town musician, into suicide. Accepted by Baron von Dalberg, the director of the Mannheim Theater, the play was an even greater success than *The Robbers.* Schiller received a one-year appointment as the theater's official playwright.

Shortly after his arrival in Mannheim Schiller suffered the first attack of a disease (a combination of chest trouble with an intestinal disorder) that plagued him for the rest of his life and eventually killed him. His contract at the Mannheim Theater was not renewed. In ill health and almost destitute by 1785, he accepted an invitation to live with Gottfried Körner, a friend and admirer, in Leipzig. After Körner's marriage, Schiller moved with him to the Körner country estate at Loschwitz near Dresden. During this time, which must have been a most peaceful one for Schiller, he composed his famous "Ode to Joy," parts of which were later immortalized in the choral finale of Beethoven's Ninth Symphony. In this idyllic setting he also completed his first drama in blank verse, *Don Carlos,* in 1787. What he had originally planned as "a domestic drama in a royal house" evolved into a major politico-philosophical tragedy.

Not wishing to outstay his welcome at the Körner's, Schiller went to Weimar, the home of Goethe and the literary capital of Germany, in July 1787. He began an intensive study of history and completed his *History of the Revolt of the United Netherlands* the following year. It marked his departure from the "Storm and Stress" to the objectivity of history, and was the start down the path to Classicism.

In 1790 Schiller met Goethe for the first time in the house of Charlotte von Lengefeld, whom he married that year. Initially, Goethe

167

was aloof, but after a chance meeting in 1794 the two dramatists began to exchange letters. Ultimately, Goethe succeeded in getting Schiller an appointment as a professor of history at the University of Jena.

From 1791 to 1793 Schiller wrote his *History of the Thirty Years War,* which provided him with the material for his most ambitious drama, *Wallenstein,* a trilogy in eleven acts. He completed it in 1799, the year he moved to Weimar to be close to Goethe and the court theater there. Goethe found *Wallenstein* "so great that there is no second work that could be compared with it."

On a visit to Swabia in 1793-94, Schiller had met Johann Friedrich Cotta, one of Germany's leading publishers, who became a close personal friend and adviser. Cotta published a periodical edited by Schiller, called *Die Horen,* in which several of Schiller's philosophical essays appeared.

Schiller's preoccupation with the philosophy of Immanuel Kant influenced his essay "On Grace and Dignity" of 1793 and his "Letters Concerning the Aesthetic Education of Mankind" of 1794. Schiller's treatise "On Naive and Sentimental Poetry," written between 1795 and 1796, discussed the contrast between ancient and modern poetry, between nature and idea, subject and object. Specifically, it was an attempt by Schiller to prove to himself and his contemporaries that his poetry could co-exist with Goethe's as separate and distict art forms. In Schiller's view, Goethe was a "naive" or classic poet, at one with nature as the ancient Greeks had been. Schiller considered himself a "sentimental" poet who had lost this immediate contact with nature and had to regain it through a reasoned effort of the will.

Now that Schiller's classical ideals had caught up with Goethe's, the two became close friends who helped each other and influenced each other's works. Both had an extremely productive year of writing ballads in 1797.

But Schiller's health had begun to worsen. Working against time, he produced several historical dramas in quick succession after *Wallenstein.* In 1800 his *Maria Stuart* was first performed. Schiller compressed the last three days in the life of Mary, Queen of Scots, into the plot. Mary, with whom Schiller's sympathies lie, turns the outward disaster of her conviction into an internal triumph by accepting the unjust verdict and transcending it. Schiller did not stick to the historical facts, but created a powerful drama in conformance with his theory of tragedy: the moral rebirth of the hero through an act of voluntary self-denial.

Schiller's *The Maid of Orleans* appeared in 1801. He called it a "romantic tragedy." The heroine, Joan of Arc, dies after a victorious battle instead of at the stake, as was the fate of the real Joan in 1431. *The Bride of Messina,* completed in 1803, is a heroic play in the classical Greek manner with a chorus of wise men. It concerns an evil prophecy from which there is no escape, but the tragic guilt of the leading characters – two brothers in love with their own sister – has its source in their own human failings.

Schiller's last complete play, *William Tell* (1804), about the beginning of Swiss independence and Tell's personal struggle for human rights, ultimately became his most popular one. Schiller was working on a play called *Demetrius* when death caught up with him in his 46th year on 9 May 1805. His remains were exhumed 22 years later and placed in a tomb in Weimar, where Goethe is also buried.

The Schiller monument by the Danish sculptor Bertel Thorwaldsen (1768-1844) was erected at Schiller Square *(Schillerplatz)* in Stuttgart in 1839. A statue of Schiller created by sculptor A. Donndorf in 1909 stands to the left of the main entrance to the Baden-Württemberg State Theater. Two streets *(Schillerstrasse* and *Schillerpassage),* a section of the city along the *Neue Weinsteige* called *Zur Schillereiche,* and a square (with monument) in Stuttgart-Vaihingen are also named in honor of Swabia' a most famous poet and dramatist.

So also are a variety of literary prizes awarded in Schiller's name since his 100th birthday anniversary in 1859. In May 1955, the 150th anniversary of the poet's death, the Baden-Württemberg Government established a foundation to present the "Schiller Commemorative Prize" to a deserving author, preferably a dramatist. The prize was awarded for the first time on 10 November 1955 (the anniversary of Schiller's birthday) to Rudolf Kassner (1873-1959); in 1957 to Rudolf Pannwitz (1881-1969); in 1959 to Wilhelm Lehmann (1882-1968); in 1962 to Werner Bergengrün (1892-1964); in 1965 to Max Frisch (1911); in 1968 to Günther Eich (1907-1972); in 1971 to Gerhard Storz (1898); in 1974 to Ernst Jünger (1895); in 1977 to Golo

Mann (1909); and in 1980 to Martin Walser (1927). The next Schiller Commemorative Prize of the State of Baden-Württemberg will be presented in November 1983.

In the year 1480 Count Eberhard "in the Beard" had a wall built around the city of Tübingen. Part of that wall is a tower facing the Neckar River. During the first half of the 19th century people began to call it the "Hölderlin Tower." It was the last home of a restless, insane Swabian poet named FRIEDRICH HÖLDERLIN from 1807 until his death in 1843. The tower still stands today (and can be visited from 10-12 am and 3-5 pm Mondays through Fridays, from 3-5 pm on Saturdays and 10-12 am on Sundays).

Although Hölderlin's lyric poetry was hardly appreciated by his contemporaries, it is regarded today as both unique and unsurpassed in beauty and style. Hölderlin's depth of thought and discipline of form make his elegaic odes landmarks in German literature.

Hölderlin's poems were collected and published by the poets of the so-called "Swabian School" – Gustav Schwab, Ludwig Uhland, and Justinus Kerner in 1826. (I'll come back to them shortly.) But it took a fellow genius and admirer of classical Greece, the controversial philosopher Friedrich Wilhelm Nietzsche (1844-1900), to recognize their real importance. Hölderlin's poetry, he wrote to a friend in October 1861, "lifts us to the heights of idealism," which was the poet's "native element." Today Hölderlin scholars the world over make the pilgrimage to the Baden-Württemberg State Library *(Landesbibliothek),* next to the American Consulate General in Stuttgart, to do research where Hölderlin's manuscripts are stored.

Although Hölderlin used ancient Greek metrical forms for his poetry, the wealth of subjective feeling it expresses rendered it more romantic, perhaps, than classic. A forerunner of German Romanticism, Hölderlin breathed an intensity of passion into his poems in the attempt to reconcile the Christian faith with the gods of ancient Greece. He was a pure and noble spirit with a weak body, wholly devoted to his art but unable to cope with the realities of his environment.

Friedrich Hölderlin was born in Lauffen on the Neckar on 20 March 1770. There is a memorial plaque in the garden of his birthplace, but the house itself no longer stands. (A small Hölderlin museum is in the old city hall.)

Two years after the death of Hölderlin's father, his mother married the *Bürgermeister* (mayor) of Nürtingen, where Friedrich attended the Latin School and befriended Friedrich Wilhelm Joseph von Schelling (see chapter XIII). Hölderlin's mother, widowed again in 1779, wanted him to become a minister. Accordingly, she sent him first to the "Lower Cloister School" in Denkendorf in 1784, and then to the Cloister School at Maulbronn.

Founded by monks of the Cistercian order in 1147, Maulbronn is the only cloister of its kind in Germany that survived the centuries intact. (The proceeds from annual summer concerts held there go to charities for handicapped children.) In 1557 it became a Protestant preparatory seminary for the study of theology. There Friedrich Hölderlin suffered from the rigid discipline from 1786 to 1788, just as did Hermann Hesse a century later.

In 1788 Hölderlin began his studies of philosophy and theology at the theological seminary in Tübingen, where Eduard Mörike spent four years from 1822 to 1826. His schoolmates were Schelling (again) and the young Georg Wilhelm Friedrich Hegel (see chapter XIII). Intellectually Hölderlin tried to transcend the confining walls and petty "spy system" of the seminary, which he endured only to please his mother. A good musician, he played the violin, piano, and the flute. His poetic inclinations were strongly influenced by two older student-poets, Ludwig Neuffer and Rudolf Magenau, and especially by C. Philipp Conz, one of his teachers, who was an avid devotee of classical Greece. In September 1790 Hölderlin received his master's degree, but he did not feel called to become a Lutheran pastor.

In 1789 Hölderlin had met Gotthold Friedrich Stäudlin, who was a dozen years his senior. A Stuttgart lawyer, Stäudlin was the "High Priest of the Swabian Muses." As editor of the *Musenalmanach,* a poetry annual, he published Hölderlin's poems for the first time in 1792 and again the following year. Of greater importance was Stäudlin's introduction of Hölderlin to Friedrich Schiller in the summer of 1793. Schiller recommended Hölderlin as a private tutor of the ten-year-old son of his friend Charlotte von Kalb in Waltershausen near Jena. The two poets met while Schiller was visiting Ludwigsburg. Hölderlin accepted the job, which was not an easy one. Charlotte's son turned out to be a most difficult pupil. Nevertheless, Hölderlin was able to study with the philosopher Johann Gottlieb Fichte (1762-1814) at the University of Jena, to associate with Schiller (who published a fragment of a later work called *Hyperion* in his periodical *Neue Thalia,* and to meet Goethe and the cultural philosopher Johann Gottfried von Herder. Hölderlin's early poems show the influence of Schiller. They reflect the spirit of the early stages of the French Revolution, praising freedom, humanity, brotherhood, and harmony.

In January 1795 Hölderlin left the service of Charlotte von Kalb, travelled extensively, and spent an unhappy summer in Nürtingen. On 28 December he arrived in Frankfurt to become the private tutor for the children of Jakob Friedrich Gontard, a rich banker. Hölderlin fell in love with Gontard's beautiful wife Susette, whom he immortalized in his poetry and in his novel *Hyperion,* which was published in two volumes (1797 and 1799). He called her his "Diotima." Unhappily married, she not only returned his affection but released in him poetic powers that had been slumbering. In a letter to his old school friend Neuffer he wrote of his "everlasting, happy, sacred friendship with a being who has really strayed into this miserable century." Their relationship led to a confrontation between Hölderlin and his employer. In September 1798 Hölderlin had to leave Frankfurt. He went to stay with his friend Baron Isaac von Sinclair in Bad Homburg near Frankfurt but corresponded with his Diotima from October 1798 until May 1800. These letters are among the finest in the German language.

Hölderlin tried to regain his balance after the breakup with Susette. Despite a nervous irritability and profound melancholy, he was extremely productive, writing some of his finest odes and elegies. His attempt to start a journal failed, and his wanderings began anew: to Stuttgart, to Switzerland (where he worked briefly as a tutor), to Nürtingen, to Jena (where he tried in vain to obtain a job teaching Greek at the university). In January 1802 he made a journey on foot through the High Auvergne to Bordeaux, where he worked for a few months as a tutor for the German Consul and winemerchant Daniel Christoph Meyer. In June he left Bordeaux suddenly, returning to Nürtingen in a mental state that alarmed his friends. Susette Gontard died of consumption on 22 June.

From 1804 to 1806 Hölderlin lived again with his friend Sinclair, who obtained for him a position as librarian to landgrave Friedrich V of Hessen-Homburg. But in September 1806 Sinclair was alarmed by Hölderlin's mental state. He took him to a clinic in Tübingen, where he was treated by Dr. Autenrieth and his assistant Justinus Kerner. A carpenter and fruit-grower named Ernst Zimmer cared for Hölderlin in his own home, after the poet was released from the clinic and given three years to live. (The "Hölderlin Tower" was part of his house on top of the old city wall.) Hölderlin lived there for 36 years until his death on 7 June 1843.

A secondary school, a square, a street and a high-rise apartment building in Stuttgart bear his name.

One of Hermann Hesse's most touching stories, *Im Presselschen Gartenhaus,* is about two young poets who visit Hölderlin during the last years of his life in Tübingen. They talk of poetry in an animated fashion. Hölderlin seems to take an interest in their conversation. He goes off to his room and paces up and down restlessly for a long time. By the last light of the waning day, he writes on the bottom of a piece of paper cluttered with insane scribbling:

> "The pleasures of this world were mine to know,
> My childhood days passed by, long, long ago.
> The summer months, how quickly did they fly!
> I'm nothing now. I only wish to die."

A Swabian joke, recorded by Thaddäus Troll in one of his books, defines a Swabian as one who can pronounce *oag'nehm* (uncomfortable) and thinks Uhland is a real poet.

That's a rather unfair critique of the poetry of LUDWIG UHLAND (1787-1862), much of which survives today in the songs of Brahms, Schubert, Schumann, Liszt, Reger, Humperdinck, and Richard Strauss. A total of 2,139 of Uhland's poems were set to music.

Born in Tübingen, Uhland studied law and languages at the university there. A liberal with a strong political conscience and a firm belief in democracy, he refused to swear an oath of allegiance to Friedrich, the first King of Württemberg, in 1805. As a result, he was not permitted to become a civil servant. After working as a legal clerk in the Ministry of Justice in Stuttgart from 1810 to 1814, he practised as a lawyer.

In 1815 the former German Empire was replaced by the German Federation of 35 sovereign princes and four free cities with the central government in the house of representatives *(Bundestag)* in Frankfurt (Main). King Friedrich of Württemberg wanted no part of it. He feared that a single constitution for the Federation with a representative assembly of the people would severely limit his royal privileges and prerogatives. Consequently, he announced to the members of his parliament in January 1815 that he intended to give his kingdom a separate constitution reflecting his will. A written protest with 572 signatures was presented to the King. The author was Ludwig Uhland. The King punished all who had signed it. As a reward for his liberalism and his courage, however, Uhland was elected to parliament in 1819 as a delegate from Tübingen. (King Friedrich died on 30 October 1816.)

In 1822 Uhland published a monograph on Walther von der Vogelweide, Germany's most important poet of the Middle Ages. His studies of Old- and Middle-High German, his knowledge of German sagas, legends and poetry qualified him superbly for the professorship he received at Tübingen University in 1829. There he helped to found the science of Germanic Philology *(Germanistik)* – the study of Germanic languages and literature.

King Wilhelm I of Württemberg (1781-1864), who succeeded his despotic father in 1816, was not as liberal as he pretended to be. When Ludwig Uhland was elected to parliament in 1832, a motion he had drafted annoyed the King so intensely that he dissolved the old parliament and refused to grant Uhland a leave of absence from the University of Tübingen to serve in the new diet. Uhland promptly gave up his professorship. A grateful city of Stuttgart presented him with a heavy silver trophy. It is hardly surprising that he was chosen as one of 28 delegates from Württemberg to serve in the German National Assembly in Frankfurt in 1848.

Uhland wrote poetry only in his youth, and some scholars call him the best writer of ballads after Schiller. Most of his ballads have medieval backgrounds, such as "Count Eberhard," "The Curse of the Minstrel," and "Bertram de Born," reflecting his deep knowledge of early German history. His historical dramas *Duke Ernest of Swabia* (which had its premiere on 29 September 1819 in the Stuttgart Castle Theater) and *Ludwig the Bavarian* reflect his noble outlook and mastery of language, but they lack dramatic impact.

The lyric poetry of Uhland, much of which is very beautiful, expresses romantic feelings with a clarity and simplicity of form. It is no wonder that so much of it has been set to music. Particularly noteworthy are his "Spring Faith," which Franz Schubert turned into a song published on 10 April 1823, and his "Good Comrade," which soon became a popular, if melancholy folksong.

In 1844/45 Uhland published his collection of *Old High and Low German Folksongs.* He died in Tübingen on 13 November 1862. A school in Stuttgart-Rot and two streets in Stuttgart bear his name.

The "folk-and-fatherland" freshness of Uhland's poetry made him the founder of the "Swabian School of Poets" *(Schwäbischer Dichterkreis).* Its main representatives, Justinus Kerner, Gustav Schwab, and Ludwig Uhland had been students together at the University of Tübingen. They got together frequently at the home of JUSTINUS KERNER in Weinsberg, near Heilbronn, where he had his medical practice. He had a large flower garden and his house was at the base of a famous old fortress. It must have been a very pleasant place to gather, to judge by a painting that shows Uhland, Schwab, and Kerner in the latter's garden. A *"Viertele"* is on the table – one of many that inspired Kerner's drinking and wandering songs. He is best remembered for his political poem "Praising with many beautiful speeches," which was sung a few years ago at the *Cannstatter Volksfest* and which Thaddäus Troll selected as a title for one of his books.

Kerner was born in Ludwigsburg (Marktplatz 8) on 18 September 1786. A trace of sadness, of melancholy runs through much of his poetry. But Kerner was also capable of expressing fine humor, as in his legend "The Fiddler from Gmünd." He wrote a satirical novel, *Travel Shadows,* which was published in 1811.

Kerner was fascinated by the supernatural. (A tower on his property was supposedly haunted.) He devoted considerable time and attention to sleep-walking and hypnosis. Based on his observations of a sleep-walker named Friederike Hauffe, who lived in his house for several years, he wrote a novel called *The Clairvoyante of Prevorst,* which was published in two volumes in 1829 and reprinted in 1894.

Kerner died in Weinsberg on 21 February 1862. There is a small statue of a boy with an open book in his right hand and a guitar slung over his left shoulder on Kerner Square *(Kernerplatz)* in Stuttgart. I pass it frequently on the way to Robinson Barracks from my office on Olgastraße.

When I look at it, I don't think of Kerner the poet, or Kerner the novelist, but Kerner the young doctor who attended to Friedrich Hölderlin in Dr. Autenrieth's clinic in Tübingen in 1806.

A Stuttgart tunnel and street are named in honor of GUSTAV SCHWAB (1792-1850). As a poet of the Swabian School he was less gifted than Uhland or Kerner, but his three-volume recreation of *The Most Beautiful Sagas of Classical Antiquity* (1838-40) earned him a permanent niche in the history of German literature. It has been reprinted many times as a one-volume edition. Schwab also collected and published German ballads and folksongs.

Of his own poems, the best known are "The Thunder Storm" and "The Rider of Lake Constance."

His grave is in the *Hoppenlau* cemetery north of the Liederhalle.

The most beloved of the Swabian poets, even today, is EDUARD MÖRIKE, who was born at Kirchstraße 2 in Ludwigsburg on 8 September 1804. He grew up in the house at Obere Marktstraße 2. After finishing secondary school in Urach, he studied theology at Tübingen from 1822 to 1826.

Following several migratory years as a curate, Mörike became the pastor of the little town of Cleversulzbach (about 15 kilometers northeast of Heilbronn) in 1834. His mother and sister kept house for him there.

In 1832, while still a curate, Mörike published a two-volume novel called *Nolten the Painter.* In 1838 his collected poems were printed. Imbued with simple beauty and an unsurpassed clarity of expression, his verse is the best of the German Romantic School. In his *Outline of German Literature* published in 1926, Karl Heinemann called Mörike a "life-long child" whose poems were overrated. But they have stood the test of time through their immediate appeal and kinship to folksong. Frederich Bruns of the University of Wisconsin found in them "a gamut of tones," ranging from "tragic pathos to exuberant joy and rollicking humor, from the sweetly idyllic to festal solemnity." Curt von Faber du Faur, one of my professors at Yale and a man with impeccable artistic taste, called Mörike the greatest and most genuine lyric poet after Goethe and Hölderlin, "blissful within himself," to quote one of Mörikes own poems.

Mörike's inner harmony and peace of mind, which he did not acquire easily, are best expressed in his poem "Prayer," which I have tried to translate from German as follows:

Lord, send here below
Some joy or some pain.
I'm content just to know
In Your hands both have lain.

Joy or pain, what You deem,
Please don't overwhelm.
Somewhere in between
Is love's modest realm.

Close to 600 of Mörike's poems have been set to music, 53 of them alone by Hugo Wolf between 16 February and 26 November 1888.

Mörike gave up his parsonage in 1843 for reasons of health. He set about his wanderings again, settling down finally in Stuttgart in 1851 as a teacher of literature at the *Katharinenstift,* a private school for girls, from 1851 to 1866. During this time he wrote his much-loved fairy tale *The Shrivelled Little Stuttgart Man* (1853) and the short novel *Mozart's Journey to Prague* (1856). Portraying a single day in the composer's life, just before the performance of his opera *Don Giovanni,* the contemplative, gentle story foreshadows Mozart's early death. It was Mörike finest prose work.

In the fall of 1863 the director of the girls' school in Stuttgart invited the ill and ageing Mörike to recuperate at his country home in Bebenhausen. The poet accepted. While at Bebenhausen he examined carefully the old Cistercian cloister, dating from the 12th century, which is situated on the edge of the Schönbuch Forest on the way to Tübingen (via B-27 today). Mörike described the cloister in a cycle of eleven elegaic poems calles *Pictures of Bebenhausen.*

Eduard Mörike died in Stuttgart on 4 June 1875, the last and best of the Swabian School of Poets. His grave is in the Prague Cemetery north of the railroad station. Karl von Gerok conducted the funeral. A library and a street in Stuttgart bear his name.

Stuttgart has honored a prolific native son, WILHELM HAUFF, with a side street. Born in 1802, he produced 36 volumes of poetry, short stories and novels before his death in Stuttgart at age 25 in 1827. He was educated at Tübingen University, worked as a tutor, and finally became the editor of an important journal for the last ten months of his life.

Hauff's historical novel *Lichtenstein,* showing Duke Ulrich of Württemberg (1487-1550) from his better side (he was the one who killed his stallmaster), was one of the first to be influenced by Sir Walter Scott's *Waverley Novels.* The setting is the Lichtenstein Castle and the so-called "fog cave" near Honau (which you must also visit), where Ulrich spent the time of his banishment from 1519 to 1534. The novel was published in three volumes in 1826. That same year Hauff's novel *The Man in the Moon* also appeared. His *Communications from the Memoirs of Satan* (1826-27) show great fantasy and wit, yet the prose that made him immortal is found in his marvellous fairy tales. *Nosey the Dwarf, The Cold Heart,* and *Caliph Stork* are stories within the stories entitled *The Inn in the Spessart* and *The Caravan.* More sophisticated readers claim that Hauff's best work was his *Fantasies in the Bremen Ratskeller,* a gruesome yet extremely humorous glorification of wine and its effects on the intellect and the mood of the drinker. His best-known short story is *The Beggar Woman from Pont des Arts,* his best-known poems "I Stand in Darkest Midnight" and "Rosy Dawn, Rosy Dawn."

Hauff was buried in the *Hoppenlau* cemetery.

For the sake of completeness, if only to identify the origin of some of the names of Stuttgart's streets, I should mention some of Swabia's minor poets:

FRIEDRICH SILCHER (1789-1861) wrote Swabian songs sufficiently memorable to have a room in the Stuttgart *Liederhalle* named after him. He taught choral and instrumental music at Tübingen University.

WILHELM FRIEDRICH WAIBLINGER (1804-1830), a precoccious classical poet and friend of Mörike and Schwab, was born in Heilbronn. Inspired by Hölderlin's *Hyperion* and classical civilization, he went to Italy as a young man and died in Rome.

HERMANN KURZ (1813-1873) wrote novels about Swabian life in the latter part of the 18th century, such as *Schiller's Years at Home* and *The Innkeeper of the Sun.*

KARL VON GEROK (1815-1890) was a Protestant theologian

Schiller

Hölderlin

Mörike

Hesse

179

who wrote religious and patriotic poems, such as "A Boy's Grace" and "The Steeds of Gravelotte."

GEORG HERWEGH (1817-1875) was such a radical, revolutionary poet that he spent much of his life in exile in Switzerland and in France. He wrote a collection of vitriolic verse published under the title "Poems of a Live Man" in 1841.

WILHELM GANZHORN (1818-1880) is remembered especially for one of his poems called "In the Most Beautiful Meadow Ground."

Poet-engineer MAX EYTH (1836-1906) wrote short stories but remained a local literary talent. A school and a lake in Stuttgart bear his name.

CAESAR FLAISCHLEN (1864-1920) wrote the plays *Martin Lehnhardt* and *Toni Stürmer,* a novel *Jost Seyfried,* and a collection of poems called *Everyday and the Sun.* Written in rhythmic prose, these poems praise the sun as a source of power for life. The best known is "Keep the Sun in Your Heart."

In 1948 a friend of mine talked me into attending Harvard Summer School, which had just reopened after World War II. I needed to make up some credits in French in order to finish my B. A. at Yale the following year, so I agreed to go. It turned out to be the best summer of my life.

I was majoring in German Literature at Yale. In order to graduate I had to write a so-called senior essay, but I hadn't found a topic that really appealed to me. My friend advised me to audit a course he was taking on German "Neo-Romanticists" with Professor Karl Vietor, an authority on Hölderlin and Goethe.

The course opened a new world to me. I began to read the novels of a Swabian writer named HERMANN HESSE (1877-1962) on the broad granite steps of the Widener library and was enthralled by his lucid style, his outlook on life, his addictive message. By the end of the summer I had devoured everything he had ever written. And I had found a suitable topic for my senior essay: *The Dream as a Literary Device in Five Novels by Hermann Hesse.*

Not quite 19, I was incurably romantic, terribly impressionable. A girl I met at the Harvard Summer School by the name of Bernice had spent her Bryn Mawr junior year abroad in Switzerland in 1946-47. I found her enormously sophisticated. She called Hesse's writings "poison," at least for the influence they were having on me.

Once I began to think about my essay back in New Haven, a thousand questions popped into my mind. I decided to write a letter to Hesse. I mentioned this in a letter to Bernice, who was living in New York City. Our one-sided campus romance was coming to an end, but we still corresponded. My diary entry for November 27, 1948, recorded her reaction: "Do you really think Hesse is important enough to spend all that time on him? Why don't you write on someone who is completely purged of fuzz in his writing, someone less sensuous than Hesse – it might be good discipline for you to try an author who is Hesse's opposite." That same entry reflected the opinion of the friend who was responsible for my having discovered Hesse in the first place. "How do you know," he asked me, "if Hesse will last? Twenty years from now he might be completely unheard of."

I mention this because both critiques were typical of what young people of the immediate post-war generation, who were more mature than I, thought of Hermann Hesse.

The fascination of Hesse for American youth in the 1960s struck me as ironic until I realized that their Hesse was the author of *Steppenwolf,* not my lonely, sensitive, introspective Swabian whose "heroes" could not cope with their surroundings.

Hermann Hesse was born in Calw on 2 July 1877. He suffered from the discipline in the Protestant theological seminary at Cloister Maulbronn, as did Friedrich Hölderlin a century earlier.

Hesse began writing poetry when he was very young. (I have seen a dozen unpublished poems he wrote at age 15. The originals belong to an acquaintance of mine in Calw.)

After leaving Maulbronn, Hesse tried his hand as a mechanic and then as a book-seller. Finally, he turned to writing. His early novels are largely autobiographical. *Under the Wheel* of 1906 recaptures his unhappiness at Maulbronn. The novels written before 1919 – *Peter Camenzind, Gertrud, Roßhalda* – are eminently readable but limited in depth.

Shocked by the militant nationalism of Germany on the verge of World War I, Hesse moved to Switzerland in 1912. During the war years he steeped himself in psychoanalysis, reading the works of Freud, Jung, Bleuler and Stekel. He also studied the writings of Friedrich Wilhelm Nietzsche and continued his age-old preoccupation with eastern philosophy.

In the spring of 1919 Hesse moved to Montagnola in the Tessin canton of Switzerland, where he spent the rest of his life. That spring and summer he wrote two of his most important short novels, *Klein and Wagner,* and *Klingsor's Last Summer.* He also began to write *Siddhartha,* a story set in India, that winter, but did not complete it until almost two years later. This story, coupled with the novel *Demian* published that year, reflect a life-long theme: the search for the inner self, the urge to explore the ego while striving to fulfill one's destiny, to complete one's personality. Hesse calls this process "the way inward." It requires introspection and deep meditation, which Hesse indulged in himself in order to complete his *Siddhartha.*

The prose is so beautiful and the setting so sublime that many of Hesse's readers wished he might have continued to write in that manner.

An abrupt change of pace came with his *The Wolf of The Steppes,* or *Der Steppenwolf* of 1927. It was unlike anything Hesse had ever done before. Just as in *Demian* it deals with a split personality who lives in a "light world" of cultured refinement, but also in a "dark world" of evil. But the form is unusual – an "editor's" introduction, a diary, and a tract within the diary – as is Hesse's use of the healing balm of humor as an antidote to frustration, a means to escape from the chaos of the ego by not taking oneself too seriously. After reading *Steppenwolf* for the first time I noted in my Yale diary with considerable frustration: "For a while I thought that Hesse was becoming clear to me, but I find it impossible because he has experienced so many changes in his lifetime. His mind has undergone all sorts of metamorphoses; in fact, one might call him the chameleon of German literature."

Hesse felt the need to explain this to his readers himself. In an epilogue to a 1932 edition of *The Way Inward,* a collection of four long stories including *Siddhartha,* he wrote: "That I did not remain longer in this world of Indian philosophy, like a convert in the religion of his choice, that I often left this world again, that *Steppenwolf* followed *Siddhartha,* is something held up to me often with regret by readers who love *Siddhartha* but have not read *Steppenwolf* with sufficient care. I have no answer for that; I stand by *Steppenwolf* no less than by *Siddhartha.* For me, my life and my work are a natural unity which I don't feel obliged to prove or defend."

Harry Haller (= Hermann Hesse), the schizoid hero of *Steppenwolf* discovers that he has not just two, but a thousand souls. The other "reality" he seeks lies only within himself. At the time I was struggling to understand the novel, I got a lot of interpretative help from Joe Mileck, a graduate assistant whom I had met at Harvard. He called *Steppenwolf* Hesse's "storm and stress" writing back then. Joe and I corresponded regularly after I began to write my senior essay. He helped me to bring many aspects of Hesse's thinking into proper focus.

Joe and I lost track of each other around 1950, but the first edition of this book renewed the contact, if only by mail, after 30 years.

Joe had done what I wanted to do: he is devoting his life to the study of Hermann Hesse. A longtime Professor of German at the University of California at Berkeley, he is the author of *Hermann Hesse and His Critics; Hermann Hesse: Biography and Bibliography;* and *Hermann Hesse: Life and Art,* which was recently published in German. Joe's ancestors were Swabians who settled in the eastern end of Hungary (now Rumania) in 1730. We hope to meet again on his next sabbatical to Stuttgart.

The first novel of Hesse's that I chanced to read was still my favorite after I had read all of the others. In my view it is the best written, perhaps even the finest novel in the German language. *Narziss und Goldmund* was written in 1923 and translated into English in 1930 with the title *Death and the Lover.* The setting is Maulbronn in the Middle Ages, the plot reminiscent at the start of *Under the Wheel.* Goldmund is brought to the cloister by his father, who wants him to become a monk. But while there he comes under the influence of Narziss, a novice on the faculty, who makes Goldmund aware of his true, artistic nature.

Goldmund leaves the cloister and goes out into the world. He experiences the struggle between nature and spirit, sensuality and asceticism, death and immortality. He learns to appreciate the human being's capacity for extreme pain and for unbounded ecstasy. Only late in life do the two friend truly understand each other's nature. Narziss, the intellectual, lives in a world of concepts. Goldmund, the artist, lives in a world of pictures.

Hesse's two-volume *The Glass Bead Game* of 1943, with its quiet, intellectual asceticism, is a quantum jump from the sensuality of *Narziss und Goldmund* and the surrealistic sexuality of *Steppenwolf*. The hero of the story, Josef Knecht, forsakes an elite, intellectual society courting its own doom by devoting itself solely to the sterile manipulation of glass beads. In so doing, Knecht represents Hesse's view of the proper role of the intellectual: to maintain and cultivate high ideals and values, not for their own sake, but to help society aspire to them. The intellectual is not the organizer of society, but rather its shaper and its conscience.

Hermann Hesse won the Nobel Prize and the Goethe Prize for Literature in 1946 and the peace prize of the German book trade in 1955. He died in Montagnola, Switzerland, on 9 August 1962.

XX　　　Swabian America

Christian Münzel, the energetic director of the travel bureau of Schwaben International in Stuttgart, has taken many German tour groups around the United States. He told me about a Swabian couple in the last group he escorted.

As the aircraft was making its final approach to JFK, Herr Münzel reminded the passengers over the PA system: "Remember, US customs laws prohibit taking foodstuffs into the States." The Swabian couple called Herr Münzel aside and confided to him that they had 15 rolls stuffed with ham and wurst in their luggage.

"You better start eating them before we land," Herr Münzel advised.

"We can't," the couple said. "We packed them in our suitcases, not in our carry-on luggage."

"That's too bad," Herr Münzel sympathized. But as he shepherded his flock through the Port of New York Authority, he spotted the couple cramming those rolls into their mouths with both hands as they pushed their luggage along the counter with their knees.

The true *Schwob* throws nothing away, much less allow it to be confiscated.

Swabians have been going to America ever since the 17th century. The ravages of the Thirty Years' War, in particular, prompted many to migrate to the New World. In 1626 Jakob Fuchs from Baden is mentioned in old records, and in 1653 winegrowers from Heidelberg and evirons who settled in New York colony. Early settlers imprinted the names of Heidelberg, Mannheim, German Flats, Germantown, Oppenheim, Neu Durlach, Fuchs Dorf, Brunnen Dorf, Weisers Dorf, Wirtemberg, Palatine, Oberweisers Dorf, and New Paltz Landing on the map of New York, but not indelibly.

In his classic, two-volume book, *The German Element in the United States,* published in 1909, Albert Bernhardt Faust quotes Louis Hennepin's claim that the first German in Texas was a *Schwob* by the name of Hiens, who was a member of La Salle's fateful expedition of 1687. The invasion of the Palatinate by King Louis XIV of France in 1688, resulting in the destruction of the Heidelberg castle and the cities of Mannheim, Speyer, and Worms, left nearly a half a million Palatines *(Pfälzer)* homeless. War, famine, religious persecution, and the tyranny of petty princes were the main causes for the first mass migration from southwestern Germany. The War of the Spanish Succession in 1707, and the particularly severe winter of 1708/9, prompted some 13,000 southwestern Germans to assemble in London by October 1709. A large contingent sailed to the Carolinas, and an even larger one to New York colony. Of that latter group of 3,000 in ten crowded ships, 2,227 survived the voyage. The exact number of Swabians in their midst has not been recorded, but it must have been sizeable. (Since the first group came from the Palatinate, ship manifests and other records simply referred to all subsequent German emigrants as "Palatines" *(Pfälzer)* until the middle of the 18th century.)

One of the most prominent Swabians in that exodus of 1709 was Johann Konrad Weiser (also spelled Weisser), the mayor of Großaspach, who took 13 of his 15 children – two were married and stayed behind – with him to America after the death of his wife. His son Konrad, with his father's consent, lived with the Mohawk chief Quagnant at age 16 and learned the Mohawk language and customs. After Konrad's return to the white settlement in Schoharie, New York, he was the interpreter and mediator between the settlers and the Indians. The Weisers were unyielding champions of the rights and the independence of the German colonists, frequently locking horns with Governor Robert Hunter of New York, who was suspicious of their good relations with the Mohawks. Unable to obtain a clear title to their possessions in New York, the Weisers and about 60 other families moved to Pennsylvania in 1733. Konrad was soon recognized as the head of the new settlement at Womelsdorf in Berks county. Reports of peace and prosperity in Pennsylvania soon diverted the stream of German immigration from New York to Pennsylvania. Within two decades there were 50,000 Germans in that state alone, and by 1775 they constituted about one-third of the entire population.

Israel Daniel Rupp's collection of 30,000 names of German, Swiss, Dutch, French, Portuguese, and other immigrants in Pennsylvania, chronologically arranged from 1727 to 1776 (2d revised and enlarged edition with German translation, published in Philadelphia in 1872) calls all of them "Palatines" at first, then "Palatines" and "Swiss," and finally, as of 1749 specifically identifies

"Württemberger."

Baron Stiegel from Mannheim established the first iron foundry in Pennsylvania, naming it the Elizabeth Iron Foundry and Smelters after his wife. He founded the city of Manheim (with one *n)* in Lancaster county around 1758, laying it out in the checkerboard pattern of his home town in Germany. The town flourished. Stiegel diversified his products, manufacturing stoves and then starting a glassworks. The Revolutionary War wiped him out and left him destitute. He died in poverty.

In 1796 Jacob Böhm and his fellow Pietists from Württemberg established a Swabian colony called "New Germany" on the Ohio river. A Swabian named Johann Georg Rapp from Iptingen (now called Wiernsheim, east of Pforzheim) founded the religious colony of Harmony in Butler county, Pennsylvania, in 1805. The founder of a religious sect called "Harmonists," Rapp was a successful farmer whose followers were extremely loyal to him. Thanks to successful farming at Harmony, the Rappists increased the value of the colony, which Rapp sold for $100,000. He used the money to by 30,000 acres of land on the Wabash river in Indiana. From 1814 to 1824 the members of his Harmony Society carved a prosperous town out of the wilderness of the Indiana Territory called "New Harmony." Rapp sold it to Robert Owen, the founder of English socialism, in 1825. According to Faust, Owen's socialist community failed two years later. According to a pamphlet published by the Visitors' Bureau of Historic New Harmony, Inc., New Harmony, Indiana, "Owen made New Harmony the site of an ambitious utopian experiment, which brought together a group of eminent naturalists and educators" who made "New Harmony an American center for scientific and intellectual inquiry from 1825 to 1860." At least it hasn't grown in size much over the past 150 years.

After selling New Harmony to Owen, Rapp (who died at age 90 in 1847) and his followers returned to Pennsylvania and established his third colony, Economy, in Beaver county. It was the most successful of the three, and the value of the properties of the sect increased to millions.

In 1817 Josef Bäumler and a group of 150 fellow-Swabians settled in Lawrence township in Tuscarawas county in Ohio. They were members of the Zoarite religious sect. Bäumler was a weaver. Under his leadership, the Zoarites became successful farmers in the area. In 1827 the brothers Christian, Friedrich, and Wilhelm Schmidt from Dunsbach near Kirchheim/Teck established the town of Weinsburg, Ohio, made famous by Sherwood Anderson's book by that name.

In June 1839, John Augustus Sutter, one of the most famous men in the history of California, arrived in Monterey from Hawaii. Having gone bankrupt in Switzerland, he emigrated to the United States in 1834 to escape the law and the wrath of his wife. He went to New York first and then made his way across the United States to Santa Fe and Oregon. From there he went to Alaska and finally to Hawaii, before settling in California.

Readers of earlier editions of this book asked me why I had not included Sutter in the chapter on Swabian America.

"Because he was a Swiss and not a *Schwob,*" I argued for the life span of two editions.

My authority was my favorite historian of the American West, Ray Allen Billington, who refers to Sutter's "native Switzerland" in his superb and scholarly *Westward Expansion: A History of the American Frontier* (4th edition, New York, 1974). I knew that Sutter had spent his youth in Switzerland, and that he was born in Kandern, a town in the Black Forest about 15 kilometers (as Tell's arrow flew) from the Swiss border. I vaguely recalled from my patchwork study of history and geography that in the early 19th century a tip of Switzerland near Basel protruded into territory that is part of Baden, Germany, today.

Was it possible that Kandern belonged to Switzerland in 1803, the year of Sutter's birth?

Historians may often be wrong, but they are never in doubt. Uncertainty began to plague me like a loose filling. Recalling the extensive collection of historical maps I had seen in the Baden-Württemberg State Library, I went to see its director, my friend Dr. Hans-Peter Geh. He turned me over to Herr Henning, a cadaverous cartographer who can find any hamlet in this hemisphere quicker than you can say Rand McNally.

In a moment he had Stieler's *Hand-Atlas* of 1829 open for my inspection of a map of Switzerland. Sure enough, Kandern was clearly in Baden. Just as quickly he fetched a volume that traced Kandern's lineage to the year 790, when it was called Chandro. Elevated to a city in 1810, Kandern belonged to the municipal authority *(Stadt-amt)* of Lörrach in the early decades of the 19th century.

So Sutter was an "Upper" Swabian after all.

Billington describes him as "a rotund adventurer who blended bluff, deceit and ability so expertly that no man ranked higher in influence."

In June 1839 California still belonged to Mexico. With his winning ways and a wad of letters of introduction, Sutter persuaded Governor Juan Bautista Alvarado to grant him Mexican citizenship and 97,648 acres of land in the Sacramento Valley near the junction of the Sacramento and American rivers.

With the help of the Kanakas he had brought with him from Hawaii and local Indian labor, he built an adobe fort with 18-foot walls around his colony of "New Helvetia." He tilled the soil, planted crops and orchards, raised cattle, sheep, horses, mules, and hogs. Sutter was a farmer, a trapper, a stock raiser, a merchant, and a semi-official representative of the Mexican Government with the authority to administer justice. He described the rapid growth of his colony, which soon became a hospitable gathering point and a trade center for trappers and explorers, in his diary: "I found a good market for my products among the newcomers and the people in the Bay district... Agriculture increased until I had several hundred men working in the harvest fields, and to feed them I had to kill four or sometimes five oxen daily. I could raise 40,000 bushels of wheat without trouble, reap the crops with sickles, thresh it with bones, and winnow it in the wind. There were thirty plows running with fresh oxen every morning. The Russians were the chief customers for my agricultural products. I had at the time 12,000 head of cattle, 2,000 horses and mules, between 10,000 and 15,000 sheep, and 1,000 hogs."

Since the 1780s the Russians, moving steadily southward from Alaska, had been operating the Russian-American Fur Company in California. Just north of San Francisco they built Fort Ross. It soon became the chief outpost of the Russian colony in California. But mismanagement of the Fur Company and the difficulties of transporting supplies across Siberia prompted the Czar to withdraw his subjects in 1841.

Sutter bought Fort Ross--together with its chattels, livestock, and the 20-ton schooner *Constantine*--for $30,000. He made a cash downpayment of $2,000 and agreed to pay the balance in yearly installments of produce. Then he dismantled the fort and shipped everything he could take with him to New Helvetia on the *Constantine.* It must have been a second Noah's Ark with 1,700 head of cattle, 9,000 sheep, and 940 horses and mules on board. His purchase included French cannons and muskets which the Russians had gathered up as Napoleon retreated from Moscow.

The Mexican War with America ended on 17 September 1847 with the surrender of Santa Anna, and Mexico ceded its former possession to the United States the following year. That event, memorable enough in itself, was overshadowed in 1848 by the discovery of gold in California.

That discovery, by Sutter's carpenter/foreman James Wilson Marshall, should have made both him and Marshall rich, but it was the beginning of the downfall of both of them.

Born in New Jersey in 1810, James Marshall learned his father's trade as a millright. He went west to seek his fortune and arrived at Sutter's fort in 1845. While building a sawmill for Sutter near Coloma, on the south fork of the American River, he discovered a gold flake in the tailrace on 24 January 1848, nine days before Mexico signed the Treaty of Guadalupe Hidalgo, ceding California to the United States. Sutter's title to his land under American law was questioned, and when Sam Brannan, a San Francisco publisher, spread the news of Marshall's discovery, the Gold Rush was on. Hordes of gold-seekers overran Sutter's fort, stole his cattle, drove off his Indians, and disputed his right to his land. By 1852 Sutter was bankrupt again. In the meantime, the population of California had swollen from 15,000 in 1847 to 92,497 in 1850.

John Sutter spent the rest of his life appealing for his rights to state and federal authorities. From 1864 to 1878 he received a pension of $250 from the state of California. Bills were introduced in Congress on his behalf in 1876 and again in 1880, but no action was taken on them. In 1873 he moved to the Moravian village of Lititz in Pennsylvania. He died in Washington, D.C., on 18 June 1880--allegedly on the steps of the White House--while still seeking to reclaim his property rights.

James Marshall, his carpenter/foreman, fared no better. Miners drove him off his land, posting armed guards to keep him away while they prospected his claim. When he appealed to the courts, he discovered that the jury was made up of the trespassers' friends. In 1872, responding to the pressure of public opinion, the California legislature appropriated a $200-a-month pension for him, but it was cut in half in 1874 and eliminated in 1876. In his final years Marshall lived off odd jobs and whatever people were willing to pay him for his autograph. He died in poverty on 10 August 1885 and was buried within sight of the spot where he found the flake of gold that ruined his life and Sutter's.

Apart from a bronze statue of James Marshall, and an 18-foot-high stone monument erected by the Society of California Pioneers to the memory of Marshall in 1924, the biggest structure in Coloma today is the reconstruction of Sutter's Mill, which is electronically operated in fair weather around two p.m. for visitors on Saturdays and Sundays.

A complete restoration of Sutter's fort is located in downtown Sacramento on the original site. It is open daily from 10 a.m. to 5 p.m. Sutter's quarters have been turned into a museum with relics of early California days.

Swabian settlers of the 19th century clung to Swabian customs in the United States, and especially to their dialect. M. Bürkle from Plattenhardt wrote in Swabian dialect after founding the town of Stuttgart, Arkansas. The Swabians founded their own schools and used the power of their votes to insist that German was taught in public schools attended by their children.

Cleveland, Ohio, is the home of the "Schwäbischer Sängerbund," a male chorus founded by August Benz and several other men of Swabian origin in John Starr's saloon on the corner of Scovill Avenue and Greenwood Street on 14 August 1885. It is still very much alive and well today (despite anti-German sentiment during two World wars). The present address is 1400 East 55th Street in Cleveland.

There is a Swabian men's chorus in Bridgeport, Connecticut; a *Schwäbischer Sängerbund,* a *Schwaben* Athletic Club, a *Schwaben Frauen-Verein,* and a *Schwäbischer Unterstützungsverein* (booster club), and a *Schwaben-Verein* in Chicago; a Swabian booster club, a

Schwaben-Verein, and a Swabian Men's Chorus in Detroit; a *Schwäbischer Sängerbund* in St. Louis (the partnership of city Stuttgart); a *Schwäbischer Sängerbund* in Newark, New Jersey; a Swabian Club in Elizabeth, New Jersey; a *Schwäbischer Sängerbund* and ladies' chorus of the *Schwäbischer Sängerbund* of Brooklyn, New York; a *Schwaben-Verein* and a men's chorus in Buffalo; a Murray Hill *Schwaben* club, a *Schwäbischer Frauenbund,* a *Cannstatter Damenverein,* the United Swabians from Gross, N.Y., and the *Schwabenverein New York* in New York City; a *Schwabenverein* in Rochester; (the original) *Schwäbischer Sängerbund* and *Vereinigung der Donauschwaben* (Association of the Swabians from the Danube) in Cleveland; a Swabian booster club and *Verein der Donauschwaben* in Cincinnati; a *Cannstatter Volksfest-Verein,* a *Schwarzwald* Quartett, and a *Vereinigung der Donauschwaben* in Philadelphia. Folk festivals à la Bad Cannstatt are held annually in the United States in New York, Chicago, and Philadelphia.

Ann Arbor, Michigan, and Tübingen enjoy a very active partnership, which is best exemplified by the student exchange program of the universities of both cities. Besides the Tübingen-Ann Arbor, and the Stuttgart-St. Louis partnerships, others in Baden-Württemberg are: Crailsheim-Worthinton (Minn.), Esslingen-Sheboygan (Wis.), Freiburg-Whittier (Cal.), and Freiburg (Pa.), Hechingen-Valley Forge (started by your author), Heidelberg-Milwaukee, Karlsruhe-Phoenix, Mannheim-Manheim (Pa.), Offenburg-Easton (Pa.), Friedrichshafen-Peoria (Ill.), Ulm-New Ulm (Minn.), Walldorf-Astoria (Oregon), Wiesloch-Sturgis (Mich.), Wolfach-Richfield (Ohio), Weinheim-Lynchburg (Va.), and Meßstetten-Toccoa (Ga.). Baden-Baden and La Jolla (Cal.) are gradually getting together as of this writing.

XXI   Swabian Proverbs

I have saved these for last because there is no better way to sum up the Swabian's philosophy, and perhaps even his mentality.

Was ma hot, des hot ma. (What you've got, you've got, or: a bird in the hand is worth two in the bush.)

Solang mr sengt, isch d'Kirch net aus. (As long as we're singing, church is not over, or: the ball game's not over until the last man is out.)

Besser a Glatze als gar koine Hoor! (Better bald than no hair at all, or: it's six of one and half a dozen of the other.)

Wenn's sei muaß, no kommet Se halt rei! (Come on in, if it can't be avoided.)

Em Arme fehlt viel – em Geizige älles! (A poor person is missing much – a miser everything. This is most un-Swabian, and must be the exception that proves the rule.)

Am Verdeane isch no keiner z'Grond gange! (No one has perished from earning money.)

Wenn ois von onz zwoi stirbt, no ziag i nach Merklingen. (If one of the two us dies, then I'm moving to Merklingen.)

Elend gleabt isch ällweil besser als schee gstorba. (A miserable life is always better than a beautiful death.)

Mancher stirbt ganz leicht, ond mancher wird fascht he derbei. (Some die quite easily, and some almost expire in the process.)

Omesonst isch dr Tod, ond der kost au noh Leba. (Death is for nothing, and it even costs life.)

Em'e hongrige Mage isch net guat predige. (You can't preach well to a hungry stomach.)

Liaber meh essa als zwenig trinka! (It's better to eat more than to drink too little!)

Bei de Reiche lernt mr's Spara, bei de Orme s'Kocha. (We learn how to save from the rich, and how to cook from the poor.)

Was em Bauch verdaut, wird niht vom Staat geklaut. (What digests in the stomach won't be stolen by the state.)

Dr Bauer frißt nix oagsalza. (The farmer eats nothing unsalted.)

Liebr a Laus em Kraut als gar koi Floisch. (Better a louse in the cabbage than no meat at all.)

A Gosch voll glufa, dem ghört Zong gschabt. (The tongue in a

193

mouth full of pins deserves to be scraped.)

Wer Bildungs- ond Zahnlücken hat muß d'Gosch zulassa. (He who has gaps in his education and his teeth must keep his trap shut.)

Dr Schwob, dr wird mit 40 gscheit, d'andre net en Ewigkeit! (The Swabian gets smart at age 40, but others never!)

S'gibt sodde ond sodde, aber meh sodde! (There's this kind and there's that kind, but more that kind!)

Erst s'Om-de-Romm ond s Lass-mi-ao-mit machts Leba schee! (It's the contact with others and the let-me-join-in that really make life beautiful.)

Nuie Besa kehret guet, aber se langet net in d'Wenkel. (New brooms sweep well, but they don't reach into the corners.)

Dr bescht Bauer ackret emol e kromme Furch. (The best farmer plows a crooked furrow on occasion.)

Der siehts dr Kuah am Euter a', was z Paris dr Butter kost. (By looking at the cow's udder he can tell the price of butter in Paris.)

Ma' ka' vome Ochse net maih verlange als e Stückle Rendfloisch. (You can't expect more from an ox than a piece of beef.)

Gspäßig, daß oin a leerer Beutel ärger druckt als a voller. (It's funny that an empty purse weighs one down more than a full one.)

Mer ka net älle Müka derschlaga. (You can't kill all the flies.)

A hausigs Weib is d'best Sparbüchs. (A thrifty wife is the best piggy bank.)

En Zau oms Gärtle
s Auto en dr Garasch
D Rolläda ronder
ond Hausdiir zua

Was ma hot
des hot ma

A fence around the garden
The car in the garage
The shutters closed
And the front door shut

What you've got
You've got

Georg Holzwarth

Swabian Sights

This book was not intended to be a travel guide, but many American readers have told me that it has been helpful to them while exploring the Swabian countryside. History really comes alive when you are able to see the places where it took place. Without this opportunity, history is often little more than a collection of dull and inert facts.

Accordingly, this chapter is a checklist of interesting places to visit and explore for a fuller appreciation of Swabian history and culture. It is far from complete, and I apologize for any sins of omission. (There are about 400 museums in Baden-Württemberg!)

The inspiration came from my daughter Miriam. Impressed by the live coverage of the wedding of the Prince Charles and Lady "Di" on television, she took me up to the top floor of the Old Castle in Stuttgart shortly thereafter to view the crown jewels of Württemberg. (The Old Castle is the home of the Württemberg State Museum, or *Landesmuseum.*)

Miriam led me by the hand up to the magnificent crown of the kings of Württemberg on display in a transparent glass column in the center of the room.

"That's what I want to wear when *I* get married," she said.

I had been inside the Württemberg State Museum in the Old Castle several times, but I was always in such a rush that I never got beyond the second floor. From previous visits in less haste, Miriam had explored the place fully. She knew that the crown jewels were in that little room on the top floor, but I didn't.

There was a lesson in that for me, and for all of my fellow Americans in Swabia: if you don't know what's there, chances are you will pass it by.

☐ **AALEN,** 22 kilometers northeast of Schwäbisch Gmünd, is famous for its Roman Limes Museum, and for its Schubart Museum on the second floor of its 17th century city hall *(Rathaus)*. Born in Obersontheim, southeast of Schwäbisch Hall, on the 24 March 1739, Christian Friedrich Daniel Schubart was a Swabian Tom Paine. His liberal newspaper *Deutsche Chronik* and his blasts against Duke Karl Eugen earned him ten years imprisonment in Hohenasperg from 1777 to 1787. A great admirer of Frederick the Great, he finally gained his freedom through the influence of the Prussian monarch. Schubart was a theater director, a musician, and a writer of poetry calling for political liberty. He died in Stuttgart on 10 October 1791. In 1907 a Schubart scholar and honorary citizen of Aalen, Wilhelm Jakob Schweiker, made his Schubart collection available to the public in a museum which was moved to the city hall in 1935. The Limes was a Roman boundary road, partially fortified by guard towers and strongholds (castella), from Rheinbrohl on the Rhine to Lorch, and from Lorch to the Danube. Castella discovered in and around Aalen showed its role in the defense system. The Limes Museum in Aalen, at St. Johann Straße 5, is located on the site of a former Roman castellum. It is a branch of the Württemberg State Museum in Stuttgart and contains armament of Roman soldiers, a model of the Limes, a diorama with tin figures depicting Roman life along the Limes, plus many other exhibits. If you are interested in the history of the Romans in Württemberg, here is the place to start looking. The Limes Museum is open from Tuesday to Sunday, 10–12 am, 2–5 pm. Admission is DM 0.50 for adults, DM 0.30 for students, DM 0.20 for pupils and students accompanied by their teacher.

☐ **BAD MERGENTHEIM** is a resort town or spa. If you know German, read Carlheinz Gräter's delightful book *Bad Mergentheim – Portrait einer Stadt* before *and* after you go there. Take his advice and have a bird's eye view of the city from the steeple of the Church of St. Johann first and then begin your explorations at the market place. It abounds in half-timbered houses. The Rathaus (city hall) was built in 1564, the Church of St. Johann between 1250 and 1274. The design of the Schlosskirche (church in the castle) is attributed to Balthasar Neumann and François Cuvilliés. In 1526 Mergentheim was selected as the residence of the head of the Order of the German Knights *(Hoch- und Deutschmeister)*. Founded in 1190, the so-called *Deutscher Ritterorden* was dissolved by Napoleon in 1809. The Castle at Bad Mergentheim, begun in 1568, was the residence of the *Hoch- und Deutschmeister*. Master builder Blasius Berwart of Stuttgart constructed the remarkable circular staircase in the northern tower. Have a good look at the museum inside the castle. From 1844 to 1851 the Swabian poet Eduard

Mörike (see chapter XIX) lived in Bad Mergentheim, where he met and married his wife, Margarethe Speeth. His houshold account book from 1844 to 1848 is in the museum at the castle.

☐ **BAD SCHUSSENRIED,** a small town of 5,500 residents southwest of Biberach, is noted for its former Premonstratensian Abbey (1183–1803) which is used today as a clinic for the mentally ill. Be prepared for the most magnificent library you have ever seen when you view Dominikus Zimmermann's creation (1754–61). Its carvings and light pastels make it Rococo as it should be: "purely picturesque and decorative, playful and ornamental," to quote the Austrian cultural historian Egon Friedell, who committed suicide four days after Hitler marched into Vienna in March 1938.

☐ **BAD WIMPFEN,** just 15 kilometers northwest of Heilbronn, has only belonged to the state of Baden-Württemberg since 1952. From 1945 until 1952 it was a part of Baden. In the museum in the *Steinhaus* (stone house), which was built around 1200, you will find models of a Roman camp and bridge across the Neckar (with actual timbers discovered in 1957), weapons from Merovingian times, and a model of the imperial fortress-palace *(Kaiserpfalz)* which Emperor Friedrich Barbarossa had built after visiting Wimpfen on 9 February 1182. The so-called *Burgviertel* (fortress quarter) is all that remains of the *Kaiserpfalz* today. A visit to the museum in the *Steinhaus*, located in the *Burgviertel*, is a good place to begin your walking tour. Just follow the yellow arrows marked *"Rundgang"* for an hour's walk. The *Roter Turm* (red tower) at the end of Schwibbogengasse is a massive, windowless bulwark of limestone blocks,where the Emperor took refuge in case of danger. It is probably the oldest part of the *Kaiserpfalz*. Renovated in 1976, it is used for cultural events today. Four coats of arms on the *Rathaus* (city hall) mark the most important periods of Wimpfen's history. Behind the *Rathaus* is the *Blauer Turm* (blue tower), which also dates from around 1200. It got its name from the blue shell lime used to construct it. In both the blue tower and the stone house you will discover corner toilets. No longer in use, these one-holers give you an interesting view of medieval sanitation. House number 16 on Schwibbogengasse is the oldest domestic residence in Wimpfen. At the end of this cobblestone alley is the Hohenstaufen Gate. From there it is an easy walk to the *Löwenbrunnen*, a Renaissance fountain from the 16th century, and then to the artillery bastion, designed by Albrecht Dürer, at the end of Bollwerkgasse. Bad Wimpfen has ten churches, but the most important ones are just four. The Protestant parish church *(evangelische Stadtkirche)* was St. Mary's Catholic church during the Middle Ages. The foundations of the towers are Romanesque (ca. 1210) and the rest of the church Gothic.

The churches in Bad Wimpfen have locked glass doors inside to prevent theft, but you can still have a good look at the interiors. If you are fortunate enough to get inside the parish church (on a tour or during Sunday services), you can see the northern side altar with the miracle cross of 1481. The head and arms move, and the hair is human. The Dominican church *(Dominikanerkirche)* near the artillery bastion dates from the 14th century but was given the Baroque style in the 18th century. A purist at heart, I normally shudder at the results of such mayhem, but in this case the transformation was probably beneficial. The *Pfalzkapelle* (palace chapel) is worth a glance (and that's all you get). You can look through the glass door in the west wall at the Emperor's gallery, where he attended Mass. From there he had a quick escape route along the inside of the fortress wall to the safety of the red tower. One of the oldest Gothic churches in southern Germany is the Collegiate Church of the Knights *(Ritterstiftskirche St. Peter)* in the part of town that lies in the valley, as you drive toward Heilbronn and the Autobahn. A Roman camp once occupied this site. The oldest part of the church is Romanesque.

☐ **BEBENHAUSEN,** as you know from several references in this book, is famous for its former Cisterian monastery dating from 1190. It is located on the edge of the Schönbuch Forest on route B-27, about one kilometer north of Tübingen. The austere basilica was built from 1188 to 1227. The Cloister with its tracery windows (each one has its own pattern) is late Gothic. Following the Reformation, the monastery was converted into a Protestant school. Around 1650 the headmaster was Johan Valentin Adreä (1586–1654), the founder of modern Rosicrucianism. During the last century part of the monastery was remodelled as a royal castle for the King and Queen of Württemberg. The State Museum of Württemberg has a branch museum of medieval art in the three refectories and hall of the brothers in the monastery. The museum is open from April to September (Monday to Sunday, 9–12am; 2–5pm) and from October to March (Monday to Sunday, 10–12am; 2–5pm). When we took our friends Jim and Arlyn Culpepper from Marietta, Georgia, around Bebenhausen in August 1981 on a Saturday afternoon, we decided to come back for the Protestant service at 11 o'clock in the basilica the next morning. Four children pulled the bell ropes dangling from the ceiling in front of the altar. The ornate pulpit is so high on the left wall that you get a stiff neck if you try to maintain eye contact with the minister during his sermon. (I can't get used to seeing a microphone in a real Gothic pulpit.) A baptism was part of the service that morning, so the Culpeppers got to see how it's done in Swabia. They were particularly impressed by the floral decorations on the altar and the floral design on the baby's baptismal gown.

☐ **BIBERACH** on the River Riss is best known to my friend Richard Kurman, an American artist and art historian who has been living there for many years. An expert on Baroque art and architecture, Richard also did the English text for the tri-lingual book *Biberach an der Riß im Herzen Oberschwabens*. (He lent me the materials, but not his eyes, for the chapter on Swabian Baroque.) On a memorable walking tour of "his town", he showed me Biberach's one large church, the basilica of St. Martin on the market place. The outside has retained its late-Gothic appearance, dating from the 14th century. But the interior was "Baroqued" by Johannes Zick from 1746 to 1748. We looked at Biberach's "old" city hall, an alemannic half-timbered house built in 1432, and the "new" city hall of 1503. We viewed the late Gothic facade of the hospital of the Holy Ghost, which houses one of the largest art collections in Baden-Württemberg (the Braith-Mali Museum) as well as memorabilia of Christoph Martin Wieland (1733–1813), who was born in nearby Oberholzheim. (The Wieland Archive is in Biberach at Marktplatz 17.) Wieland is a big name in German literature of the Enlightenment. He studied law at Tübingen University and lived in Switzerland (Zurich and Berne) for six years before moving to Weimar in 1772 to become the tutor of the sons of Duchess Amalia of Sachsen-Weimar. He wrote several novels, one of which, *Die Abderiten* (1774), pokes fun at the narrow-mindedness of the people of Biberach, where he lived from 1760 to 1769. Spanish, French, and English literature influenced him. From 1762 to 1766 he translated twenty two of Shakespeare's plays into German. In the theater in Biberach in 1761 he produced and directed the first German-language version of a Shakesperian drama. Elegant, witty, graceful and urbane, this man of the world never struck me as a Swabian poet, which is why I did not mention him in the first two editions of this book. But writing about Biberach without mentioning Wieland is tantamount to an essay on Frankfurt without Goethe or about Calw without Hermann Hesse.

☐ **BRACKENHEIM,** just eight kilometers southwest of Heilbronn, is a town with many Renaissance houses. Its most famous house could have been the birthplace of Theodor Heuss (see chapter XV), the first President of the Federal Republic, but he had it torn down in 1950. A year later a new wine press of the winegrowers' association was erected on the site. Heuss had said in 1950: "Go ahead and tear the old house down. A place to cultivate good Brackenheim wine seems to me to be far more important than romantic fame in storage." In 1968, a year after Heuss' death, a Theodor Heuss memorial site was opened in the old guardhouse at Obertorstraße 25, just across from the place where his birthplace once stood. Established by the city, the memorial contains photographs, letters, and documents reflecting the most important events in the life of Heuss, including his childhood Brackenheim.

☐ **ESSLINGEN** on the Neckar has a history that spans 1,200 years. Originally the site of a monk's cell, "Ezzelingen" was the second German city to receive permission to conduct a market (in 866). A century later coins were minted in Esslingen, which was first mentioned as a city in 1212. In 1215 Emperor Friedrich II erected the guard towers around the city wall. The Romanesque parts of the east spire of the parish church of St. Dionys date from the time of this Hohenstaufen emperor. For centuries, Esslingen's bridge over the Neckar was part of the imperial highway from Antwerp to Venice. (One of its original towers from the 13th century is still standing.) Emperor Karl V (1519–1556) gave the imperial city of Esslingen a constitution that remained in force until 1803, when the city became part of Württemberg. The old city hall was built in 1430 as a mercantile and customs house and was used for commercial purposes for 400 years. It is used as a district court today and has an interesting museum on the top floor. Heinrich Schickhardt built the beautiful Renaissance gable facing the market place between 1586 and 1589. The astronomic clock dates from 1592. The city council meets in the citizens' hall of the old city hall where carved figures of the 15th century decorate three octagonal columns. Esslingen's hallmark is the *Burg* (citadel) overlooking vineyards, the spires of St. Dionys and the bell tower of the old city hall. The thick tower (*Dicker Turm*) got its wooden roof in the 19th century and contains a restaurant. You can explore the old wall and take superb photos of the city from that lofty vantage point. The cathedral of St. Paul, formerly the Dominican church, is Germany's oldest church of the order of mendicant friars and the first Gothic church of central Swabia. It was completed as a basilica without a transept in 1268. Secularized in 1830, it was reconsecrated as a Catholic church in 1864. The *Frauenkirche* (Church of Our Lady) is Gothic in style and dates from 1321. The south portal contains scenes from the life of the Virgin Mary carved in 1350 and the jaws of hell opening for the damned from all walks of life. Be sure to spend some time window shopping on the inner bridge, which is now a pedestrian zone in the heart of the city. The shops on the bridge continue a tradition from the beginning of the Middle Ages. In 1694 the old medieval shops were replaced by beautiful little Baroque houses which are a joy to every passerby today.

☐ **GÖPPINGEN** has a Renaissance Protestant parish church built in 1618/19 according to plans drawn by Heinrich Schickhardt. The painted wooden ceiling separates the nave from the spacious frame which was intended to be used as a granary. If you missed the big Hohenstaufen (*Staufer,* in German) exhibit in Stuttgart in 1977, you will find its mobile displays and a comprehensive documentation on the Hohenstaufen dynasty (1138–1254) in the Documentation Center for Hohenstaufen History *(Dokumentationsraum für staufische Geschichte)* in Kaiserberg-steige in Göppingen-Hohenstaufen. It's open Monday through Sunday, 10–12 am, 2–5 pm from 15 March until 15 November and the admission is free. If you're interested in tree trunks and root stocks from 6000 BC to 500 AD, visit Johann Weber's collection of them at Heininger Straße 20 in Göppingen. Admission is free, but phone ahead of time (07161) 7 45 76. The municipal museum *(Städtisches Museum)* at Wühlestraße 36 has Hohenstaufen artifacts, including a collection of coins stamped on one side only, and a documentation of the city's history as well as other interesting exhibits. It is open on Wednesdays, Saturdays and Sundays from 10–12 am, 2–5 pm. Admission is free. If geology and palentology are your bag, be sure to visit the collection of Pastor Dr. Theodor Engel, a leading Swabian geologist and palentologist which the city of Göppingen acquired in 1925. It is housed in the museum of natural history in Göppingen-Jebenhausen, Boller Straße 102. It can be seen from April to November on Wednesdays, Saturdays and Sundays from 10–12 am, 2–5 pm. Admission is free.

☐ **HAIGERLOCH,** a lovely little town in the valley of the meandering Eyach River, sits between two cliffs. On top of one of them is the pilgrimage church of St. Anna, one of the loveliest Baroque masterpieces in Germany. On top of the other cliff is the Haigerloch Castle, begun in the late 13th century. It sits on top of the cave where Professor Dr. Werner Heisenberg and Germany's top nuclear physicists experimented with nuclear fission in the last months of World War II. All of this and lilacs in the spring, too! Haigerloch is 60 kilometers southwest of Stuttgart, 8 kilometers east of the Empfingen exit on the Singen Autobahn (A-81). It was first settled about 900 years ago. The hallmark of the city (also the trademark of the local brewery) is the so-called *Römerturm* (Roman tower). It has nothing to do with the Romans but was probably the belfry of the citadel of the Counts of Zollern who lived in Haigerloch from the middle of the 11th to the middle of the 12th century. The balustrade and octagonal top were added in 1746. The tower offers a splendid view of the town. The oldest church in Haigerloch is the "Lower Town Church" *(Unterstadtkirche),* the oldest part of which is the choir with ribs from the 12th century. The high altar and Gothic vault date from the 15th century. The church is located inside the old cemetery between the market place and the Eyach River. If you walk up to the castle from the center of town, the castle church *(Schloß-kirche)* will be on your right. It was built by Count (Graf) Christoph of

Haigerloch between 1584 and 1607. The exterior appears to be late Gothic, but the interior is in the style of the Baroque, a result of the renovation ordered by Fürst (Prince) Joseph Friedrich von Hohenzollern-Sigmaringen in 1748. Have a good look at the beautiful side altars and the pulpit before you approach the wrought iron screen in front of the most beautiful Renaissance altar you will ever lay eyes on. Consecrated in 1690, its 60 carved wood figures date from 1604. In front of the screen are a late Gothic crucifix above a life-size Mater Dolorosa by Johann Georg Weckenmann of 1755. Andreas Meinrad von Aw did the ceiling paintings. Two pilasters in the nave have statues of Graf Christoph and Fürst Joseph standing on them with paintings of Haigerloch and Sigmaringen behind them. At the feet of Graf Christoph is a model of his *Schloßkirche.* The Haigerloch Castle is a complex of several buildings in addition to the church. Around 1580 Graf Christoph expanded the medieval castle toward the north and added a south wing. In 1662 Fürst Meinrad I von Hohenzollern commissioned master builder Michael Beer to add another story with three gables to the main building. In 1975 Paul Eberhard Schwenk, a manufacturer of timing devices and a patron of the arts, bought the Haigerloch Castle from Fürst Friedrich Wilhelm von Hohenzollern for DM 300,000. Since then he has invested six million Marks into converting part of it into a hotel, a restaurant, and a cultural center with art galleries and a small theater. The food is excellent, but the restaurant is closed on weekends. If you walk down the steps past the church into town, you will see a sign marked Atom Keller Museum. It was opened in May 1980 to mark the site – a cave inside the cliff underneath the castle church – where Professor Dr. Werner Heisenberg, Professor Dr. Walter Bothe, Professor Dr. Carl-Friedrich von Weizsäcker and Professor Dr. Karl Wirtz (who spoke at the opening ceremony) experimented with nuclear fission in March and April 1945 by suspending a ton and a half of uranium cubes in heavy water in a reactor surrounded by graphite bricks. The experiment was successful in principle, but the scientists lacked sufficient materials to bring about a critical mass. The story of their experiments, of the capture of Haigerloch on 23 April 1945 by Colonel Boris Pash and the 1279th Engineer Combat Battalion, and of his subsequent rounding up of the German scientists has been told in many history books. One of the best accounts is in Lieutenant General Leslie R. Groves' *Now It Can Be Told: The Story of the Manhattan Project* (New York, 1962, 1975). The museum contains the remains of the original reactor and a complete reconstruction of it, as well as models and documentary material. It is open from March through April on Saturdays, Sundays and holidays from 10–12 am, 2–5 pm, and from May through September every day, 10–12 am, 2–5 pm. What I love most about Haigerloch is the pilgrimage church of St. Anna, designed by Johann Michael Fischer of

Munich with stucco work on three altars by Johann Michael Feichtmayr of Augsburg – both of them left their mark at Zwiefalten (see Chapter XI) – frescoes by Andreas Meinrad von Aw, wood carvings by Johann Georg Weckenmann and other embellishments by great masters of the Baroque style. St. Anna was built between 1752 and 1755 at the instigation of Fürst Joseph Friedrich von Hohenzollern-Sigmaringen. Tiny on the outside, the church's decorative interior looks surprisingly large. Von Aw's ceiling painting over the nave shows Fürst Joseph dedicating the church. The magnificent high altar has a sculpture of the Holy Mother Anna and two allegorical figures, a wood-carving from the second half of the 14th century. Side altars are devoted to St. Fidelis and St. Meinrad. Their statues by Weckenmann are flanked by cherubs considered to be the best of the entire German Rococo. Two stone pillars with capitals carved by Weckenmann support the Prince's Loge at the rear of the church and the Baroque organ of 1755 with its original pipes still in working condition. The organ was repainted in vermillion on silver in 1955. This sacred Baroque jewel is on a par with Birnau and Zwiefalten. Amen.

☐ **HECHINGEN,** 24 kilometers southwest of Tübingen, is noted for the Hohenzollern Castle on the "Zoller Mountain" *(Zollerburg)* overlooking the city. The oldest citadel, built early in the 11th century, was destroyed in 1423. The second was started in 1454 and expanded into a massive fortress during the Thirty Years' War, in the course of which it was twice conquered. Destroyed at the end of the 18th century, it was replaced by a late romantic castle designed by Stüler and Prittwitz and erected between 1847 and 1867. The 15th century Catholic chapel of St. Michael is the oldest part of the present castle. The *Zollerburg* rests (that's a poor choice of verb) on a geological fault that is subject to frequent earthquakes. The most recent one, in the fall of 1978, did damage that is still being repaired. The treasure chamber *(Schatzkammer)* contains a small collection of medieval weapons and armor and a large display of personal belongings of Frederick the Great (1712–1786), including a snuffbox with a bullet imbedded in it from the battle of Kunersdorf (1759). The crown of Prussia, reconstructed by order of Kaiser Wilhelm II in 1889 (the original of 1701 no longer exists), is also on display. In 1956 seven of Frederick the Great's snuffboxes (he had about 1,200 of them) at the castle were smashed by a thief and the jewels in them stolen. Four have been reconstructed from the remains of the originals. On display, as well, are loan exhibits from the Steuben Society of America which I arranged to have shipped to Hechingen from New York City in 1970. They are memorabilia of Baron Friedrich Wilhelm von Steuben (1730–1794), trainer of the American Continental Army, who was a captain in Frederick the Great's Prussian Army and later the Lord Chamberlain to the Prince of Hohenzollern-Hechingen for 12 years before going to America in 1777 to join George Washington. In the Protestant chapel you will see the coffins of Frederick the Great and his father, Friedrich Wilhelm I (1688–1740), "the Soldier King". Once kept in the Garrison Church in Potsdam (near Berlin), they were hidden in a salt mine at Bernterode near Erfurt in 1944. Master Sergeant Louis C. Travers and six men of the 350th Ordnance Depot Company discovered them there, together with the caskets of Chancellor Paul von Hindenburg and his wife, and many other Hohenzollern treasures, on 27 April 1945. A large collection of paintings, including works by Lucas Cranach, was also discovered. Captain Walker Hancock of the 1st US Army had these treasures and the caskets transported to Marburg on 9 May 1945. The caskets remained in the Gothic church of St. Elisabeth in Marburg after the war. In 1952 the coffins of Frederich the Great and his father were brought to the Hohenzollern Castle at the request of His Imperial Highness, Dr. Prince Louis Ferdinand of Prussia, the grandson of Kaiser Wilhelm II. Born in 1907, he is the head of the Prussian House of Hohenzollern today. Prince (Fürst) Friedrich Wilhelm von Hohenzollern is the head of the Catholic, older line of the Hohenzollern family. He owns the castle in Sigmaringen and one-third of the castle in Hechingen. In the name of his deceased wife, Princess Kira (1909–1967), Prince Louis Ferdinand gives annual charity concerts at the castle in Hechingen with Professor Karl Münchinger and the Stuttgart Chamber Orchestra. The proceeds enable underprivileged Berlin children to spend summer vacations at the castle. The concerts are held in the beautiful *Grafensaal* (Hall of the Counts), the foyer of which has the family trees of the Catholic and the Protestant Hohenzollerns painted on the walls. The builder of the first castle was probably Graf Friedrich, presumably the father of Burchardus de Zolorin, whose death in battle on 29 August 1061 is recorded in the *Death Register of St. Gallen.* Inside the castle, which is open the year round, you will find historical wall paintings showing events involving the two earlier castles. Around the perimeter are huge statues of Prussian kings from Friedrich Wilhelm von Brandenburg (1620–1688) to Kaiser Wilhelm I (1797–1888). Parking is ample at the base of the *Zollerburg.* You may either continue up the winding road on foot or transfer to a VW shuttle bus and ride up for a small fee. The Stuttgart USO runs an excellent tour of the Hohenzollern Castle. (See THE KIOSK for dates and times. The price – DM 10 for adults; DM 8 for children – includes bus transportation from pickup points in the greater Stuttgart area, admission to the castle, and a guided tour in English.)

☐ **HEILBRONN's** name comes from an old pagan site of worship called the "holy well" *(Heiliger Brunnen* = Heilbronn), but as the hardest hit Swabian city in World War II there are only a few edifices still standing to reflect the city's long history and cultural past. The Kilian's church is a late Gothic edifice of the 13th century, two spires of which are original. The west spire, built between 1513 and 1529, is the hallmark of the city. The altar is the work of Hans Seyfer (1498). The Renaissance additions were the first to reveal the full impact of this style on German ecclesiastical architecture. The city hall *(Rathaus)* on the market place has a high Gothic hip roof with a Renaissance gable. The clock has an angel turning an hour glass while another one plays the trumpet, and every four hours a golden rooster crows while flapping its wings. A model inside the city hall shows how much of the old city was destroyed by air raids in World War II. The city has museums at Eichgasse 1 (the *Deutschhof),* at Kramstraße 1 (the former *Fleischhaus),* at Gymnasiumstraße 64 (Neckar River Traffic Museum), and at Frankfurter Straße 65 (a beautiful exhibit of Ludwigsburg and Nymphenburg porcelain can be viewed there by calling Dr. Heim, the museum director, ahead of time at 07131 – 56 22 95, but never on Mondays!) Heilbronn is famous for Heinrich von Kleist's play *Das Käthchen von Heilbronn* (Catherine of Heilbronn), a medieval folks' drama which was finished in 1808 and printed in 1810. Even though it deservedly added to Kleist's posthumous fame, Goethe threw it into the oven. The historical model for Käthchen in real life was Lisette Kornacher, who allegedly lived in the "Käthchenhaus" next to the city hall during the 18th century. Heilbronn is equally famous for its fabulous wines. At the annual wine festival in September, the best receives the coveted label *Käthchenwein.*

☐ **HOLZMADEN** is a small town just off the Stuttgart–Munich Autobahn (E 11) as you approach the Aichelberg, better known to Americans as "Alligator Mountain". And thereby hangs a tail – the sign with the "alligator" is actually a fossil advertising the site of one of the world's most important collections of prehistoric creatures. The fossils were discovered more than 200 years ago in slate quarries of the Swabian Jura mountain range (thus the Jurassic period in palentology). In the Hauff Museum, the property of Dr. Bernhard Hauff who made some of the more recent discoveries himself and opened his collection to public view in 1936, you will find ichthyosauri (fish), plesiosauri (marine reptiles), bird fossils and invertebrates. The colony of enchinoderms ("water lilies"), measuring 6 x 18 meters, is the largest interrelated group of fossilized invertebrates in the world. The Hauff Museum is open Tuesday through Sunday, 9–12 am, 1–5 pm. Admission is DM 2.00 for adults, DM 1.00 for children and students.

☐ **LEINFELDEN-ECHTERDINGEN,** due south of Stuttgart and Autobahn E-11, is the place where Pastor Philipp Matthäus Hahn, the famous *Tüftler* and clockmaker (see Chapter XVII), died in 1790. His diaries and other memorabilia are in the *Heimatmuseum* at Hauptstraße 79 in Echterdingen (and one of his clocks in the Württemberg State museum in Stuttgart). My friend Rudi Melters, Director of Culture and Schools for Leinfelden-Echterdingen, and a Toastmaster who speaks perfect English, is expanding the museum's holdings at present. It is open on Sundays from 10–12 am by special arrangement. (Call Rudi at 0711 – 7 98 61). In the elementary school at Schönbuchstraße 32 you will find the German Playing Card Museum that used to be housed at the ASS factory Americans smile at whenever they pass the sign with a red ASS inside a red heart on a white circle on the green wall of the *A*ltenburger und *S*tralsunder *S*pielkartenfabriken just off the Autobahn. (Now you know what ASS stands for and why the company markets its products in the United States under the trade name of ACE.) The collection is fascinating and fabulous and a must on your list of things to see near Stuttgart. It is open from Tuesday to Friday from 2–5 pm, and on Sundays and holidays from 10 am to 1 pm. Admission is DM 1.00 for adults and DM 0.50 for students and children.

☐ **LICHTENSTEIN,** about a dozen kilometers southeast of Reutlingen on route 312, boasts the little fairytale castle overlooking the town of Honau. The castle owes its fame to an author of fairy tales, Wilhelm Hauff (1802–1827), about whom you will find more on page 177. The original medieval castle on this lofty site was acquired by Count Wilhelm of Württemberg in 1837. It was torn down and replaced by a romantic castle designed by Victor Heideloff and J. G. Rupp between 1840 and 1842. Many claim their plans were influenced by the castle imagined and described by Hauff in his historical novel published in 1826. Duke Karl Gero von Urach owns the contemporary castle which contains armor and weapons of the late Middle Ages, as well as a valuable collection of glass and wood paintings of Swabian masters of the 14th and 15th century. The castle is open from April to October (Monday through Sunday, 8:30–12 am, 1–5:45 pm) and on Saturday and Sunday from 9–5 am from November to March. Admission is DM 1.50 for adults, DM 0.50 for children. The interior is small, and you are not allowed to climb to the top of the tower, but it is worth looking at, and the view of the valley below is marvellous. Nearby is the fog cave where Duke Ulrich hid from 1519 to 1534. Southwest of Honau, on a country road to Erpfingen, you will pick up a sign to the *Bärenhöhle* (bear cave). Discovered early in this century, this stalactite cave was a place of hibernation for bears for more than 2,000 years. Near the exit is a small amusement park for children. The Stuttgart USO will show

you the castle and the bear cave and provide your transportation for DM 10 (adults), DM 8.00 (children), but you need to brown bag your lunch.

☐ **MARBACH on the Neckar** is just a few kilometers east of the Pleidelsheim exit on the Stuttgart–Heilbronn Autobahn (E-70). Swabia's greatest poet, Friedrich Schiller, was born there on 10 November 1759. (See Chapter XIX for a sketch of his life and works.) His parents lived in two rented rooms with kitchen on the ground floor of a half-timbered house facing the market place. It is open to the public. His mother's birth house is also in Marbach. A Schiller Foundation was established in 1895 to perpetuate his name and fame. In 1903 a Schiller National Museum was built high above the Neckar (Schillerhöhe 8–10) in the style of Schloß Solitude (near Leonberg). It was expanded in 1934 and its contents evacuated during World War II. It was reopened in 1947 and the holdings of the museum greatly enlarged. In 1955 an archive for German literature was established at the museum and a separate annex built to accommodate the archive in 1973. The main hall of the museum is devoted to the life and works of Schiller. There you will see such memorabilia as his portable pen and ink well, his pocket watch, snuff box and rings, as well as manuscripts and letters. There is also a permanent exhibit devoted to other Swabian poets, all of whom are mentioned in this book. The archive has manuscripts, letters, and diaries of Swabian poets and of German writers since 1880. The library has some 200,000 volumes. The museum also contains a special collection of newspapers, dust jackets, phonograph records, theater programs, and literary posters. The Schiller National Museum is open from Monday to Sunday from 9–5, but closed on 25 and 26 December. Admission is one DM. The Stuttgart USO does this tour as part of a cruise on the Neckar River.

☐ **Cloister MAULBRONN,** 20 kilometers northeast of Pforzheim, is a superb one-hour, on-site lesson in German architecture from the Romanesque to the Renaissance style. You turn off at the Pforzheim Ost Autobahn exit and take B-10 towards Mühlacker. At Enzberg you pick up a country road that is well marked to Maulbronn. Drive on through the little town until you see a black-and-white sign marked *Kloster.* You have the right-of-way through the narrow aperture in the massive gate that is part of the walled fortification surrounding the cloister. Inside that gate there is plenty of free parking space. You find yourself in a different world, in a different century: a cluster of half-timbered houses inside the walls that once served as bakery, smithy, barn, mill, servants quarters and a seven-story grainary – buildings that were added in the course of the cloister's expansion to serve the logistical needs of the monks. It is a little town unto itself. (The royal stable has been the city hall of Maulbronn since 1839.) It all began more than 800 years ago when monks of the Cistercian Order, who worked as hard as they prayed, started to build a church on the site in 1147. By 1178 they had completed the original basilica. The reticulated vaulting was added around 1424. The original roof was flat and made of wooden beams. The Cistercians dedicated the church to the Virgin Mary. The nave is truncated by a solid stone chancel barrier with arches in it. Just in front of this barrier is a life-size crucifix carved out of stone around 1473, probably by the sculptor Conrad von Sinsheim. If you chance to see it during the summer solstice in June when the sun is shining through an upper window, the crown of thorns glows blood red. Behind the crucifix and chancel barrier are wooden choir stalls of solid oak, dating from the 13th century, with seats for 92 ordained monks. They were carved decoratively around 1450. (In later centuries the monks themselves carved their names and a date into the wood.) The ordained monks were rigorously segregated from the lay brothers, who sat in front of the crucifix in the rear of the church. You may explore the spacious rooms and the smaller ones surrounding the courtyard and see the *Herrenrefektorium,* where the ordained monks took their meals, the *Laienrefektorium* (where the lay brothers ate), the *Parlatorium,* where the monks were allowed to meet and talk briefly every day, and the *Kapitelsaal* (chapter hall), where a chapter a day from the rules of the order was drilled into them. In 1534, shortly after the Reformation, Duke Ulrich of Württemberg made the cloister Protestant. In 1556 his son, Duke Christopher, established the boarding school in the upper rooms of the cloister which Kepler, Hölderlin, and Hesse attended. The hallmark of the cloister is the Fountain Chapel *(Brunnenkapelle)* in the courtyard where the monks washed their hands before and after meals and had their tonsures and beards trimmed. A painting in the vaulted arch shows a mule drinking from a well, which may give credence to the legend that the monks intended to build their church at Mühlacker, but having found little water and not much sandstone, sent a mule in search of water and decided to build where he found some. Thus the conection between mule *(Maultier)* and well *(Brunnen)* resulting in the contracted name Maulbronn. Admission to the church and cloister is DM 1.50 for adults and DM 0.50 for children. An 18-page, illustrated guidebook in English sells for 2.50 at the ticket window. Be sure to walk around the exterior of the church, starting from the so-called *Paradies* (Paradise). This vestibule, built in 1220, has Romanesque ribs in its vaulting and early Gothic windows. Walk up the hill to the right of it for a fine view of the church from the outside and of the decorative Faust Tower, named after the alchemist Dr. Johannes Faustus, who allegedly tried to make gold in the kitchen of the cloister to help out an abbot who had run out of money due to bad management. A walk around the walls behind the half-timbered houses will show you how well fortified the cloister was and how deep its former moat. A small musem in the "Fireplace House" (called *Frühmesserhaus*) near the main gate has a fine scale model of the cloister and a display of books about it, some written by the famous men who attended the Maulbronn Cloister School.

☐ **NECKARSULM** lies 5.5 kilometers due north of Heilbronn. Its former Castle of the Order of the German Knights *(Deutschordenschloß)*, built around 1530, was heavily damaged in World War II. Restored after the war, it was been the home of the German Two-Wheeler Museum since 1956. Forty bicycles on display enable you to trace the history of the two-wheeler, from Karl Friedrich Drais' wooden model of 1817 to the modern folding types. Drais (1785–1851), Baron von Sauerbronn, was a forestry commissioner in Karlsruhe. His bike, propelled by the rider's feet, was so sensational at the time that it became popular in England as the "Dandy Horse" in 1818, as well as in the United States later on. The motorcycle section contains 90 of the most important types produced by German industry, including the first mass-produced Hildebrand and Wolfmüller models and those of NSU (1902), as well as 25 racing motorcycles, some of which set world records.The museum is open from March through November, Monday to Sunday, 9–12 am, 1:30–5 pm. Admission costs DM 2.50 for adults, DM 1.50 for children.

☐ **NERESHEIM** (See Chapter XI)

☐ **OBERKOCHEN,** a few kilometers south of Aalen just off route 19, is the location of a optical museum that belongs to the world-famous optical firm of Carl Zeiss. Here you will find original optical instruments – eyeglasses, telescopes, microscopes, surveying equipment and cameras – from their prototypes to the present, including camera models and lenses used by our Apollo XI astronauts to photograph the moon. Opened in 1971, the museum is located Am Ölweiher 15. It is open from Monday to Friday, 10 am to 1 pm, 2–4 pm, and on Sundays from 9–12 am. It is closed on holidays and during the school holidays in Baden-Württemberg (see a German pocket calender for these exact dates, as they vary from year to year). Admission is DM 1.00 for adults, DM 0.50 for children.

☐ **PFORZHEIM** is famous for its jewelry – that is, goldsmith's artistry – and its great humanist son and scholar Johannes Reuchlin. He was born in Pforzheim on 22 February 1455. Reuchlin began to study Hebrew in 1492. His *Rudimenta Hebraica* (1506) was the first Hebrew grammar to be written by a Christian. He taught Hebrew, Greek, and law at Heidelberg and Tübingen universities. When Johannes Pfefferkorn, a Jew turned Christian, recommended that all books in Hebrew be destroyed, Emperor Maximilian asked Reuchlin for his opinion. Reuchlin advised suppressing only those Hebrew books that attacked Christianity and proposed two chairs of learning for Hebrew in all German universities. A storm of controversy resulted. Reuchlin rose to his own defense with his *Augenspiegel (Mirror of the Eye)* in 1511, attacking Pfefferkorn and distinguishing between classical works in Hebrew and anti-Christian propaganda. The Dominican clergy in Cologne defended Pfefferkorn while the humanists sided with Reuchlin. Crotus Rubianus and Ulrich von Hutten published their *Letters of Obscure Men (Epistolae obscurorum vivorum)* in Reuchlin's defense, but the Curia suppressed his writings against Pfefferkorn in 1521. An opponent of Luther's Reformation, Reuchlin remained a Roman Catholic in spite of his controversy with the Church. He died at Bad Liebenzell on 30 June 1522. The Reuchlin house at Jahnstraße 42 in Pforzheim was bombed out and its contents destroyed in an air raid in 1945, but the building was restored and reopened in 1961. Today it is a jewelry museum covering four thousand years, from the earliest Egyptians to modern times. The museum is open on Tuesdays, Thursdays, Fridays and Saturdays from 10 am – 1 pm, and 3–5 pm. Admission is free.

☐ **RAVENSBURG** is 45 kilometers south of Biberach on route 30. An imperial city in the 13th century, it was one of the leading trade centers of Europe during the 15th century. The *Waaghaus* at the *Blaserturm* was built as a trade and storehouse in 1498. Three of the city's churches – the Protestant parish church, the Church of Our Lady, and the Church of St. Jodok – date from the 14th century. Today Ravensburg is known for the games and jigsaw puzzles of Otto Maier's publishing company, but he hasn't started a puzzle museum yet! –The *Heimatmuseum* on Charlottenstraße has coins, paintings, sculptures, period furniture, Gothic, Renaissance, and Baroque rooms, and coats of arms of the guilds, as well as ample other evidence of the city's history. It is open from Monday to Saturday, 3–5 pm, on Sundays from 10–12 am, 3–5 pm. Admission is free.

☐ **ROT on the Rot** River, 20 kilometers southeast of Biberach, was the earliest settlement of Premonstratensian monks in Upper Swabia. The monks themselves built the original cloister there between 1120 and 1150. It was completely rebuilt in the Baroque style between 1760 and 1782 with decorations by Januarius Zick, Franz Xaver Feuchtmayer, and Michael Schuster. It has a delightful array of onion bulb towers.

☐ **SCHWÄBISCH GMÜND** was an imperial city of the Hohenstaufen dynasty. Founded in the 12th century, it has several impressive buildings reflecting those times, such as the Romanesque *Johanniskirche* (Church of St. John) and the beautiful *Heiligkreuzmünster* (Cathedral of the Holy Cross). The Parler family from Gmünd, Heinrich and his son Peter, were famous for their Gothic architecture. Heinrich worked on the *Heiligkreuzkirche,* the oldest so-called *Hallenkirche* (literally, church of halls or aisles) in southern Germany. Unlike a basilica, a *Hallenkirche* has several aisles of the same height, so that the middle aisle (nave) receives only indirect lighting. The high hall choir (apse) built by Heinrich Parler in 1351 marked the beginning of the late Gothic style in southern Germany. Schwäbisch Gmünd has an exellent municipal museum *"im Prediger"* at Johannisplatz 3 where you can learn a great deal about the history of the city while enjoying exhibits of sculpture, jewelry, and arts of the 19th and 20th century. The *Museum im Prediger* is open from Tuesday to Friday, 2–5 pm, Saturday and Sunday, 10–12 am, 2–5 pm. Admission is free.

☐ **SCHWÄBISCH HALL** is an old imperial city. Hall = salt and its abundance at Schwäbisch Hall accounted for its prosperity and power in earlier times. Coins were minted there, and *Heller,* the German word for farthing, supposedly was "coined" in Schwäbisch Hall, too. The city lies in the valley of the Kocher River in a beautiful setting. The market place is one of the most attractive in Germany. Noteworthy is the Cathedral of St. Michael with its open staircase of 1507 in front of the west steeple, where festivals are held in the summer. The figure of the archangel Michael killing a dragon in the portico dates from 1300. The first four levels of the steeple are all that survives from the Romanesque period around 1150. The Gothic aisle with reticulated vaulting dates from 1427–56. The carved high altar was done around 1470 and the side altars in the 16th century. The *Rathaus* (city hall) , in the Rococo style of the late Baroque period, originally built between 1732 and 1735, burned down in 1945 and was completely restored after the war. The Keckenburg Museum at Untere Herrengasse 8 has Roman and Merovingian artifacts, a display showing the history of salt mining in the area, a large collection of implements of punishment, works of art in wood and stone, rustic furniture, and costumes from the Hohenlohe area. It is open from Tuesday to Sunday, 9–12 am, 2–5 pm. Admission is DM 3.00 for adults, DM 1.00 for pupils and students.

☐ **STUTTGART** has so many places of interest that I shall simply list them and urge you to go and look for yourself (or with the downtown Stuttgart USO walking tour for DM 7, which includes a guide and transportation from pickup points at US facilities in the Stuttgart area):

☐ Linden Museum (ethnology), Hegelplatz 1, Tue–Thur 10–5, free.

☐ Porsche Museum, Porschestraße 42, Stuttgart-Zuffenhausen, Mon–Fri 9–12, 1:30–4, free.

☐ Museum of Natural History, Schloß Rosenstein, Tue–Sat 10–4, Sundays and holidays 10–5, free.

☐ Municipal Art Gallery *(Staatsgalerie)*, Konrad Adenauer Straße 32, Wed, Fri–Sun 10–4, Tu & Thur 10 am – 9 pm, free.

☐ Hohenheim University Museum, Exotischer Garten 1, Sundays & holidays, 10:30–12:30, free.

☐ Württemberg State Museum *(Landesmuseum)*, Old Castle, Schillerplatz 6, Tue, Thur–Sun 10–4, Wed 10 am – 8 pm, free.

☐ Stuttgart City Archive, Konrad Adenauer Straße 2, Tue–Fri 11–6, Sat 10–4, free.

☐ Württemberg Artist's Association, Bolzstraße (near the New Castle, off the *Schloßgarten*), where the expressionist work of Otto Dix is on permanent display, plus roving exhibits, free.

☐ Daimler-Benz Museum, Mercedes Straße, Stuttgart-Untertürkheim, Mo–Fri 8:30–4, Sat 8:30–1, free.

☐ Württemberg State Library, Konrad Adenauer Straße 8 (bibles, manuscripts, maps, incunabula and rare books of later vintage), free.

☐ TV Tower, one of the hallmarks of Stuttgart, 217 meters high, built in 1954. Restaurant and observation platform 136 meters up.

☐ *Leonhardskirche* is a 3-aisle *Hallenkirche* built by Aberlin Jörg between 1470 and 1474.

☐ *Schloß Solitude,* near Leonberg, started in 1763 and finished in 1767. Architects: Johann Friedrich Weyhing and Philipp de la Guêpière. From its spacious lawn you can see the Ludwigsburg Castle on a clear day.

☐ *Stiftskirche zum Heiligen Kreuz* (Collegiate Church of the Holy Cross) was built by Aberlin Jörg between 1436 and 1495. The choir is older (1327–1347). Destroyed in WW II, it was rebuilt between 1953 and 1958.

☐ *Liederhalle,* at Berliner Platz, built between 1955 and 1957 by Rolf Gutbrod, who showed it to me in 1958. Eugene Ormandy told him it had the finest acoustics in the world, after a performance there.

☐ *Hauptbahnhof,* built between 1914 and 1917 by Paul Bonatz (1877–1956), a professor of architecture at Stuttgart University.

☐ **TRIBERG** in the Black Forest is one of the oldest health resorts in Germany and the site of Germany's largest waterfall (163 meters or 535 feet high). The *Heimatmuseum* at Wallfahrtsstraße 4 is known to Americans as the "cuckoo clock museum". It also contains a model of the Black Forest railway, woodcarvings and native costumes. In summer it is open Monday to Sunday, 8 am to 6 pm, during the winter on the same days but from 9–12 am, 2–5 pm. Admission is DM 2.00 for adults, DM 0.70 for children.

☐ **TÜBINGEN,** mentioned so often in this book, can be easily explored on foot. First mentioned in 1078, it reflects several centuries of Swabian history. Graf Eberhard im Bart founded the university on 9 October 1477. (There is a large equestrian statue of him in the courtyard of Stuttgart's Old Castle.) The older parts of the university are near the *Stiftskirche,* the newer parts on the edge of town along Wilhelmstraße and Nauklerstraße (where the Office for Foreign Students or *Akademisches Auslandsamt* is located). Peter von Koblenz did the choir of the *Stiftskirche* (collegiate church) in 1470. In 1550 it became the final resting place for the Dukes of Württemberg until 1593. Hans Augstaindreyer did the nave in 1478. Three windows have statues instead of tracery. In one oval window you will find a symbol of the city: a stone carving of a man tied to a wheel, reflecting a miscarriage of justice during the 15th century. A spectacular sight during your walking tour is your first glimpse of the *Rathaus* on the market place (which is not square, by the way) with its beautiful painted facade and portraits of some of the city's VIPs of yore. Built in 1435, it has been remodeled several times since then. The fourth story was added in 1543, the gable in 1598. Johannes Stöffler added the astronomic clock in 1511. Duke Ulrich was responsible for the construction of the Renaissance castle *Schloß Hohentübingen* (and high up it is, giving you a magnificent view of the city from its ramparts). The round corner towers were added as of 1507, the residence starting in 1525, the massive portal in 1604, a creation of Christoph Jelin by order of Duke Friedrich. The French destroyed the castle in 1647. It was rebuilt 20 years later and the living quarters 200 years later in the neo-classic style. The University of Tübingen has a valuable archive of its history (Wilhelmstraße 32) and a collection of coins and medaillons (Wilhelmstraße 9). At Osianderstraße 2–8 you can sink your teeth into a museum of dentistry (Monday to Friday, 8–12 am, 2–5 pm) at no charge. Buried in the old cemetery (*Alter Friedhof*) are the poets Hölderlin and Uhland. The Hölderlin Tower at Bursagasse 6, overlooking the Neckar, has an austere display about the poet's life and works which can be visited from Monday to Friday, 10–12 am, 3–5 pm, Saturdays from 3–5 pm, and Sundays from 10–12 am. Admission is DM 1.00 for adults, DM 0.50 for students and children.

☐ **ULM** on the Danube was first mentioned in a document of 854 as the royal palace-fortress of "Hulma". The colony was surrounded by a wall around the year 1000. Henry the Proud of Bavaria burned it down in 1134, but the Hohenstaufens rebuilt and expanded the imperial city. By 1316 it was four times its original size, surrounded by a wall 3,350 meters long. At the start of the 16th century the fortifications were rebuilt and strengthend using a system developed by Albrecht Dürer, only to be replaced by the bastions of the 17th century which are best seen in Matthäus Merian's engraving of the city as it looked around 1650. Ulm has 100,000 residents today, and just about that number of tourists from all over the world climb the 740 steps of the world's tallest steeple on the Ulm cathedral every year. Designed to accommodate almost 30,000 people, the cathedral was the work of many architects (the Parlers from Gmünd, Ulrich Ensinger, and Burkhardt Engelberg) and artists (Hans Multscher, Jörg Syrlin, and Martin Schaffner). The steeples were not finished, however, until 1890, using original plans but the construction methods of the late 19th century. During the night of 17 December 1944, two-thirds of Ulm was destroyed in an incendiary air raid, including part of the cathedral. The *Metzgerturm,* also called the "leaning tower", on the bank of the Danube is one of the oldest structures of the city. On the "wine courtyard" in front of the so-called "swearing house", the citizens of Ulm gather annually to hear the Lord Mayor repeat a rite that goes back to the 14th century. He gives an account of his stewardship for the previous year, ending with the oath from the democratic constitution of 1397 "to be a common man for all citizens, whether poor or rich". A pediment on the 16th-century *Rathaus* (city hall) has frescoes showing the history of Ulm, but you can learn a great deal more about that subject in the Ulm Museum at Neue Straße 92. It is open from Tuesday to Saturday, 10–12 am, 2–5 pm, and on Sundays, 10 am – 1 pm, 2–5 pm. Admission is free. The significant role that bread has played in the history of mankind can be traced in the unique *Deutsches Brotmuseum* (German Bread Museum) at Fürsteneckerstraße 17. It is open from Monday to Friday and on Sunday, 10–12 am, 3–5:30 pm. Admission is DM 1.00 for adults, DM 0.50 for children, and DM 0.20 for school classes.

☐ **VAIHINGEN an der Enz,** 29 kilometers northwest of Stuttgart on route B-10, has a wine museum at Alte Keltergasse 3 (Horrheim suburb) showing the development of wine over the past two centuries. It contains implements used in the vineyards and goblets of the 18th and 19th century. If you come in a group, you can also arrange for a wine-tasting. The museum is open from Monday through Sunday, but you must call in advance (07042 – 54 63) or the city administration (07042 – 60 55

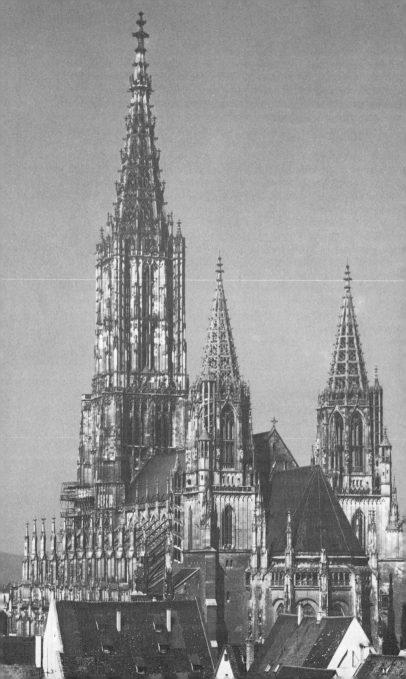

showing the development of wine over the past two centuries. It contains implements used in the vineyards and goblets of the 18th and 19th century. If you come in a group, you can also arrange for a wine-tasting. The museum is open from Monday through Sunday, but you must call in advance (07042 – 54 63) or the city administration (07042 – 60 55 or 50 81). Admission is DM 1.50 for adults, DM 0.50 for children, DM 1.00 for groups of 20 and up.

☐ **WEINSBERG,** near Heilbronn, is noted for the house of Justinus Kerner (see Chapter XIX), which you can visit at Öhringer Straße 3 from Tuesday to Sunday from 10–12 am, 2–5 pm (DM 1.50 for adults, DM 0.70 for children). It contains memorabilia of Kerner and the Swabian School of Poets. Kerner's avid interest in parapsychology is evident in the writings on display, plus the doctoral diploma and portrait of Franz Anton Mesmer (1734–1815), the inventor of hypnosis (mesmerism). You can also stroll in the garden and see the Spook Tower *(Geisterturm)* where Nikolaus Lenau (1802–1850), a passing member of the Swabian School of Poets although a Hungarian by birth, wrote his *Faust*.

Vacation Spot
SONNENMATTE

Rustic and Cozy   **Vacation in Your Own House!**

In an extraordinary vacation area - between the mighty Hohenzollern Castle, the mysterious Bear Cave and the legendary Lichtenstein Castle - lies Schwaben International's vacation village of "Sonnenmatte" (Sunshine Meadow).

Fifty fully furnished chalets, a community center with library, a guest house with swimming pool and a restaurant guarantee a relaxing vacation all year round.

A Facility of Schwaben International for Families with Lots of Children

Information and Registration:
**Schwaben International
Charlottenplatz 6, 7000 Stuttgart 1
Telefon (0711) 21 39-0**